Arab Americans in Film

Critical Arab American Studies
Carol W. N. Fadda, *Series Editor*

CRITICAL ARAB AMERICAN STUDIES

Syracuse University Press is pleased to announce the launch of a new series, Critical Arab American Studies. The series features cutting-edge scholarship that adopts interdisciplinary, intersectional, feminist, transnational, and comparative frameworks of inquiry to develop the study of Arab Americans across various fields of research, including history, gender and sexuality studies, critical race and ethnic studies, anthropology, literature, film and media studies, and sociology, among others.

Breaking Broken English: Black-Arab Literary Solidarities and the Politics of Language
Michelle Hartman

Interrogating Secularism: Race and Religion in Arab Transnational Literature and Art
Danielle Haque

Arab Americans IN FILM

From Hollywood and Egyptian Stereotypes to Self-Representation

Waleed F. Mahdi

SYRACUSE UNIVERSITY PRESS

Material from chapter 1 reprinted with permission from "Post-Oriental Otherness: Hollywood's Moral Geography of Arab Americans," *Mashriq and Mahjar: Journal of Middle East Migration Studies* 3, no. 2 (2016): 35–61.

Material from chapter 2 reprinted with permission from "Representation without Recognition: A Survey of Arab American Images in Egyptian Cinema," *JCMS: Journal of Cinema and Media Studies* 59, no. 1 (2019): 89–111.

Syracuse, New York 13244-5290

First Edition 2020
20 21 22 23 24 25 6 5 4 3 2 1

∞ The paper used in this publication meets the minimum requirements of the American National Standard for Information Sciences—Permanence of Paper for Printed Library Materials, ANSI Z39.48-1992.

For a listing of books published and distributed by Syracuse University Press, visit https://press.syr.edu.

ISBN: 978-0-8156-3671-7 (hardcover) 978-0-8156-3681-6 (paperback)
978-0-8156-5496-4 (e-book)

Library of Congress Cataloging-in-Publication Data
Names: Mahdi, Waleed F., author.
Title: Arab Americans in film : from Hollywood and Egyptian stereotypes to self-representation / Waleed F. Mahdi.
Description: First edition. | Syracuse : Syracuse University Press, 2020. | Series: Critical Arab American studies | Based on the author's dissertation (doctoral)—University of Minnesota, 2015. | Includes bibliographical references and index. | Summary: ""Arab Americans in Film" explores the representation of Arab Americans in Hollywood and Egyptian films that results in a unique and striking revelation of identity, belonging, and cultural citizenship"— Provided by publisher.
Identifiers: LCCN 2020003897 (print) | LCCN 2020003898 (ebook) | ISBN 9780815636717 (hardcover) | ISBN 9780815636816 (paperback) | ISBN 9780815654964 (ebook)
Subjects: LCSH: Arab Americans in motion pictures. | Stereotypes (Social psychology) in motion pictures. | Identity (Psychology) in motion pictures. | Motion pictures—United States—History—20th century. | Motion pictures—United States—History—21st century. | Motion pictures—Egypt—History—20th century. | Motion pictures—Egypt—History—21st century.
Classification: LCC PN1995.9.A67 M34 2020 (print) | LCC PN1995.9.A67 (ebook) | DDC 791.43/629927073—dc23
LC record available at https://lccn.loc.gov/2020003897
LC ebook record available at https://lccn.loc.gov/2020003898

Manufactured in the United States of America

To my wife Bassma, my daughters Lana and Lilian, family, friends, and individuals fighting prejudice, discrimination, and exclusion

Contents

Illustrations

Acknowledgments

THIS BOOK would not have been possible without support from many individuals and institutions. First and foremost, I would not have been able to commit to an academic career without the many sacrifices of my parents, Farea Mohammed Mahdi and Aman Alhitar, and my siblings in Yemen. My achievement as a first-generation author is in fact a realization of my parents' challenge of their Yemeni peers in daring to have faith in education for my individual fulfillment. I would also like to thank my wife Bassma Alqubati and her family for their love. Bassma dedicated her time generously to this work by watching and discussing with me hundreds of films and morally supporting me throughout the researching, writing, and revising phases of the project.

I am grateful to Alex Lubin, Rebecca Schreiber, Walter Putnam, Pamela Cheek, and Katrin Schroeter for supporting me through my MA program in cultural studies and comparative literature at the University of New Mexico, and for instilling in me the desire to pursue comparative and transnational research at the doctoral level, effectively laying the foundation for this book. I am grateful for the dedication of my advisor, Roderick Ferguson, and dissertation committee members Donna Gabaccia, Evelyn Alsultany, and Bianet Castellanos during my PhD program in American studies at the University of Minnesota, for believing in the premise of my topic and for their insightful feedback on my research, writing, and plans to develop my doctoral project into this book.

I would like to recognize the mentorship and support of David Noble, Lary May, Patricia Lorcin, Cawo Abdi, Kevin Murphy, Erika

Lee, Karen Brown, Jennifer Pierce, Riv-Ellen Prell, David Karjanen, Elaine May, and Shaden Tageldin at the University of Minnesota. I would also like to recognize the support of many colleagues at the University of Oklahoma: Janet Ward, Mitchell Smith, Samer Shehata, Ping Zhu, Afshin Marashi, Miriam Gross, Eric Heinze, Joshua Landis, Dylan Herrick, Jill Irvine, Julia Abramson, Pamela Genova, Michael Winston, Logan Whalen, Robert Lemon, Karin Schutjer, Joseph Sullivan, Emily Johnson, Bruce Boggs, Robert Lauer, Luis Cortest, Nancy LaGreca, Jonathan Stalling, Aqil Shah, Joshua Nelson, Man Fung Yip, Victoria Sturtevant, Rita Keresztesi, Mohammad Al-Masri, Amel Khalfaoui, Amit R. Baishya, Manata Hashemi, Alexander Jabbari, Julie Ward, Dina Hassan, Marjaneh Seirafi-Pour, and Hossam Barakat. And many thanks go to Karen Rupp Serrano, Liorah Golomb, and Lauri Scrivener at the University of Oklahoma's libraries and to the staff in my affiliated departments for their valued support: Beth Young, Stephanie Sager, Rhonda Hill, Sheila Dickerman, Terri Smith, Natalie Tobin, Mona Springfield, James Ratcliff, Morgan Brokob, and Genevieve Schmitt.

My research has been enriched through conversations with scholars and researchers in other institutions. So, due credit goes to Jack Shaheen, Melani McAlister, Louis Cainkar, Amal Amireh, Caetlin Benson-Allott, Jeff Menne, Kristian Petersen, Pauline Homsi Vinson, John Mowitt, Jaap Kooijman, Nathaniel Greenberg, Eid Mohamed, Mounira Soliman, Maha el Said, and Walid El Hamamsy. I have been fortunate to receive critical feedback from several anonymous peer reviewers of my work and the many scholars engaging with my conference presentations at the American Studies Association, the Middle East Studies Association, the Arab American Studies Association, the American Comparative Literature Association, the "Cinema of the Arab World" conference organized at the American University in Cairo, and the "Transnational American Studies" conference organized by the American University of Beirut. A word of thanks goes to Karen Broyles, Elizabeth Crowley Webber, Kim Greenwell, Martha Ash, Claire A. Kempa, Marcia Hough, indexer Debbie Olson, and other editors and copyeditors who similarly enriched this work.

I would like to recognize Syracuse University Press for instituting the Critical Arab American Studies series and including this book in the series. I appreciate the thoughtful comments of the series editor, Carol W. N. Fadda, throughout the process of writing, evaluating, and revising the book. Many thanks to the series advisors Evelyn Alsultany, Sarah Gualtieri, Amira Jarmakani, Sunaina Maira, Nadine Naber, Steven Salaita, and Theri Pickens for believing in my work. I also appreciate the dedication of Deborah Manion, Suzanne E. Guiod, Mona Hamlin, Mary Doyle, Lisa Kuerbis, Victoria Lane, Kay Steinmetz, Nora Luey, Meghan Cafarelli, Abbey Metzler, and others in the editorial, design, and marketing teams at the press and their various contributions to the publishing process.

My students and colleagues (both faculty and staff) at the University of New Mexico, the University of Minnesota, George Mason University, and the University of Oklahoma have been integral to my success. I am indebted to them for thinking critically with me and lifting my spirit in my down moments. A word of thanks goes to Arab and Muslim American communities for offering me a space to think critically about my own sense of belonging as a first-generation immigrant. I am grateful for all the support of my Yemeni American communities in Minnesota and across the United States. I am also thankful for the many wonderful experiences that I have had with relatives, neighbors, friends, and acquaintances across the United States and the globe.

Finally, yet importantly, I would like to acknowledge the collegial support that I have received from the University of Oklahoma's Department of Film and Media Studies in addition to the financial and collegial support that I have received from the Department of International and Areas Studies; the Department of Modern Languages, Literatures, and Linguistics; the College of International Studies; the College of Arts and Sciences; and the Humanities Forum. Financial support was also provided from the university's Office of the Vice President for Research and the Office of the Provost. Also, this work would not have been possible without early support from the Fulbright Program and Taiz University in Yemen, which enabled me to travel to the United States and pursue my graduate studies. I am also indebted to the Department of American Studies, the Interdisciplinary Center for the Study of Global Change, the Immigration History Research Center, the Community of Scholars Program, and the Graduate School at the University of Minnesota for sponsoring my research through a number of fellowships including but not limited to the ICGC-MacArthur Fellowship, the Doctoral Dissertation Fellowship, and the Francis Maria Graduate Fellowship in Arab American Studies.

Note on Transliteration

IN TRANSLITERATING the Arabic terms in this project, I have adopted the system approved by the *International Journal of Middle East Studies.* Throughout the book each Arabic word, except proper nouns, is italicized; the first occurrence is followed by an English translation in parentheses. Arabic words signifying personal names (e.g., Layla) require no translation. Whenever possible, Arabic words are prioritized over translations to preserve their authentic cultural connotations. In the case of Arabic films, the translation is accompanied by the release date, separated by a comma. In rendering Arabic names with no known preferred spelling, I have exercised discretion in using the most common spelling. When mentioning fictional characters in a particular work, I have made sure to include in parentheses the full name of each actor to the extent available.

Transliterated Terms

adab al-mahjar. Diaspora literature
akh. Brother
al-huwwiyya al-'arabiyya. Arab identity
al-nahḍa. Cultural awakening
al-qawmiyya al-'arabiyya. Arab nationalism
al-Rābiṭah al-Qalamiyah. Pen League
al-'uruba. Arabism
awlad el-balad. Sons of the country
Daesh. ISIS
el-ghorba. Alienation and foreignness
el-Ikhwān el-Muslimūn. The Muslim Brotherhood

el-Jamā'ah el-Islamiyyah. The Islamic Group
***fatwa*.** Islamic ruling by a recognized authority
***hawala*.** Money transfer
***infitah*.** Open door policy
***intifaḍa*.** Uprising
***khawagāt*.** Western foreigners
Maglis el-Sha'b. The People's Assembly
Maglis el-Shura. The Consultative Council
***mulukhiyya*.** A type of mallow leaf used in Arabic cuisine
***nakhwa*.** Generosity
***rafiq*.** Comrade
***raqabat el-shari'*.** Street censorship
***rijal el-kheer*.** Men of goodness
***salafi*.** Ultraconservative
***shahamah*.** Chivalry
***shari'a*.** Islamic way of life
***shika bika*.** Abracadabra
***Tamarod*.** Rebellion
***ummah*.** Transnational Muslim community

Arab Americans in Film

Introduction

TWO MOMENTS collided and produced this work. The first is personal, the second is political. The personal moment draws from my experience as an Arab American of Yemeni background constantly wrestling with American, Yemeni, Arab, and Muslim narratives of belonging and citizenship. In my travels I have encountered conflicting public attitudes and government policies preconfigured to define me and confine my identity within a specific national, ethnic, or even religious frame. During trips to Malaysia, Turkey, Lebanon, Egypt, Qatar, United Arab Emirates, Morocco, and Yemen over the past few years, people would often question me about US foreign policy toward Arabs and Muslims. The impetus for such questions, in most cases, was not so much interest in my scholarship but rather a desire to read my responses through the prism of allegiance. My interlocutors sought to package me as either an American or a Yemeni—identities implicitly presumed to be incompatible. The "Yemen place of birth" line in my American passport presents a special challenge for government officials in many of these countries because they are forced to treat me simultaneously as a Yemeni and an American.

In the meantime, my return to the United States in the aftermath of every overseas trip has involved an additional layer of security, whether before boarding in Tokyo, London, Dubai, Doha, and Amman, or when landing at Chicago's O'Hare Airport. The "SSSS" designation on my boarding passes, which stands for Secondary Security Screening Selection, speaks of an institutional anxiety around my ethnic background and conflates it with a potential act of terrorism. This anxiety stretches across the globe via a US mandate of national security, which locates individuals like me at the periphery of American citizenship. That mandate grows out of a post-9/11 paranoia that continues to shape the experiences of first-generation immigrants and Americans of Middle Eastern and South Asian backgrounds. The transnational nature of my personal encounters made me curious to explore meanings of Arab American citizenship and belonging in a globalized but fractured world. But it was a political moment that solidified my interest in examining these issues.

September 11, 2012, not only marked the eleventh anniversary of the tragic attacks of September 11, 2001, but also served as a violent testimony to the failure of a decade-long US-led "war on terror." Motivated by a mixed sense of frustration and anger, hundreds of Egyptians, Libyans, Yemenis, and Tunisians—to name only protesters in Arab revolutionary spaces—swarmed US embassies to decry a sensational film titled *Innocence of Muslims* (2012), written and produced by US-based and Egyptian-born Coptic Christian, Nakoula Basseley Nakoula (also known as Mark Basseley Youssef). The film's satirical, if not cynical, imagery advanced conceptions of the prophet of Islam that were perverse and sadistic. Violating Muslims' taboo against the pictorial depiction of the prophet, not to mention vilifying his spiritual message, the work rendered the United States a breeding ground for anti-Islam narratives. The film's charged content, along with its decontextualized circulation through social media, left no room for recognition of the American actors, who categorically condemned it and denied their previous knowledge of the director's true intentions. It was easy to label the film as an American product and embed it in a post-9/11 Islamist critique of the United States as a neocolonial religious entity bent on what President George W. Bush once called a "crusade" against, as what many Muslims would say, Islam. Protests against the film and, more broadly, against its perceived endorsement by the United States, turned violent and opened doors for extremists to dominate the scene. Crucially, these extremists were now positioned to transform earlier grievances against a poorly composed Islamophobic film into a sociopolitical statement of a Muslim identity in crisis.[1]

The significance of this moment is threefold. First, it embodied the state of insecurity following the peaceful calls for change celebrated as the "Arab Spring" in Western media, and the emergence of extremist groups like al-Qaeda and Daesh (the Arabic name for ISIS) as de facto geopolitical alternatives in unstable states. Second, it raised questions about the transnational modes surrounding these alternatives, whether in terms of their ability to produce high-quality propaganda materials, employ alternative media to recruit Western-raised Muslims, or generate Islamophobic reactions across Europe and the United States. Third, the moment spoke of the power of film, however poor and underfunded, to spur transnational cultural politics; equally important, it underlined how an independent work by an Egyptian immigrant could circulate globally out of context to become symbolic of America's Islamophobia. It is this instrumentality of film imagery specifically and its relation to identity and representation that is this book's critical site of inquiry.

The confluence of my personal struggle to navigate East-West efforts to gauge my allegiance and my realization of the importance of film in visualizing difference and producing changes beyond the screen forced me to ask several questions. What are the discourses shaping the mutual construction of Arab American Otherness in US and Arab collective memories? What is the role of cultural producers in perpetuating images of inclusion and exclusion? How is the interstitial experience of my Arab American community codified in the two spheres? Is it possible to renarrate the Arab American story beyond the imperatives of suspicion and patriotism? What does it mean to develop a complex sense of Arab American identity in film? In order to make sense of these questions, this book explores both the construction of Arab American subjectivity in US and Egyptian cinemas and the role of Arab American filmmakers in the process.

Arab Americans in Film directly engages with the questions raised above by examining how Arab American belonging is constructed, defined, and redefined in a transnational context (i.e., US and Arab realms of cinematic imagination). The book explores the representation of Arab Americans in Hollywood, Egyptian, and even Arab American filmmaking, comparing the politics of portrayals in each. It unsettles the "national" as a theoretical category of analysis as it seeks out alternatives for deeper understanding of the Arab American image at the crossroads of US and Arab sociocultural and geopolitical encounters. This comparative framework, therefore, presents an intervention in the field of Arab American Studies by simultaneously critiquing and transcending the nationalist rhetoric of cultural producers that mediate sensational narratives of Arab American Otherness to American and Arab audiences.

Arab Americans in Film pursues two main objectives. The first is to theorize how Arab American Otherness cannot strictly be viewed as a mere by-product of US Orientalist and racialized histories, but as an outcome of the polarized cultural imaginations of "Self" and "Other" that exist in both US and Arab state nationalist narratives. Current conceptualizations of Arab American Otherness engage primarily with the parameters of US cultural citizenry. US-based scholarship often conceptualizes Arab Americans as a minority wrestling with assimilation, acculturation, alienation, and exclusion. Many scholars locate the root of Arab American experience in US Orientalist yearnings that render Arab Americans as the racialized, gendered, and sexualized Other.[2] This understanding of Arab American identity is critical and enriching. It is, however, predicated on a theoretical limitation imposed by using the "national" as the primary category of analysis. What happens when this category is unsettled?

Important studies on Arab American identity and anti-Arab sentiment have proliferated since 9/11, but to date, there have been few works theorizing Arab Americanness in a transnational context of East-West competing narrations of identity. Since the early 2010s, scholars in the field of Arab American studies have increasingly sought to locate questions of Arab American identity and belonging in a transnational context.[3] Nadine Naber's calls for collapsing of "time-space distinctions" in conceptualizing Arab American experiences in the United States and the Arab region underscore the importance of this transnational trend in Arab American studies.[4] And Carol Fadda-Conrey's analysis of the transnational configurations of citizenship and belonging in Arab American literature serves as an important illustration of this trend.[5]

There is, however, a lack of scholarly research related to the simultaneous articulations of Arab American citizenship and belonging in both US and Arab societies and their relevant popular cultures. A major theoretical contribution of *Arab Americans in Film*, therefore, is in suggesting that Arab American Otherness cannot only be conceived as an outcome of US Orientalist and racialized histories. It rather imagines Arab American Otherness as an outcome of the polarized cultural imaginations of "Self" and "Other" that exist in both US and Arab state nationalist narratives, examined in this book through Hollywood and Egyptian cinematic experiences.

There is a double-layered, institutionalized process of alienation of Arab Americans in both the United States and the Arab world. The first layer is governmental. The US government has screened out many Arab Americans through its racial profiling practices at airports, policing of places of worship, or mapping of ethnic communities; it has also screened out critical Arab American voices and projected them as undesired citizens—whether legally as in the denaturalization case of Rasmea Odeh or rhetorically as in President Donald Trump's tweet for Congresswomen Rashida Tlaib and Ilhan Omar to "go back" to their ancestral homelands, Palestine and Somalia, respectively.[6] Equally important, many Arab governments, guided by perceived threats of Western-based mobilization of their own public revolutionary demands of regime change, have also screened out dissidents among Arab diasporas in the United States and elsewhere, tortured some, and sentenced others to death in absentia; the Egyptian case since 2014 is a notorious example.[7]

The second layer in the alienating process of Arab Americans occurs on both US and Arab silver screens. Hollywood films have fostered reductive imagery of Arab Americans since the 1970s, while Egyptian filmmakers since the 1990s have used polarizing images of Arab Americans to communicate their nationalist critiques of the United States. Despite major differences between the two cinematic industries in power, production, and circulation, I argue that the filmmakers in these filmic sites have subjected their imagery of Arab Americans to binaristic modes of Othering in their glorification of Americanness and vilification of Arabness in Hollywood and vice versa in Egyptian cinema, leaving no imagination of Arab Americans as complex communities defined by a multitude of individualistic experiences at the intersections of nation, race, ethnicity, class, religion, gender, and sexuality, to name prominent identity particularities.

The second objective of *Arab Americans in Film* is to identify post-9/11 filmic efforts in Hollywood and Egyptian cinemas, as well as the filmmaking of Arab Americans themselves, that challenge the aforementioned restrictive representation strategies. To move beyond the nationalist cultural politics that have divided Hollywood and Egyptian filmmakers and denied Arab Americans their own distinct space, I focus on films that offer representations with alternative narratives of Arab American citizenship and belonging, ones that defy mapping according to the reductive binaries of Hollywood and Egyptian cinemas. The selected films for analysis in this regard challenge the nationalist rhetoric of belonging in Hollywood and Egyptian cinemas, which presupposes a chasm between Arab Americans and their American and Arabic identities. Unlike mainstream films in Hollywood and Egyptian cinemas, which overstate the nation as the locus of identity and citizenship, the films present their Arab American characters with complexity, realism, and fluidity.

Overall, *Arab Americans in Film* examines film as a critical site of inquiry given the power of the visual image to reflect and shape both collective memory and national identity. Existing scholarship illustrates the role of films in exploring the interplay between identity and culture.[8] Communicating mass-oriented messages to national and international audiences, films rely on existing cultural codes and frames of references, especially regarding cultural Others. For decades, Hollywood has played a major role in mediating the American collective imagination and manufacturing sensational conceptions of cultural Otherness, particularly of minorities. In this context, Hollywood's conflated articulation of Arabness and Islam diminishes and enunciates cultural difference through a series of binary oppositions. Matthew Bernstein and Gaylyn Studlar's *Visions of the East* (1997), Jack Shaheen's *Reel Bad Arabs* (2001), Tim Semmerling's *"Evil" Arabs in American Popular Film* (2006), and Evelyn Alsultany's *Arabs and Muslims in the Media* (2012) investigate the history of Hollywood's reductive binary codes and criticize its repertoire of stereotypes and images. Such contributions have laid a solid foundation for this work, which seeks to balance their analysis with attention to the cinematic representation strategies of the Arab American community itself.

Alongside this analysis of Hollywood filmmaking, this work investigates Egyptian cinema as similarly essential to the mainstream cross-cultural consumption of the Arab American image. Since the silent era, Egyptian cinema has played an important role in challenging the hegemonic constructions of Arabness in Western cultural productions. The significance of this industry lies in its engagement with certain Arabist and Islamist postcolonial discourses, primarily in ways that serve the sociocultural dictates of the Egyptian nationalist narrative. But whereas Arab cinema scholarship has generally shied from such inquiry, this book analyzes the imagery of Arab Americans in Egyptian filmmaking as a by-product of an Egyptian filmic postcolonial consciousness, which, I argue, still generates a limited and limiting mode of representation that reverses Hollywood's images but reproduces similar reductive binaries.

In its third angle of analysis, this book explores a burgeoning direction of Arab American filmmaking that not only offers a counternarrative to the discursive formations of Hollywood and Egyptian cinemas, but also demonstrates a desire for diasporic agency and self-representation. The Arab American films examined here exhibit certain "accented" elements, to borrow Hamid Naficy's description of exilic and diasporic filmmaking, with their distinct images and spectatorial environment.[9] Self-representation enables Arab American actors and directors to transcend the respective tropes of "evil" in Hollywood representations and "allegiance" in Egyptian cinema. Arab American films capture efforts to negotiate identity across nationality, religion, gender, and generation. Such films also project

Arab Americans beyond the confluence of terrorism and geopolitics, thus constituting critical interventions in the filmic representation of Arab American subjectivity.

Thus, *Arab Americans in Film* captures the multilayered articulations of Arab American subjectivity across US and Arab collective memories and filmmaking industries. The book does not purport to provide a comprehensive catalogue of American, Arabic, and Arab American films. Rather, it selects films for analysis that reveal diverse, often conflicting narratives of Arab American belonging. The films produce socially constructed meanings defined by linguistic constraints, social formations, and monopolies of power.[10] The analysis draws on established literature and considers the spatial and temporal dimensions of the three cinematic sites' history of production and filmmakers' investments. Although I consider audience reactions to the selected films, I do not operate from a reception studies framework, nor do I claim to measure this engagement. Instead, I chart the established links between the "real" and the "reel" by connecting the examined films to critical events and incorporating government records and scholarly sources into the analytical framework of the book. Throughout, I seek to capture the heterogeneity of Arab Americans' consciousness and locate their narratives at the crossroads of the individual and the collective, the local and the national, and the national and the transnational.

Hollywood's Repertoire of Arabness

"I can't trust Obama," declared seventy-five-year-old Gayle Quinnell, in a tone of anger and frustration. Quinnell was voicing her suspicion of the 2008 Democratic presidential candidate, Barack Obama, at a town hall meeting largely in support of Republican presidential candidate John McCain. Quinnell went on to explain, simply: "He is an Arab." Realizing the problematic nature of such a statement, McCain quickly took the microphone and responded, "No ma'am. No ma'am. He is a decent family man citizen that I just happen to have disagreement with on fundamental issues."[11] Though some lauded McCain for "defending" his political opponent, a deeper reading of this globally mediated unscripted scene reveals a polarizing rhetoric—one that has dominated the US cultural imagination for decades, if not centuries. For all their seeming opposition, both Quinnell's identification of Obama as an Arab and McCain's rejection of that identification reveal the assumed incompatibility of Arabs with American citizenship.

Of course, this assumed incompatibility is hardly new. We need only reflect on the history of popular constructions casting American and Arab as mutually exclusive identities. Cultural perceptions of Arabs and Muslims in the United States date back to the post–Revolutionary War era (1775–83). The period of 1785 to 1815 marked a prolonged process of negotiation for power and dominance between the United States and what Europeans once called the "Barbary Coast."[12] The Algerian capture of Boston-based ship *Maria* in July 1785 and the subsequent trend of subjecting American prisoners to slavery or ransom threats sparked an American interest in translating European constructs of East versus West for the United States. "Despots and slaves, taken as signifiers of the 'Barbary' Orient," Malini Schueller contends, "generated an imperial narrative based on raced distinctions between Oriental tyranny and US American freedom, a narrative that drew both on the immediate historical moment and on long-standing Western philosophical distinctions between European and Eastern forms of power."[13] Royall Tyler's *The Algerine Captive* (1797), David Everett's *Slaves in Barbary* (1797), Susanna Rowson's *Slaves in Algiers* (1794), James Ellison's *The American Captive* (1812), and Jonathan Smith's *The Siege of Algiers* (1823) were early American literary works that contributed to this dichotomy. Peter Markoe's *The Algerine Spy in Pennsylvania* (1787) was one of the earliest literary texts to imagine the triumph of American values in the life of an Arab Muslim living in the United States. The thriller illustrates a process of disillusionment for Mehemet, an Algerian spy, who eventually converts to Christianity and renounces his commitment to the "despotism" of the East. The book, in the words of historian Timothy Marr, "symbolically enacts a multiple conversion through which Islam bows to Christian truths, despotism dissolves into democracy, and ethnic differences are assimilated into national character."[14]

The US cultural imagination of Arabs and Muslims prior to the Civil War era mirrored a nationalist anxiety that transcended encounters with the Barbary and spoke to deeper religious power dynamics. This anxiety was most vividly expressed through depictions of Ottoman rule that were devoid of accuracy. "Americans who used the Muslim world as a reference point for their own society," the author of *The Crescent Obscured* observes, "were not concerned with historical truth or with an accurate description of Islam, but rather with this description's political convenience."[15] The coincidence of Americans' desire to escape the pains of the Civil War and the booming steamboat industry prompted a fascination with tourism and exploration beyond US shores. The Orient, particularly the Holy Land and Egypt, attracted flows of missionaries, pilgrims, Egyptologists, and adventure seekers. Travel writings soon followed and reproduced sensational images of the Orient to reassert Americans' sense of national identity. A wide range of literature clustered around what Hilton Obenzinger calls "Holy land Mania," as Anglo Protestants identified the United States as the "new Israel."[16] Meanwhile, Egyptomania represented a site of inquiry for Egyptology and racialized science.[17] The two trends intertwined in their manufacture of the Orient's Otherness and the newly defined cartographies of global power. The production and circulation of such imagery in this era instituted a viable US Orientalist heritage that served as a cultural frame of reference for generations to come. A leading magazine like *National Geographic*, founded in 1888, hosted one of the most important reiterations of this heritage through its reductive images of the Orient. A glimpse at its first one hundred years reveals a remarkable level of consistency in its one-dimensional portrayals of Arab men and women.[18]

This cultural history of misrepresentations from the eighteenth and nineteenth centuries provided the foundations for US cinematic imaginings of Arab Otherness. *The Dance of the Seven Veils* (1893) was one of the earliest films produced by Thomas Edison's first US film studio in West Orange, New Jersey. The film was available for public consumption through the early motion picture exhibition device of the kinetoscope.[19] This was the first of many films to follow during the

1. The Sheik (Rudolph Valentino) and Lady Diana (Agnes Ayres) experiencing the pleasures of the Orient in *The Sheik* (1921). © Paramount Pictures.

age of silent cinema, which entertained fetishized and exotic images of Arabs, inspired by a Western visualization of the classical *Arabian Nights*. The element of Arab foreignness in the Oriental genre registered the potency of the Orientalist discourse in US culture and defined difference through the prism of spatial morality: good vs. evil, civilized vs. primitive, peaceful vs. violent, etc.[20] Films like *The Sheik* (1921), among others,[21] created a buffer zone or, as Melani McAlister puts it, a "moral geography" for Americans to both experience the pleasures of the Orient (i.e., romance, exotic milieus, and harem sexual allure) while spatially and culturally distancing themselves from it.[22] A close shot of the Sheik (played by Rudolph Valentino) intimately romancing Lady Diana (Agnes Ayres) underscores the exoticization of this consumption (figure 1). In an era defined by mass consumption, the sheer volume of films produced—at least eighty-seven films during the 1920s—speaks to the power of the US film industry in mediating this moral geography.[23]

Hollywood's engagement with the Arab image has transcended this particular era, however, and contributed more than thirteen hundred films to this day—the majority of which entertain superficial and denigrating images of Arabs and Muslims. Jack Shaheen, author of the two most comprehensive surveys of Hollywood's portrayal of Arabness, comments:

> From 1896 until today, filmmakers have collectively indicted all Arabs as Public Enemy #1—brutal, heartless, uncivilized religious fanatics and money-mad cultural "others" bent on terrorizing civilized Westerners, especially Christians and Jews. Much has happened since 1896—women's suffrage, the Great Depression, the civil rights movement, two world wars, the Korean, Vietnam, and the Gulf wars, and the collapse of the Soviet Union. Throughout it all, Hollywood's caricature of the Arab has prowled the silver screen. He is there to this day—repulsive and unrepresentative as ever.[24]

Most of the films produced prior to the rise of the United States as a post–World War II superpower and its adoption of an interventionist foreign policy in the Middle East circulated this Orientalist framework. Arabs were depicted as primitive people living in tents between sand dunes or in underdeveloped cities full of dirt and chaos. Backwardness and violence were their innate characteristics. Arab women were sometimes perceived as submissive, covered from top to toe, with no choice but to abide by certain patriarchal rules. At other times, they were viewed through a lens of imagined sensuality, belly dancing seductively or bathing in harems.

The Cold War era defined by US-USSR ideological and cultural battles over the newly decolonized Arab countries fueled conflict and tensions across the Middle East, shaping a new mode of representation, or a new moral geography, that still drew from Hollywood's Orientalist and racialized histories, but was simultaneously influenced by sociopolitical realities of the time. The 1970s, I argue, constituted a critical turning point in the industry's projection of Arabness away from its Orientalist mode of distant Arabia toward another representation mode concerned with the Arab presence in the United States. To make sense of this new mode of representation, I emphasize the complex interplay between US cultural productions and sociopolitical changes of the 1970s; namely, the US interventionist foreign policy in the Middle East, the role of Israeli diasporic filmmakers in the post-1967 Arab-Israeli war to mediate conflating narratives of Arabness and terrorism to American audience, and the growing anxieties around the presence of Arab immigrant and Arab American activists within the United States.

At the core of this new mode of representation is a vision of the Arab presence in the United States as either a national security concern—as in films like *Black Sunday* (1977), *The Next Man* (1976), *Wrong Is Right* (1982), *Terror in Beverley Hills* (1989), *True Lies* (1994), and *The Siege* (1998)—or a foreign policy concern as in films like *Network* (1976), *Rollover* (1981), *Protocol* (1984), and *Power* (1986). Many of the vilified characters in such films were not depicted as Arab American per se but were denigrated as Arabs whose presence in the United States was presented as out of place. The films mediated a post-1967 US-based vilification sentiment of Arabness as distinctly different from, if not threatening to, American culture and society. Scholars have critiqued the context of anti-Arab racism since the 1970s, a decade that witnessed increasing governmental surveillance of Arabs and Arab Americans wrapped in a media and entertainment culture of vilification.[25]

The lack of interest in featuring Arab American characters in Hollywood prior to the 1970s, and the industry's persistence in portraying the Arab presence in the United States as opposed to portraying Arab American characters since the 1970s, underlines a narrative of minority elision from the nation's collective memory. This elision could be read as a symptom of Hollywood's Orientalist tradition in limiting images of Arabness to the distant Orient. But it also speaks of a troubling racialized discourse that projects whiteness as the epicenter of the American experience and denies minorities such as Arab Americans inclusion in and belonging to American culture. Even efforts to inject characters that may be seen as Arab Americans in such films as *The Siege* (1998), *The Recruit* (2003), *Five Fingers* (2006), *Traitor* (2008), and *Unthinkable* (2010) among others are limited to the characters' pledge of patriotism as American law enforcement agents or intelligence operatives in fighting terrorism. These characters appear no more than racial tokens to communicate the filmmakers' sensitivity to Arab and Muslim Americans in exchange for advancing denigrating portrayals of Arabness and Islam. This book is certainly less invested in labeling individual filmmakers as racist but is critical of how anti-Arab racism has been institutionalized in Hollywood's narrations and images, particularly since the 1970s.

It is also worth noting that the post-1970s era was punctuated by traumatic events such as the Munich attacks (1972), the Iranian hostage crisis (1979–81), the hijacking of TWA Flight 847 (1985), 9/11, and the emergence of ISIS, which served as backgrounds to Hollywood's conflation of Arabness and Islam as interchangeable identities. As this book underlines, the boundaries of religion and ethnicity are blurred in many of the films produced since the 1970s. The films are replete with representations of Arabs and Muslims that ultimately extend to Arab Americans and Muslim Americans as minorities and racialized communities whose Americanness is not recognized in the industry's narratives of American culture and citizenship. As Islam became the post–Soviet Union threat in the US media during the 1990s, to echo Edward Said's critique,[26] 9/11 opened the doors even more widely to Islamophobic portrayals that cannot be divorced from anti-Arab portrayals of the 1970s. Both forms of anti-Arab racism and Islamophobia in Hollywood appear to function within a similar nationalist continuum of alienation at the core of this book's critique. While the historical narratives of Arab and Muslim experiences in the United States are distinctly different, as Sally Howell illustrates in *Old Islam in Detroit*, the trajectories of Hollywood's conflated representations are similar. Not only do anxieties around globalization, migration, and geopolitics play a key role in such representations, but the industry also preserves a shared sense of Orientalist and racialized repertoire of a troubling imagery, albeit presented in evolved forms throughout history.

Advancing this reductive mode of representation is not exclusive to the film industry. Some scholars have critiqued the way in which news reporting cultivates Americans' fear of Arabs and Muslims,[27] while others have underlined the sensational role of television, literature, music, comics, cartoons, and other cultural forms in reducing

Arabness to a site of xenophobia.[28] What is more troubling is how the repertoire of Arabness in US collective memory has moved beyond the realm of consumerist cultural production, and normalized, if not legitimized, the government's so-called "war on terror" measures of racial profiling, preventive detention, and torture. This is the context in which both Quinnell's association of Obama with Arabness and (ironically) McCain's rejection of that association, as described at the beginning of this section, operate to locate Arab Americans outside the parameters of US belonging.

Limits of Postcoloniality in Egyptian Cinema

The popularity of the Egyptian cinema is historically rooted in its well-funded grandeur as the most established and prolific filmmaking industry in the Arab world. The country had eleven movie theaters as early as 1908 that featured foreign films, most notably works of the French filmmakers, the Lumière brothers.[29] The year 1909 saw the earliest Egyptian short film and newsreel productions. Prior to 1922, the year marking the country's independence from the British protectorate system, Egyptian full-length feature films entertained a strong European influence, especially that of French and Italian cinemas.[30] Muhammad Karim was reportedly the first Egyptian to appear in such films, specifically the Italian-produced *el-Zuhoor el-Qatila* (Deadly Flowers, 1918) and *Sharaf el-Badawi* (Honor of the Bedouin, 1918).[31] It was not until Talaat Harb, the founder of Misr Bank, established Sharikat Misr li-l-Sinima wa-l-Tamthil (Egyptian Company for Cinema and Performance) in 1925 and Studio Misr (Egypt Studio) in 1935 that cinema in the country gained local resources for film production. The full-length feature films *Layla* (1927) and *Qubla fi Esaḥra* (Kiss in the Desert, 1927) were arguably the most recognized attempts to articulate the cinema's search for independence.[32] Since then, the Egyptian filmmaking industry has produced more than four thousand films, composing nearly three-quarters of the entire Arab film repertoire. It is thus fitting that Egyptian cinema has been dubbed, variously, the "Hollywood of the East," the "Hollywood of the Nile," and "Arab Hollywood."[33]

Choosing Egyptian cinema for this book does not necessarily dismiss the tremendous growth of other Arab cinemas but serves as a case study that calls upon other researchers to similarly explore articulations of Arab Americans in other sites of Arabic cultural production. The Arab world has witnessed unprecedented growth in film festivals since 2000.[34] Although independent films presented at such forums continue to face distribution challenges that make it difficult for them to compete with the level of viewership enjoyed by mainstream Egyptian films, the full spectrum of films reveals the heterogeneity of Arab voices and perspectives. Notwithstanding the popularity of the Egyptian dialect, recent decades have also seen a growing number of films featuring other Levantine, Khaliji, and Moroccan dialects, thanks to the growth of Syrian drama, dubbing of Turkish and Indian television series, Lebanese shows, Khaliji television programs, and Moroccan music.

Yet even contemporary Egyptian cinema faces several obstacles undercutting the quantity and quality of its production and the level of its reception, especially regarding films with a critical edge. Egyptian filmmakers must grapple with licensing bureaucracy, state censorship, celebrity wage hikes, production monopoly, and copyright piracy. The country's sociopolitical conditions and the annual Ramadan competition for television shows and dramas present additional pressures for the cinema's growth. Still, Egypt retains currency in filmmaking as it continues to attract commercial production and invite state-regulated contributions from Arab actors, directors, and producers.[35] Therefore, my choice of Egyptian cinema is not so much guided by an argument that the industry is necessarily the only representative site of Arabs; rather, the industry's powerful role in making the most money, producing the most films, and attracting the most viewers warrants analysis as a visible medium with widely circulated products.

Another factor making Egyptian cinema so analytically compelling is the nature of its postcoloniality. Just as state nationalism shapes the distinct sociopolitical character of every Arab country, making the very term "Arab world" contestable, so too do Egyptian filmmakers package their postcolonial critiques in a specifically Egyptian nationalist framework.[36] Successive Egyptian governments have promoted versions of state nationalism to compete with Arabist and Islamist narratives, resulting in attempts to coerce and marginalize Islamists since the 1960s and Arabists since the 1970s. The regimes of both Sadat (1970–81) and Mubarak (1981–2011) shifted emphasis from Arabist to state nationalist interests, in contrast with the relatively more repressive anti-Islamist attitudes of Nasser's (1956–70) and Sisi's (2013–present) regimes. Two critical moments solidified state nationalism in Egypt. The first occurred when President Sadat's *infitah* (Open Door Policy) led to embracing neoliberal politics and culminated in normalizing relations with Israel. This alienated both Arabists and Islamists and positioned a minority of elites as representative of westernization in Egyptian collective memory. The second moment unfurled over the course of 2011, as Egyptians first poured into the streets to demand the ousting of Mubarak, then elected Egypt's first Islamist president Mohamed Morsi, only to see his regime toppled a year later by an outraged military entourage dedicated to promoting an exclusionary state nationalist narrative.[37]

Prior to the solidification of this state nationalist narrative in the 1970s, Egypt played a dynamic role in popularizing *al-'uruba* (Arabism), the rhetorical appeal to a pan-Arab vision of unifying all Arab nation-states into a single political entity.[38] It was in Cairo that the Arab League was first established in 1945.[39] President Nasser's defiant nationalization of the Suez Canal and resilience against attacks from Israeli, British, and French forces in 1956, in addition to his eloquent pan-Arab speeches, resurrected hopes of *al-'uruba* among Arabs as part of their postcolonial search for autonomy and independence.[40] There was even unity between Egypt and Syria in 1958 in what came to be known as the United Arab Republic. Nasser's populism impacted Egyptian cinema, which was nationalized during his rule, and presented Egypt as the champion of pan-Arab rights and rejecter of Western influence. Youssef Chahine, a distinguished Egyptian film director with a repertoire of forty-four films, captured this pan-Arab fervor in several works.

According to the author of *The Arab National Project in Youssef Chahine's Cinema*, Chahine "embodies a rich and critical survey of the

2. Ahmed Mazhar plays the role of Saladin in *el-Naṣer Salah-e-Din* (Saladin the Victorious, 1963). © Lotus Films.

social, political, and cultural history of Egypt and the Arab world in the twentieth century."[41] Chahine's film *el-Naṣer Salah-e-Din* (Saladin the Victorious, 1963) is an iconic example of his cinematic mission to appeal to the unrealized Arab dream of unity.[42] In this film, the director resurrected the inspirational story of the Kurdish Muslim warrior Saladin and his struggle to emancipate the Holy Land from the Crusaders as a means to present a glorified image of Nasser as leader of the Arab postcolonial struggle for autonomy (figure 2).[43] "We need to be cognizant of our Arab national identity," stressed Chahine. "Nasser realized that, and reminded us that being Arab is what unites us."[44] The film replaced references to the Muslim-Christian religious conflict with those of the Arab struggle for unity against Western hegemony. This appropriation of an Islamic hero through parallels with Nasser's leadership made Egypt stand in for all pan-Arab postcolonial autonomy. Although communicated in standard Arabic, the film's use of the Egyptian accent invited audiences to link Egypt (and its president) with the cause of Arab nationalism writ large.

Nasser's pan-Arab project was first shaken by disunity within the United Arab Republic in 1961, and then collapsed in the aftermath of the Arab-Israeli War (1967) and subsequent Israeli territorial expansion,[45] as did many other attempts to produce unity among Arab nation-states.[46] Still, the word "Arab" was incorporated into the official titles of several countries like the United Arab Emirates, the Arab Republic of Egypt, the Syrian Arab Republic, the Yemen Arab Republic, and the Great Socialist People's Libyan Arab Jamahiriya.[47] Although concepts such as *al-'uruba* (Arabism), *al-huwwiyya al-'arabiyya* (Arab identity), and *al-qawmiyya al-'arabiyya* (Arab nationalism) lived on, their currency retained a certain value primarily at the level of popular culture.[48] Popular culture, declares Andrew Hammond, "has finally succeeded in bringing the peoples of the region together where fifty years of politics failed."[49]

The founding of Al-Jazeera in 1994 ushered in a new era of Arabism that transcended state-nationalist media and rallied around transnational issues and concerns.[50] The rapid growth of satellite-based television networks meant unprecedented levels of access to the audience of an estimated 350 million Arabs.[51] An establishment like the Saudi-funded Middle East Broadcasting Center (popularly known as MBC), for instance, has captivated the imagination of many Arabs and their diasporas in Europe and the Americas, with such popular contest shows as *Maḥbūb al-'Arab* (Arab Idol), *Lil 'Arab Mawaheb* (Arabs Got Talent), and *Aḥla Ṣawt* (The Voice). The shows reinforce a notion of "Arab homeland" that emphasizes the interconnectedness of an imagined Arab identity.[52] A diverse field of scholars in Arab cultural studies has investigated these new interlocutors of Arabism,[53] from analyses of poetry, film, media, and television to readings of cartoons, music, and posters.[54] In short, Arab popular culture has become a rich site for Arabs to reimagine unity in an increasingly divided Arab world.

In this context Egyptian cinema, much like other sites of popular culture, echoes a pan-Arab message, primarily through critiques of Israeli and American politics in the region, and markets the Egyptian dialect as a lingua franca for resistance. Despite serious linguistic differences within the Arab world, cultural works produced in the Egyptian dialect often share a level of self-awareness regarding the dialect's role in historically mediating a sense of pan-Arab consciousness. While modern standard Arabic serves as Arabs' official lingua franca, the Egyptian dialect owes its popularity to the prominence of its music and cinema industries.[55] The popular appreciation of the operetta *el-Ḥilm el-'Arabi* (The Arab Dream, 1998), which featured the contribution of ninety-five Arab artists, was in part a result of its Egyptian lyrics.[56] Its popularity was also informed by its appeal to *al-'uruba* rhetoric, especially in light of a common grievance against the Israeli oppression of Palestinians.[57] Egyptian filmmakers rely heavily on these two elements: the linguistic fluidity of the Egyptian dialect and allegorical references to a common Arab critique of US imperialism.[58]

Similarly, Egyptian filmmakers often engage, allegorically, with Islamist critiques of the West, ever since such critiques flourished in the 1970s at the intersection of el-Ikhwān el-Muslimūn (the Muslim Brotherhood) and the ultraconservative wave of el-Jamā'ah el-Islamiyyah (the Islamic Group)—the latter of which is often seen as a movement of "postcolonial puritanism."[59] Both trends shared a common interest in promoting Islam as a viable sociopolitical alternative in the Arab world and redefining Arab Muslims as part of the Muslim *ummah* (transnational Muslim community).[60] Unlike the anticolonial critique of late nineteenth-century Islamic liberalism spearheaded by intellectuals like Muhammad Abdu (1849–1905) or even the subsequent Islamist critique of the 1920s–1940s that led to the el-Ikhwān el-Muslimūn's foundation, Islamist critique in Egypt since the 1950s has had to contend, sometimes violently, with internal corruption, hypocrisy, and betrayal often framed as a proxy for neocolonialism.[61]

Since the 1970s, Egypt has witnessed an increase in religiosity that has challenged the country's liberal and secular forces and produced Islamist echoes across the Arab world. Estimates of mosques built by *rijal el-kheer* (men of goodness) rose significantly from around 20,000 in 1970, to 46,000 in 1981, and then 140,000 in the mid-1990s.[62]

Nasser's prosecution of Islamists only fueled religious-based sociopolitical grievances and facilitated the radical rhetoric popularized by Sayyid Qutb (1906–66), whose death sentence assured his status as a martyr, at least among his followers. Radical circles embraced Qutb's sensational writings as authoritative calls for Muslims in Egypt and other Arab countries to adopt political Islam as a revolutionary defense against the corrupt forces of Western liberalism and secularism.[63] The Arab military defeat to Israel in 1967 contributed to the rise of political Islam as a resolution to Israeli aggressions. Later, the success of the Islamic Revolution in Iran in 1979 offered hope for Islamists in Egypt engaged in antistate struggles.

In the meantime, three elements of Sadat's *infitah* policy inadvertently facilitated the growth of Islamist consciousness. First, his administration curtailed the influence of Nasserites' socialist demands by leveraging the Islamist camp.[64] This was brought about by releasing prisoners, empowering student organizations, and recognizing Islamist civic and political engagement. Second, adopting neoliberal economics dealt a serious blow to state-sponsored support and left the lower classes vulnerable. This forced many Egyptians to seek refuge in the religiously conservative Gulf labor market, particularly Saudi Arabia, and return with money and passion to change their society.[65] Third, Sadat's policy inaugurated an era of openness to Western political, economic, and cultural influence. Although the Egyptian army succeeded in challenging the Israeli army by crossing the Suez Canal and advancing into the Sinai Peninsula in 1973 under Sadat's leadership, Islamists' support for Sadat fractured when he suddenly departed from Nasser's postcolonial resistance narrative by normalizing relations with Israel and siding with the United States in its Cold War against the Soviet Union.[66] This fracture not only resulted in Sadat's assassination in 1981, but also provided Islamists with the opportunity to consolidate their antigovernment protests with rhetoric that pushed for more societal religiosity. This was especially visible in their critiques of capitalism and Western commodification and consumption.

In order to resolve this inherited crisis, President Mubarak adopted a different approach. His government was forced, as Karin van

Nieuwkerk points out, to "Islamicize its policy" in order to sustain its prosecution of Islamists.[67] This formula granted the government the power to enforce stability by maintaining a secular-religious equilibrium. It constrained artistic expression to state-sanctioned portrayals of Islamists while absorbing a more discernable religious pressure codified through *raqabat el-shari'* (street censorship). Meanwhile, Egyptian filmmakers were forced to deal with concerns from repentant actors and the demands of an increasingly reserved audience to censor nudity and excessive displays of affection in commercial films that reached their peak during the 1980s.[68] This filmmaking approach was a cultural means to win "the contest over the place of Islam in the social and political life."[69] Subsequently, Egyptian cultural producers had to navigate both state and street forms of censorship in their search for autonomy amid political and religious dictations.[70] Echoes of this process materialized in Egyptian cinema through the double-layered tendency to embrace the Islamist narrative of spatial morality (i.e., allocating morality along a perceived division between Islam and the West), while also avoiding presenting Islamists as public agents of change. Fears of a rising religious power threatening to rewrite the country's social contract and reject artistic creativity pushed Egyptian filmmakers even closer to Mubarak's and Sisi's regimes.

The post–Arab Spring Islamist experience in Egypt, the most populous Arab country, galvanized much attention in the Arab world and rendered it ever more divided. The year 2012 witnessed unprecedented proliferation of Islamist political parties and media outlets ranging from moderate to ultraconservative, with all subject to rapidly shifting coalitions. The same year witnessed Islamist control of the two houses of the Parliament and the government. Islamists dominated elections to Maglis el-Sha'b (the People's Assembly) with an impressive win of 71.5 percent of the seats. Of the 180 seats available for election to the Maglis el-Shura (the Consultative Council), Islamists won by 83.3 percent. And most notably, the Muslim Brotherhood's presidential candidate, Morsi el-'Ayyat, was elected president of Egypt.

Islamist supporters demanded the drafting of a new constitution based on *shari'a* (Islamic way of life) and rallied behind emerging private media that circulated a polarizing rhetoric of citizenship and identity. Confirming fears that the rise of Islamism was a threat to artistic creativity and cultural production, popular actors like Adel Imam and Ilham Shahin faced criticism, even litigation, for their alleged role in propagating anti-Islamic messages throughout their careers. Such rapid changes intensified a sense of polarization in Egyptian society. The Supreme Council of Armed forces (SCAF), which represented a sixty-year-old military system and was responsible for ousting Mubarak, gained more influence through a series of constitutional declarations, Supreme Constitutional Court legal battles, shifting coalitions, and mass demonstrations. In response, Morsi solidified his power by dissolving the SCAF, rushing an Islamist constitution, and ignoring calls for inclusion. The military, with the support of the grassroots movement *Tamarod* (rebellion) and the country's liberal and secular political coalition, the National Salvation Front, staged a coup, effectively ending Islamist rule.[71]

The ousting of Morsi would not have been possible without the popular demonization of Islamists already established through Egyptian films—both state- and foreign-funded—since the 1990s. Unlike Hollywood, which blatantly portrays Islam as a source of terrorism and Muslims as crazed terrorists, Egyptian cinema features nuanced portrayals of terrorism by highlighting the sociopolitical conditions that foster violence in the name of Islam. Moreover, Egyptian cinema also venerates Islam as a peaceful religion that defines many of Egypt's traditions.[72] Nevertheless, even the nuanced representations in films like *el-'Erhabi* (The Terrorist, 1994), *Tuyur el-Ḍalām* (The Birds of Darkness, 1995), *el-'Abwaab el-Moghlaqa* (The Closed Doors, 1999), *Ḥein Maysara* (Until Better Times, 2007), and *el-Gezira 2* (The Island 2, 2014) are limiting and limited.[73] In these examples the filmmakers honor Muslims but vilify Islamists, who use the religion for political purposes, as primarily violent and either trapped in a dichotomy between modernity and primitivity or defined by narratives of

3. Sheik Ga'far (Khaled Saleh), the leader of a lawless group of el-Raḥalah (travelers) meant to represent Islamists in dangerous terms in *el-Gezira 2* (The Island 2, 2014). © El Massah Video Film.

lower-middle-class "misery and confusion," to quote Walter Armbrust.[74] In *el-Gezira 2*, for instance, Sheik Ga'far (Khaled Saleh) leads a lawless group whose dress and thoughts appear different from, if not threatening to, those of Egyptian urbanites and supporters of the Egyptian state narrative (figure 3). Egyptian filmmaking thus subverts Hollywood's shallow portrayals only to the extent dictated by the country's government-endorsed understandings of Muslims and Islamists. This approach is a politicized means to claim Islam while vilifying Islamists, who seek social and political change through Islam, as agents of violence.

Examining the configurations of the Arab American image in Egyptian cinema requires an understanding of the industry's national parameters of postcoloniality. Filmmakers in Egyptian cinema subject their imagery of Arab Americans to certain national imaginations of the United States, which might bear Arabist and Islamist marks but are presented through state-endorsed, Egyptian terms. This postcolonial framework reflects "the unequal and uneven forces of cultural representation involved in the contest for political and social authority within the modern world order."[75] As *Arab Americans in Film* demonstrates, this postcolonial framework, however, projects Egypt first and foremost as a national site in which Arabness and Islam collide in critiquing Americanness and celebrating Egyptianness, leaving essentially no space for complex imagery of Egyptian Americans or Arab Americans.

The Egyptian cinema, I argue, fails to navigate away from the Western colonial heritage of national narration and binaristic thinking. It fails to adopt representations that move beyond mere reversal of Hollywood's imagination of Americanness and Arabness and unsettle imaginations of Arab Americans beyond the national boundaries of the United States and Egypt. The Arab American characters in Egyptian films are mainly presented as either glorified Egyptians or denigrated Americans. While this imagery is presented through nuanced critiques of the filmmakers' perceptions of US corrupting materialism, interventionist foreign policy, and alienating culture, there remains a challenge in the industry to incorporate new imagery that complicates its audience's consumption of the images of good versus bad Arab Americans.

Arab American Cultural Citizenship

"Citizenship is both a cultural and anti-cultural institution," argues Leti Volpp, because it "positions itself as oppositional to specific cultures, even as it is constituted by quite specific cultural values."[76] Consider, for instance, the systematic forms of exclusion of minorities in a multicultural democracy like the United States in which citizenship both as a legal institution and a realm of cultural belonging has been deeply rooted in racialized hierarchies. The discriminatory nature of such hierarchies has responded to decades of minority struggles and evolved from defining American citizenship, both legally or culturally, in terms of whiteness to acknowledging the legal citizenship of minorities but not without sustaining control in defining who is to be considered an American in a cultural sense. It is in this context that the term "cultural citizenship" has emerged as an important conceptual tool that captures minority struggles for inclusion.

With the Latino/a American experiences in mind, Renato Rosaldo defines cultural citizenship as "the right to be different (in terms of race, ethnicity, or native language) with respect to the norms of the dominant national community, without compromising one's right to belong, in the sense of participating in the nation-state's democratic processes."[77] In this context, cultural citizenship is a "deliberate oxymoron," to borrow Rosaldo's word choice, since it emphasizes a minority community's right to their own cultural difference and their demand for belonging in the country's national narrative of Americanness.[78] Nadine Naber, for example, explores how the cultural citizenship of Arab Americans has been configured through four paradoxes that have rendered them as "ambiguous insiders": Arab American complex communities are presented as a monolith; they are racialized as white but are treated as a people of color; they are racialized through religion (Islam) rather than biology; and their structures of identification that often stress religion are often dismissed by the US racial-ethnic structures of identification.[79]

Anthropologist Aihwa Ong offers an important definition of cultural citizenship that further stresses how the term not only establishes distinctions between legal and cultural aspects of belonging but also serves as a reminder of how citizenship itself is a sociocultural construct. She defines cultural citizenship as a "dual process of self-making and being-made within webs of power linked to the nation-state and civil society"; the process itself, Ong stresses, is produced "out of negotiating the often ambivalent and contested relations with the state and its hegemonic forms that establish the criteria of belonging within a national population and territory."[80] While many scholars have examined cultural citizenship in the US national context,[81] some have explored ways to make it possible for our understanding of the very concept of citizenship to be transnationalized.[82] A few scholars have further engaged with what citizenship and belonging might look like for South Asian Americans or Arab Americans seeking modes of thinking, narration, activism, and cultural expression that reflect their identities and experiences—seeking, in short, cultural citizenship within a transnational sense.[83] And *Arab Americans in Film* joins this effort by mapping depictions of Arab American cultural citizenship in Hollywood, Egyptian, and Arab American cinemas, effectively adding a fifth paradox to Naber's above-mentioned conception of Arab Americans as "ambiguous insiders"—one that considers how Arab Americans wrestle with being simultaneously embraced and alienated in both American and Arabic narrations of belonging.

The contribution of this book's comparative framework in relation to the issue of Arab American cultural citizenship is twofold. First, the exercise of comparing Hollywood and Egyptian cinemas in the book's first two chapters opens the door for examining two dominant sites of cultural imagination in US and Arab collective memories. Chapter 1 critiques Hollywood's depictions of Arab American foreignness by examining two primary representation patterns since the 1970s. One pattern developed parallel to, and sometimes in coordination with, Israeli productions of "Arabs as terrorists," a trend triggered by the heavily televised tragedy known as the Munich massacre (1972). The other pattern reintroduced early images of Arabia but inflected now with new images associated with the energy crisis at the time, and the subsequent fear of Arab petrodollar investments in the United States. Chapter 2 critiques Egyptian cinema's nationalist use of classed, gendered, and generational binaries in imagining Arab Americans as either Egyptians or Americans since the 1990s. By critiquing how the two cinematic sites produce limiting understandings of Arab American subjectivity, I emphasize the importance of considering the types of alienation that Arab Americans experience in the United States and beyond. This allows for the opportunity to reconceptualize the issue of Arab American cultural citizenship as one of struggle against dominant, often dismissive, narratives of belonging in the United States and the Arab world.

Second, the book's analysis of post-9/11 films in Hollywood and Egyptian cinemas and incorporation of Arab American films offers readers the opportunity to learn about existing disruptive efforts to depict Arab American characters with a sense of cultural citizenship defined by nationalism's sustained relevance in today's globalized world and the solidifying display of hybridity in diasporic communities.

Chapter 3 analyzes the character of Samir Horn (Don Cheadle) in Jeffrey Nachmanoff's *Traitor* (2008), specifically considering his multilayered sense of cultural citizenship informed by the intersection of his Arab, Black, Muslim, and American identities in the context of the US "war on terror." His character, I argue, not only collapses the good Muslim/bad Muslim binary but also traverses Arab/African, national/international, domestic/foreign, and local/empire binaries, reflecting an important depiction of cultural citizenship that defies singular narration or categorization.

Chapter 4 offers a close reading of the two Arab diasporic characters in Adel Adeeb's *Laylat el-Baby Doll* (The Baby Doll Night, 2008): Layla Khoury (Ghada Abdulrazeq) and Hossam al-Ashry (Mahmoud Abdel Aziz). Layla is an Arab American of Jewish background who falls victim to Israeli aggressions in the occupied territories. Hossam is an Arab Muslim whose life is caught between New York and Egypt. The transnational space that Layla and Hossam occupy allows a form of diasporic activism that reflects, shapes, and intervenes in the polarizing US and Arab narratives, represented by other characters in the film. The significance of this portrayal lies in the film's lack of emphasis on these characters' Americanness but captures their experiences as disjunctures at the crossroads of US and Arab geopolitics and diasporic agency.

Chapter 5 explores a post-9/11 growing Arab American filmic trend that is invested in narratives of Arab American cultural citizenship, particularly in relation to their post-9/11 struggles and aspirations. Unlike Hollywood's films that imagine Arab immigrant characters as threatening aliens or homegrown terrorist suspects, and the films of Egyptian cinema that portray them as disillusioned with the American dream or the embodiment of an alternative "Egyptian Dream," this Arab American filmmaking trend, I argue, presents Arab immigrant characters seeking to fulfill their own aspirations in the United States but not without providing insightful critiques of the American dream notion as a celebratory site of inclusion in American society. Hesham Issawi's *AmericanEast* (2007), Cherien Dabis's *Amreeka* (2009), and Sam Kadi's *The Citizen* (2012) are the three films analyzed in this chapter. In them, the lead Arab immigrant characters strive variously to fulfill material desires (e.g., houses, jobs, cars), and while the films advance such aspirations, they are also critical of the nationalist limitations of the American dream in defining meanings of belonging to and inclusion in the United States. The films do so by pointing to the Arab immigrants' disadvantaged navigation of both a US racialized system and a post-9/11 reality that equally challenge their access to American cultural citizenship.

Toward that end, I define Arab American cultural citizenship as an ever-changing amalgamation of thoughts, attitudes, and positions that result from Arab Americans' cross-cultural and multidimensional positionality. This understanding is empowering in the sense that it defies hegemonic and homogenous understandings of Arab Americans, whether in the United States or the Arab world. What defines Arab Americans, in this case, becomes less about how others define them and more about how Arab American individuals define themselves. It is a chance to decenter nationalism and render it less important while acknowledging that nationalism is not irrelevant in today's globalized yet heavily policed borders and populist agendas. The book's conclusion speculates about how Arab American films might further capture this sense of cultural citizenship.

Far from suggesting that every Arab American ought to be understood in transnational terms, this book acknowledges that Arab American individuals retain their own agency in defining themselves in relation to the broader US and Arab spectrum they occupy. The Arab American community, after all, is a community of communities, extremely diverse in multiple respects—gender, class, sexuality, citizenship status, country of origin, migration generation, language, politics, etc.[84] In this way, not all Arab Americans necessarily consider themselves as part of a diaspora, nor do they all experience cultural citizenship in the same way. In a word, there is no singular notion of Arab Americanness since it is rooted in experience rather than geography. Of course, the very term "Arab American" implies dispersed communities across the Americas with notable presence in the United States, Canada, Argentina, Chile, Brazil, Colombia, Venezuela, and

Mexico.[85] Narrowing my focus to Arab Americans in the United States reflects, but also inadvertently reinforces, the hegemonic place of the United States in the Americas. It is important to acknowledge this as both problematic and valuable in terms of speaking to the experience of a central group. In this context, this book examines the issue of Arab American cultural citizenship in terms of possibilities of disrupture to existing nationalist narratives (e.g., US and Egyptian) in imagining meanings of Arab American belonging.

In effect, *Arab Americans in Film* is a critique of how filmmakers use limiting understandings of Arab American cultural citizenship as lenses to mediate existing national and diasporic sentiments. While dominant Hollywood and Egyptian films leverage the "national," I trace emerging attempts to disrupt this narration through an emphasis on the transnational nature of Arab Americans' experiences. The book does not claim that Hollywood, Egyptian, and Arab American filmmakers necessarily produce new modes of Arab American belonging or new experiences of citizenship for Arab Americans. Rather, the filmmakers are primarily occupied with reflecting already existing and developed sentiments about Arab American cultural citizenship.

It is also worth noting that Arab American cultural citizenship, as proposed in this book, is not necessarily predicated in nationalist legal frameworks. Holding a copy of a birth certificate, a passport, or a naturalization document, for example, is not a prerequisite for defining one's Americanness. While it is important to acknowledge the legal and national boundaries that exist around Arab Americans, as well as the articulations of power surrounding them, my use of "cultural citizenship" is primarily concerned with the full articulations of one's various cultural affiliations. So, in a sense, being undocumented in the United States does not necessarily empty one's sense of belonging to the country. While the legal challenge will always remain a barrier, it becomes possible, at least culturally, to disrupt rigid narrations of identity. That said, the terms "Arab Americans" and "Arab immigrants" will often be used throughout this book. The use of these terms does not suggest that Arab immigrants cannot be American citizens but rather underscores the overlapping yet distinctive elements of the two identities and the set of legal, social, and cultural connotations that surrounds each.

Arab Americans in Film examines Arab American cultural citizenship at the interplay of nation, culture, and politics. Rooted in the Foucauldian understanding of knowledge as political and the Gramscian notion of "hegemony" as a controlling mechanism,[86] the book's comparative framework conceptualizes the rhetoric surrounding Arab American Otherness by capturing works and narratives of US and Arab identity-based and morally defined spheres. One sphere celebrates the uniqueness of the American experience in world history and stresses its global moral distinction (read, American exceptionalism).[87] This sphere reproduces the imperative of white universality and entitlement that has confronted people of color throughout US cultural memory—and, I argue, subjected Arab Americans' cultural citizenship to alienation. The other sphere offers an imagined postcolonial space for Arabs that invokes nostalgic appeals to a triumphant and unified Arab world that resists imperialism and promotes its own nationalist as well as exclusionary imagery of Arab Americans accordingly.[88] The former sphere legitimizes US imperial advances in the Arab world, while the latter counters, though reductively, by offering Arabs the agency to voice their resistance.

As a case study that contributes to the "transnational turn" in American Studies, *Arab Americans in Film* also foregrounds the crucial role of comparison in an interdisciplinary investigation of the Arab American image and its interlocutors.[89] It examines Arab American cultural citizenship within and beyond the mutual production of discourses about Arabness in Hollywood and Americanness in Egyptian cinema. This framework acknowledges the transnational context of Hollywood's consolidation of US-Israeli economic and political anxieties into a cultural sense of fear against Arabs and Muslims in the United States. It likewise foregrounds the role of Egyptian filmmakers in disciplining the multinational nature of their market into an Egyptian nationalist narrative of Arab Americans as either glorified Arabs or denigrated Americans. In both the United States and Egypt, the respective film industries circulate forms of nationalist rhetoric that inhibit complex articulations of Arab American subjectivity and authenticity. The book points to this limitation and conceptualizes a form of cultural citizenship that transcends both the citizen-terrorist paradox in Hollywood productions and the sensational binaries of Egyptian cinema. It also recognizes Arab American self-representation as a critical, albeit too often missing, component in the US and Arab clashes of identity narratives.

1

Hollywood's Portrayals of Arab Americans

POPULAR CULTURE in the United States functions through sensational and ratings-based entertainment. It also promotes an important frame of reference for cultural citizenship and national belonging in the life of "cultural citizens."[1] It serves as an ideological state apparatus, to echo French philosopher Louis Althusser, guiding citizens through an acculturation process that homogenizes their own subjectivity.[2] Cognizant of Renato Rosaldo's demands for an emancipatory sense of cultural citizenship that acknowledges minorities' rights "to be different and to belong in a participatory democratic sense," this chapter critiques Hollywood as a site that has rather enunciated a hegemonic sense of American cultural citizenship.[3] There is a tradition in this film industry that normalizes what it means to be American in ways that alienate Arab and Muslim Americans along with indigenous Americans, Latino/a Americans, Asian Americans, Jewish Americans, and African Americans, among other minorities.[4] What is problematic, in other words, is how the industry's hegemonic conceptions of cultural Otherness contribute to its filmmakers' "cultural authority" in defining "good citizenship" and "the very meaning of national identity."[5]

Hollywood's conflation of Arabness and Islam is further exacerbated by its filmmakers' consistent portrayals of Arabs and Muslims through binaries that set them apart from Americans—good versus evil, civilized versus backward, peaceful versus violent, and so on. There is already a record of works that examines such representations and criticizes the industry's repertoire of Arab stereotypes and images.[6] This chapter contributes to this record as it delves into Hollywood's history and examines its role in defining the cultural citizenship of Arab Americans. It focuses on the 1970s because this decade, I argue, constitutes a critical turning point in the industry's projections of Arabness, building on an Orientalist heritage centered around an imagined Arabia but deeply influenced by US and Arab geopolitics at the time. This chapter does not dismiss the relevance of the US Orientalist discourse in shaping today's polarizing imagination of Arab Americans. Rather, it underscores the importance of examining the post–World War II intricate interplay of US cultural productions, geopolitical challenges in the Middle East, and US sociopolitical changes during the 1970s—phenomena that cannot be read simply through Edward Said's influential Orientalist framework.[7] The boundaries of this interplay, I argue, are shaped by the US conflation of foreign policy and antiterrorism concerns, the role of Israeli filmmakers in presenting their version of the Arab-Israeli conflict to American audiences, and the rising anxieties around the increasing presence of Arab immigrants in the United States with a deep commitment to activism and agency.

As discussed in this book's introduction, the 1970s saw a departure from Hollywood's earlier Orientalist filmmaking that consumed fetishized and exotic imagery of the Orient while simultaneously remaining distant from it. Films produced prior to the 1970s, as this chapter demonstrates, mostly advanced stereotypical images of Arabs as part of a distant landscape, often desert-like or underdeveloped. So, space played a crucial role in enunciating the contrast between Arabs and Americans, which further developed through binaristic images of Arab and American as morally opposite identities. A key characteristic of such early portrayals was that they were produced within what Melani McAlister characterized as a "moral geography" for Americans so they could both experience the pleasures of the Orient (e.g., romance, exotic milieus, and harem sexual allure) while spatially and culturally distancing themselves from it.[8]

Films of the 1970s, however, embraced new sensational images of the Arab presence in the United States and filtered them through narratives of alienness and terrorism. This transition was rooted in two primary patterns of representation. The first pattern functioned alongside Israeli productions of "Arabs as terrorists" and was sparked first by the Munich massacre (1972), resulting in racialized, often caricatured, imagery of Arabs in the United States. The second pattern retooled early images of Arabia (i.e., desert, tents, sheiks, harems, and daggers) and imparted new constructions dictated by the 1970s energy crisis and the emerging anxieties around Arab petrodollar investments in the United States.

It is worth noting that the post-1970s representation patterns surveyed in this chapter often lacked clear distinctions in their characters' identification: Arabs, Arab students, Arab immigrants, or Arab Americans. The blurring of such identities, I argue, is a troubling symptom of a chronic tendency toward minority elision from the nation's collective memory, which denies Arab Americans from belonging to American cultural citizenship. It is not that Arab Americans lack representations per se, but their representations are marred by Hollywood's stereotypes of Arabs and Muslims and presented as "abstractions," to borrow Moustafa Bayoumi's description—that is, as "a foreign-policy issue, an argument on the domestic agenda, a law-enforcement priority, and a point of well-meaning concern."[9] These abstractions, Bayoumi observes, "are floating everywhere in the virtual landscape of the national imagination, as either villains of Islam or victims of Arab culture."[10] Therefore, whether the characters portrayed in many of Hollywood's post-1970s films are meant to be a representation of Arabs, Arab immigrants, or Arab Americans per se does not necessarily invalidate my critique of the industry's problematic imagery of the Arab presence in the United States as one that limits narrations of American cultural citizenship in ways that impact the very imagination of Arab Americans in film.

Rather than offering a comprehensive textual analysis of selected films, this chapter examines the meta-narratives of the post-1970s representation patterns and shows how they confined the Arab presence in the United States between issues of national security and foreign policy. The chapter does not examine post-9/11 portrayals, not because I dismiss the importance of 9/11 in spiking an exclusionary nationalist fervor at the intersection of anti-Arab racism and Islamophobia; rather, chapter 3 engages directly with the post-9/11 changing codes of representation in Hollywood. The two chapters underscore the importance of both the 1970s and 9/11 as two moments along a continuum charting how Hollywood, like other sites of popular culture, has responded to national trauma and shaped collective memory of specific events, such as the Munich massacre (1972), the 1970s energy crisis, the Iranian hostage crisis (1979), the hijacking of TWA Flight 847 (1985), and the attacks of 9/11. All those events constitute moments when, as Marita Sturken puts it, "both the structures and the fractures of a culture are exposed."[11] When filmmakers respond to such moments by conflating Arabs, Muslims, or others mistaken as such into reductive images that deny the feasibility of imagining Arab and Muslim American communities as American cultural citizens, they certainly inscribe powerful narratives of exclusion in the American collective imagination of citizenship and belonging.

History of Arab American Invisibility

The earliest documented film featuring Arab Americans prior to the 1970s is Victor Fleming's full-length feature *Anna Ascends* (1922),[12] an adaptation of Harry Chapman Ford's 1921 play bearing the same title. Both the play and the film offered a symbolic gesture of recognition to the Syrian American community, a moment of seeming triumph that saw Syrian American composer Alexander Maloof write the music for the play and Syrian American civil rights activist Salloum Mokarzel publish the script in the early Arab American journal *Syrian World*.[13] The film's message was not unproblematic however, fetishizing the correlation between acculturation and upward mobility in the life of a Syrian American waitress, Anna Ayyob (Alice Brady). The story starts with Anna working in a coffeehouse owned by a fellow Syrian immigrant, Siad Coury (Edward Durand); both are depicted as

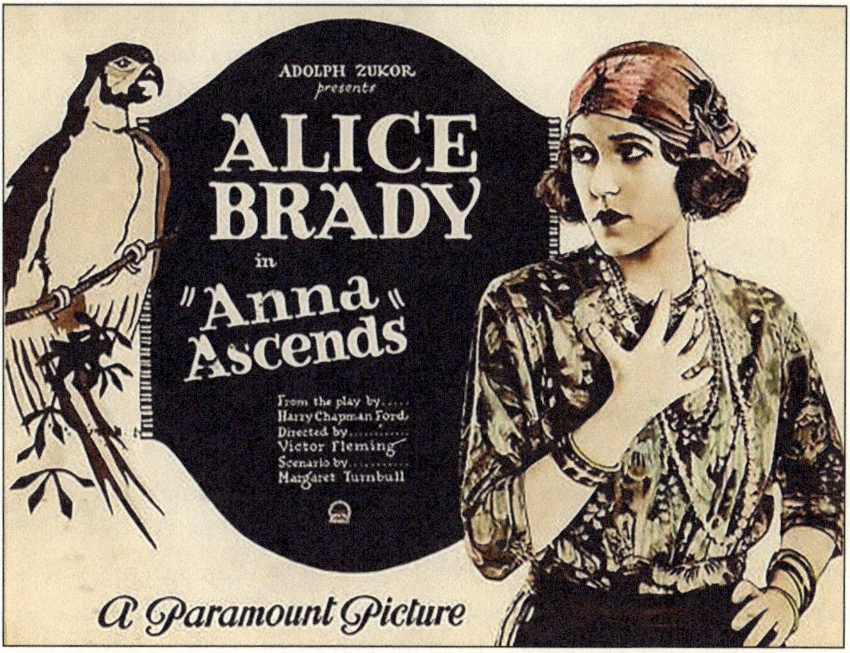

4. A poster of Alice Brady playing Syrian American Anna Ayyob in *Anna Ascends* (1922). © Paramount Pictures.

hardworking ethnics. Often presented in comical ways that enhance their differences, Siad and Anna nonetheless share a desire to Americanize their lives. Siad adopts a "patriotic" but nativist critique of his fellow immigrants while Anna eventually changes her last name to "Adams." The story focuses primarily on Anna as she escapes the "Little Syria" of New York City after a failed rape attempt at work, then emerges a few years later as an "uptown" lady. The film's poster image reveals an elegant-looking and well-dressed Anna (figure 4). Now fluent in English, she is the secretary and lover of a white, upper-class man, Howard Fisk (Robert Ellis).

As Sarah Gualtieri notes, however, Anna's "ascension into whiteness" comes only through a troubling form of assimilation:

> Anna is indeed a strong and likable character, yet her story involves the *effacement* of her Syrian identity, not the retention of it. The

> film's message was antipluralist and assimilationist: Syrians could become Americans, but they would have to lose their language, history, and culture in order to do so. . . . Not only does Anna relinquish her Syrian culture, but she is also tamed in the process. She loses her accent as well as her independence.[14]

The film's assimilation narrative inadvertently touched on one of the concerns among the first wave of Arab immigrants (1880–1924). This wave—estimated at around one hundred thousand immigrants, mostly Arab Christians from Ottoman-ruled Great Syria (modern-day Syria and Lebanon)—was mainly composed of hardworking peddlers with a deep commitment to family and religion.[15] There were some standouts, including renowned literary figures such as Gibran Khalil Gibran, Elia Abu Madi, Ameen Rihani, Mikhail Naimy, and other members of the al-Rābiṭah al-Qalamiyah (Pen League, 1915–32) whose work influenced Arabic literature through what came to be known as *adab al-mahjar* (diaspora literature). One commonality uniting Arab immigrants at the time was an effort to claim whiteness as a means to access citizenship. Fighting for whiteness was central to the US sociopolitical system for more than half a century, as fifty-two court cases were reported between 1878 and 1944 when immigrants of different backgrounds sought inclusion in the racial category.[16] The first Syrian immigrant to succeed legally was Costa Najour in 1909, when Syrians were initially included, albeit precariously, as members of the white race. This was the beginning of a forty-year battle for many Arabs in the United States, culminating notably in 1944 with the legal recognition of Arabs hailing from the Arabian Peninsula as white, in the case of Mohamed Mohriez.[17] Even such seeming victories, however, were haunted by the still "not quite white" cultural status of Arab Americans, who sought to negotiate transnational connections between their new homeland and the land of their ancestry.

Anna Ascends was a production inspired by Ford's own fascination with a Syrian family he befriended in Washington, DC. Ford came to see Syrians as a "people who could read and write probably six thousand years before the northern blue eyes" and "who had a fine culture along with the great Egyptian dynasties."[18] The film's erasure of this cultural richness and its failure to catch on with a mainstream audience, however, reflected a sense of disinterest in mainstreaming the community despite its already viable presence in American society. Only six minutes of the whole film survived. This disinterest was partly informed by the still overwhelming demand for images of the distant Orient and its mystique. "The dearth of American silent films reflecting the Arab immigrants' experience," argues Abdelmajid Hajji, "is largely due to the fact that the Arab in these films is mostly a concept, a trope, a fabrication of the imagination of Westerners."[19]

The Orientalist tropes of Hollywood films have been well documented. Most notably, Jack Shaheen's *Reel Bad Arabs* and *Guilty* provide a comprehensive catalog of images of Arabs and Muslims throughout the industry's history. Shaheen reveals an early Orientalist preoccupation with fantasy and exotic consumption of the Orient as the antithesis of Western civilization. Immediately after its inception, Hollywood entertained its audience with fantasies appropriated from the collection of *One Thousand and One Nights* (also known as *The Arabian Nights*) and its fairy tales such as Aladdin's lamp, Ali Baba's forty thieves, magic carpets, and Sinbad's travels. Silent films like *Ali Baba and the Forty Thieves* (1902), *Aladdin and His Wonder Lamp* (1907), *The Carpet from Bagdad* (1915), *Aladdin from Broadway* (1917), and *Aladdin and the Wonderful Lamp* (1917) featured stereotypes of Arabs typical in many of the adventure films of the time, usually codified through exotic images of the desert, heat, camels, harems, sheiks, primitivity, etc. In the years preceding the release of *Anna Ascends*, the US audience had already seen white men in the desert perform a variety of heroic feats, from rescuing American women held captive by Arab tribesmen in films like *Captured by Bedouins* (1912), *Fire and Sword* (1914), and *Bound in Morocco* (1918); to saving a daughter of a wealthy sheik from enslavement, as in *The Road to Love* (1916); or restoring the order of British rule, as in *Flame of the Desert* (1919). Some films were primarily invested in Western romantic adventurers in the desert, as in *The Garden of Allah* (1916, 1927, and 1936), *A Daughter of the Gods* (1916), and *Barbary Sheep*

(1917). All of these films, along with Egyptian-themed releases such as *The Egyptian Mummy* (1914) and *Cleopatra* (1917, 1934), consumed the Orient yet remained distant from it, a phenomenon that McAlister characterizes as the Orientalist moral geography of the era.[20]

The 1920s saw a solidification of this moral geography as Arabs were repeatedly portrayed as a cultural Other to the Western audience. During the 1920s alone, at least eighty-seven films were produced that underlined this sentiment.[21] One of the more notable examples was *The Sheik* (1921), which featured Rudolph Valentino in the role of sheik Ahmed Ben Hassan and his romantic relationship with British Lady Diana Mayo (Agnes Ayres). In addition to providing Valentino with one of his most popular roles—he went on to star in the sequel, *The Son of the Sheik* (1926) five years later—the film reinscribed the desert as a geography where "the children of Araby dwell in happy ignorance that Civilization has passed them by," as the first screen of *The Sheik* states.[22] Glorifying Western adventurers at the cost of denigrating Arabs was prevalent in films like *Tom Mix in Arabia* (1922), *Maid in Morocco* (1925), and *Made for Love* (1926), in addition to the adaptions of P. C. Wren's adventure fiction bearing the same film titles: *Beau Geste* (1926, 1939, 1966), *Beau Sabreur* (1928), and later *Beau Ideal* (1931), which followed the French Foreign Legion in North Africa.

Still, the industry's stubborn lack of interest in Arab immigrants' narratives during the silent era remains puzzling until one considers the entanglement between US encounters with the Middle East and the restrictive national-origin quota system of the Johnson-Reed Act (1924–65; also known as the Immigration Act of 1924). The US investment in the region's geopolitics did not fully unfold until after World War II, translating into a more sensational deployment of national politics, particularly regarding Israel. Meanwhile, the annual cap on Arab émigrés set by Congress under the Immigration Act significantly controlled the Arab presence in the United States. The numbers reported in March 22, 1929, were meager: Arabian Peninsula (100), Egypt (100), Iraq (Mesopotamia) (100), Palestine (with Trans-Jordan) (British mandate) (100), and Syria and Lebanon (French mandate) (123).[23] The modest second wave of Arab immigrants during the 1940s and 1960s, which consisted primarily of 2,924 Palestinian refugees along with limited arrivals of Arab laborers, did little to disrupt the mainstream narratives around existing Arab American and Arab immigrant communities, which were mostly compartmentalized around ethnic and religious enclaves and remained so until the Arab-Israeli War of 1967.[24]

The development of sound technology in filmmaking during the 1930s did nothing to prompt any changes in Hollywood's repertoire of Arab images. The industry was still dominated by early Orientalist imaginations of "Arabia" as a setting for heroic adventurers to save white heroines from the captivity of evil Arabs, in such 1930s films as *Chandu the Magician* (1932), *Harem Scarem* (1932), *The Mummy* (1932), and *Kiss of Araby* (1933). Even Mickey Mouse dared to rescue Minnie Mouse from her desert-dwelling kidnappers in *Mickey in Arabia* (1932). In a decade that enabled Eddie Cantor to bring democracy to Bagdad in *Ali Baba Goes to Town* (1937), it was not surprising to hear a description of "Casbah" in *Algiers* (1938) as "a melting pot for all the sins of the earth" and "the filth of centuries." Caricature of Arabs as anti-Christian "heathens" in *Another Dawn* (1937) or as anti-Western in *Adventure in Sahara* (1938) and *Chasing Danger* (1939) further built on the extremely offensive portrayals of *The Crusades* (1935).

Similarly, the advance in Technicolor during the 1940s had little effect on Hollywood's consistent practice of casting white actors and reusing the same old tropes. Indeed, if anything, new visual technology was seized upon for its ability to render exotic images of the Orient even more vividly. Distributed in the United States, the British thriller *The Thief of Bagdad* (1940) initiated the color frenzy with a theatrical trailer that invited the audience to board "a ship of adventure to meet the thief of Bagdad in the age and land of mystery, romance, thrills, and excitement." It did not take long before other Hollywood films followed suit.[25] The 1950s and 1960s were no exception, whether offering desert adventure films like *The Desert Hawk* (1950) and *Escape from Zahrain* (1962), Egypt-based adventure films like *Valley of the Kings* (1954) and *Cleopatra* (1963), or historical epics like *The Ten Commandments* (1956) and *Lawrence of Arabia* (1962).[26]

But as noted earlier, despite the ubiquity of such imagery, Arabs were still always consumed from a distance. Except for *Anna Ascends*, by the second half of the 1970s there had been no traceable serious attempt to capture narratives surrounding the lives of Arabs in the United States. The second half of the 1960s, however, brought about two key moments of change that ushered in new forms of US-based Arab visibility. The first moment was the liberalization of US immigration law through the Hart-Celler Act (1965), which facilitated the arrival of the third wave of Arab immigrants, leading to a current estimated range of 3.5 million to 4.2 million Arab Americans, more diverse in terms of religion and nationality. The second moment was shaped by the 1967 Arab-Israeli War (also known as the Six-Day War), which granted Israeli forces more access to Arab lands and sparked an upsurge in Arab American activism against the US influence in the region. The correlation of the United States' pro-Israeli stance in the Middle East and the active engagement of the third wave of Arab immigrants in Arab-Israeli geopolitics opened a space for new narratives of Arabness in Hollywood filmmaking starting in the 1970s—namely, narratives contextualizing the Arab presence in the United States in terms of national security or foreign policy.

I join historians Pamela Pennock and Salim Yaqub in describing the 1970s as a pivotal decade in the lives of Arab Americans. Pennock argues that this decade saw the emergence of an Arab American political consciousness, shaped by a rising sense of activism spearheaded by two national organizations, the Association of Arab American University Graduates and the Organization of Arab Students, both of which allied themselves with various leftist, African American, and third-world nonalignment groups. "During these years," Pennock contends, "Arab Americans were also developing new conceptions of citizenship, claiming the full rights and sense of belonging as American citizens in relation to their conceptions of themselves as citizens of the Arab world seeking justice in their homelands."[27] Yaqub argues that the decade also inaugurated a sense of recognition in "important sectors of the US intelligentsia" of Arab American perspectives and contributions to US civic life, despite their limited influence. But even if not widely influential, Arab American activists' engagement with the period's heated politics, whether national or international, afforded many of them "a greater sense of participation and belonging in the nation's civic life."[28]

The 1970s were pivotal in shaping Hollywood's new portrayals of Arabs in the United States, albeit in reductive and superficial ways. Hollywood's projections of the Arab presence in the United States shifted the industry from a passive reproduction of Orientalist imagery in films produced prior to the 1970s to a more active mode informed by the geopolitics of the time. In addition to the temporal reading of this transition, there was a spatial transition in the cinematic engagement with Arabness from a symbol of a distant Orient into a signifier of domestic anxiety—anxiety that would frame representations of Arabs and Muslims in the United States for decades to come. Examples of this trend, which I will explore further in the next sections of this chapter, include films like *The Next Man* (1976), *Network* (1976), *Black Sunday* (1977), *Back to the Future* (1985), *Terror in Beverley Hills* (1988), *Terror Squad* (1988), *The Pelican Brief* (1993), *True Lies* (1994), and *The Siege* (1998). Films produced in the post-9/11 context continued in the same vein but with distinctive narratives that seemed newly inclusive of Arab Americans, but which, I argue in chapter 3, inextricably linked their cultural citizenship to national security concerns. The Arab and Muslim American characters in such films as *The Recruit* (2003), *The Sentinel* (2006), *Five Fingers* (2006), and *Traitor* (2008) are recognized when they serve the US government in the "war on terror" context. As of the publication of this book, the industry has yet to feature Arab American actors playing lead Arab American characters in plots that do not deal with Arabness through the frameworks of terrorism or foreign policy—a narrative that I argue began in the 1970s.

My emphasis on the 1970s as pivotal should not be read as suggesting that all previous patterns and images disappeared—far from it. Hollywood continued to produce Orientalist-style fantasies with films such as *Patton* (1970), *Hawmps!* (1976), *The Wind and the Lion* (1975), *The Last Remake of Beau Geste* (1977), and *Midnight Express* (1978). This was parallel to the influx of Italian, French, German, Canadian, and

British films competing for the attention of the US audience. Most notably, British fantasies gained the most access to Hollywood's blockbuster distribution giants through films like *Blood from the Mummy's Tomb* (1971), *Antony and Cleopatra* (1972), and *Arabian Adventure* (1979).[29] Still, it should be noted that this era also made it possible for the Arab American producer and director Moustafa Akkad to create *The Message* (1976) and *Lion of the Desert* (1980), both historical films with postcolonial and anti-Orientalist narratives (see chapter 5). US films produced during the 1980s and 1990s continued the Orientalist tradition with films like *Best Defense* (1984), *Jewel of the Nile* (1985), *Ishtar* (1987), and *The Mummy* (1999).[30] Additionally, animated films like *DuckTales the Movie* (1990), *Aladdin* (1992), and *The Prince of Egypt* (1998) helped to introduce and accustom yet another generation of Americans to narrowly construed portrayals of Arabness as distant and dangerous.

Hollywood's newly introduced imagery of Arabs in the United States during the 1970s was sparked by the constant feed of hyped news about the role of Arabs in several geopolitical events at the time. The following two sections unpack this through a macro reading of two patterns of representation: Arab Americans as either a national security threat or a foreign policy issue.

A National Security Threat

On June 5, 1968, Sirhan Sirhan, a Palestinian American, shot and killed presidential candidate Robert Kennedy in a Los Angeles hotel, moments after Kennedy's speech following his win of the Democratic primary election in California. This incident concluded a decade of assassinations that claimed the lives of many political leaders, chief among them President John Kennedy (1963), Malcolm X (1965), and Martin Luther King Jr. (1968). But in contrast to these three cases, which were seen, at least primarily, as spurred by domestic politics, Sirhan's act was embedded in foreign affairs, as he reportedly declared when arrested, "I did it for my country." The specific date marked the beginning, exactly one year earlier, of the Six-Day War, which had resulted in a humiliating defeat of Egyptian-Jordanian-Syrian alliances and further expanded Israeli control over more Arab territories. Sirhan's defense team pointed to his experience of being forced out of Jerusalem by Zionists as a child in 1948 and seeking refuge in the United States. The trauma, his lawyers argued, had affected his judgment. Indeed, Sirhan himself politicized his act, while simultaneously describing it in deeply personal terms when he was interviewed at the maximum-security prison where he has since spent his life:

> To me, he [Kennedy] was my hero, he was my champion, the protector, and the defender of the downtrodden and the disadvantaged and I thought I was one. And to have him say that he was going to send fifty phantom jets to Israel, to deliver nothing but death and destruction on my countrymen, that seemed as a story of betrayal, and it was sad, it was hard for me to accept.[31]

Although it was not clear to what extent Sirhan's crime directly contributed to the already problematic portrayals of Arabs and Arab Americans in US media and popular culture at the time, it certainly forced US-based pro-Palestinian activism into a disadvantaged position, even though some Arab American activists refused to "disown" him.[32] Sirhan's act could also be seen as a historical precursor to other moments that have further shaped decades of Hollywood's association of Arabness in the United States with terrorism.

In fact, it was not until the appearance of the Black September Organization (BSO), which emerged from the ashes of the 1970 Jordanian-Palestinian clashes, that terrorism became an associated trademark of Arabness in the West. Americans were first introduced to the BSO's series of bloody operations during the Munich Olympics in September 1972. Eight members of the BSO killed eleven Israeli athletes after German and Israeli authorities failed to handle the highly publicized hostage situation. Dubbed the "Munich massacre," the incident received global coverage with support from the emerging technology of live broadcasting in commercial television.[33] "Not only were the levels of destruction and the extraordinary human casualties unheard-of for Americans in peacetime," affirms McAlister, "but the live television coverage had left the nation stunned."[34] Although

Hollywood's constructions of foreign terrorism-related plots were historically rooted in World War II films—the earliest example was Alfred Hitchcock's *Saboteur* (1942)—new portrayals of Middle Eastern terrorism in the United States and elsewhere emerged in response to the BSO's transnational operation and the suddenly marketable vision of Arabness and Islam as breeding grounds for terrorists fixated on undermining US national security.[35]

American responses to the Munich massacre, whether in government circles or the filmmaking industry, leveraged the Israeli equation of Arabness with transnational terrorism. This equation politically legitimized the Israeli's extreme responses to Munich, including a transnational assassination program, intensive airstrikes of ten Palestinian camps, and a ground invasion of South Lebanon—responses that, together, resulted in hundreds of civilian causalities. Guided by fear of another Munich-like attack in the United States and a concern that Israel might intensify its reaction and provoke "a wider war," the Nixon administration initiated policies that directly targeted US-based Arabs, regardless of whether they were visitors, immigrants, or citizens.[36] The code for those policies was "Operation Boulder," which came into existence through the newly established Cabinet Committee to Combat Terrorism.[37] Operation Boulder referred to the practice of subjecting visas for Arab visitors to additional background screening through CIA and FBI records, the Immigration and Naturalization Service, and even the US Secret Service. This procedure, which significantly delayed the visa process, targeted ethnic Arabs, defined as "anyone who had been born in an Arab country or whose parents had come from one."[38] Although Operation Boulder was short-lived, lasting from 1972 to 1975 before the State Department ruled it out as costly and ineffective, the Immigration and Naturalization Service simultaneously conducted additional screenings of non-US citizens to verify the legality of their stay, make arrests, and accelerate the deportation of violators. Meanwhile the FBI surveilled and investigated Arab students and Arab American activists, prompting the latter to label all anti-Arab government-sponsored policing as Operation Boulder, thus ascribing to the term more meaning than intended by its originators.

The foundation of the American-Arab Anti-Discrimination Committee in 1980 and its documentation of civil liberty violations of Arabs and Arab Americans indicated that such practices in the 1970s were only the beginning of sustained discrimination based on national security concerns. This history challenges any presumptions of 9/11 as marking the start of the government's aggressive treatment of various Arab and Muslim communities in the United States; rather, 9/11 led to an escalation of already existing practices of suspicion and policing. President Donald Trump's Executive Order 13769 in 2017 (also known as the "Muslim ban"), which effectively barred millions of Arab and Muslim visitors and immigrants from entry to the United States, speaks of this continuity.[39]

Parallel to the government's response to the Munich massacre, Hollywood filmmakers rushed to capitalize on public fears by producing plots that linked all symbols of Arabness in the United States with alienness and terrorism; in effect, denying Arab Americans any sense of cultural citizenship in the United States. In 1977 Paramount Pictures released *Black Sunday*, an adaptation of Thomas Harris's novel (1975), which echoed the Munich massacre and gave visual form to Americans' newly stoked fear of Arabness. The film presents an Arab woman, Dahlia Iyad (Marthe Keller), characterized by US intelligence agents as a foreign threat linked to the targeting of eighty thousand Americans, including the US president, attending the Super Bowl in Miami. The Arab presence in the United States, the film suggests, invokes a certainty of civilian massacres in the name of political grievances against the US support of Israel. The film's theatrical trailer portrays Arab terrorists as ready to strike the American public with violence at a moment's notice. "Black Sunday," the narrator's voice warns ominously, "It could be tomorrow!"

Unlike Steven Spielberg's contextualized portrayal of the massacre in *Munich* (2005), John Frankenheimer's *Black Sunday* tells its audience that the United States and Israel are aligned in their war against Arabs' "acts of terror." Throughout the film, Israeli Mossad agent David Kabakov (Robert Shaw) and FBI agent Sam Corley (Fritz Weaver) track BSO terrorists and ultimately emerge as saviors of US security and order. In fact, aligning Israel and the United States as a front against Arabs—not just Arab presence in the United States—was already a central theme, dating back to 1960, when films dramatized the Arab threat to the creation of Israel. *Exodus*, the award-winning epic (1960) based on Leon Uris's eponymous best-selling novel, introduced millions of Americans to sympathetic portrayals of Zionism by humanizing the Jewish settler narrative and aligning Arabs with Nazis. Desperate Jewish characters searching for a homeland in Palestine are warned that the Grand Mufti of Jerusalem, who "sat out the war as Hitler's guest in Berlin," is plotting with other Arab nations to "coordinate action against Palestinian Jews" in case of partition. Whether in the first Israeli feature film *Hill 24 Doesn't Answer* (1955), the Israeli–West German coproduction *Blazing Sand* (1960), the British war film *Foxhole in Cairo* (1960), or the American-British coproduction *Judith* (1966), the presumed Arab-Nazi alliance was projected as the antithesis of Israeli-Western support for Jewish freedom.

Prior to the Munich massacre, sympathetic portrayals of Israel were already well-developed in films like *Cast of a Giant Shadow* (1966), *Sands of Beersheba* (1966), *Journey to Jerusalem* (1968), and *Sinai Commandos* (1968). Following the Arab-Israeli War of 1967, portrayals of Arabness in US popular culture were marked by a favorable view of Israel as a self-declared Western state with a unique US alliance. In "The Arab Portrayed," Edward Said examines the sentiment at the time:

> During and after the June war [1967] few things could have been more depressing than the way in which the Arabs were portrayed. Press pictures of the Arabs were almost always of large numbers of people, mobs of hysterical, anonymous men, whereas photographs of the Israelis were almost always of stalwart individuals, the light of simple heroism shining from their eyes. . . . What is extremely important here is how the official Israeli view of the Arab as a kind of troublesome non-person feeds the common and accepted view of the Arab that is currently held in America.[40]

Many films during the 1970s staged American and Israeli characters fighting Arab terror. In *The Jerusalem File* (1972), a naive American,

David Armonstrong (Bruce Davison), befriends his Palestinian classmate, Rashid (Ze'ev Revach), at Yale—not realizing that Rashid is part of a terrorist network that has increased their violent attacks in Jerusalem by "100 percent." In *Rosebud* (1975), the CIA undercover agent Larry Martin (Peter O'Toole) coordinates with Israeli intelligence to save kidnapped girls from a "Palestinian Liberation Army" hostage situation. The film ends, however, with other Palestinian terrorists hijacking an airplane and demanding that Israeli authorities release their fellow terrorists, thus gloomily suggesting the attacks will only continue. In *Warhead* (1977), US Air Force Colonel Tony Stevens (David Janssen) is on a mission to deactivate a nuclear weapon in a Middle Eastern desert but finds himself trapped in a battle between Palestinians and Israelis, moments after the former blow up a school bus of Jewish children. Having learned about the terrorists' intent to use the weapon on a civilian airplane, Stevens saves the day by joining the Israeli soldiers in eliminating the terrorists. In *The Fury* (1978), an American father, Peter (Kirk Douglas), and his son, Robin (Andrew Stevens), are attacked while at an Israeli beach by Palestinian-looking individuals, leading Robin to develop animosity toward Arabs in Chicago.

Mediating pro-Israeli and anti-Arab images through the context of terrorism was made possible, to some extent, by Israeli director Menachem Golan. *Eagles Attack at Dawn* (1970), which he both wrote and directed, initiated a trend of Israeli films marketed to the American audience. In this film, an Israeli soldier who is captured and tortured in a Syrian prison escapes, then returns to liberate the other Israeli soldiers. In 1977 Golan directed and coproduced with his cousin, Yoram Globus, *Operation Thunderbolt*, a film about a rescue mission to save Israeli hostages from a Palestinian airplane hijacking. Two years later, the Israeli cousins purchased the US-based production company Cannon Films and proceeded to make around thirty low- and medium-budget B-movies, some of which recycled negative stereotypes of Arabs and Muslims. In the words of filmmaker Andrew Stewart, Cannon produced "some of the most blatantly racist and sexist exploitation films of the period."[41] *The Delta Force* (1986), a Golan-Globus

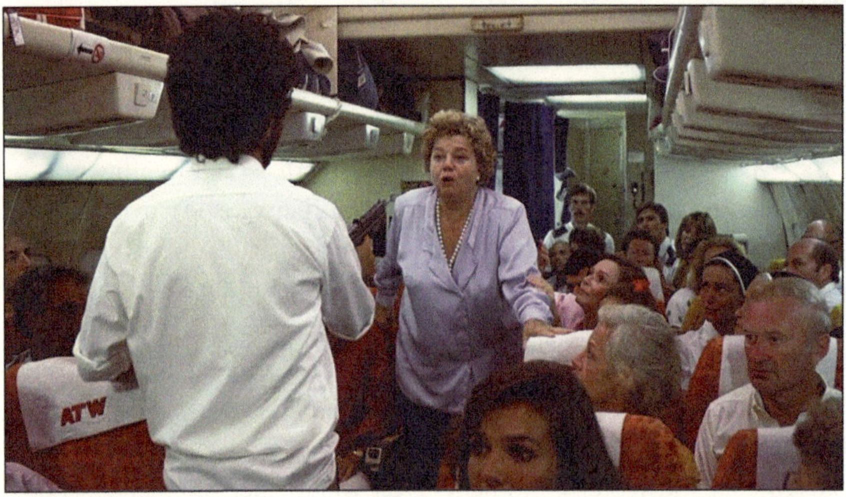

5. A terrorist singles out a Jewish passenger for persecution in *The Delta Force* (1986). © Cannon Films.

Production distributed by Cannon Films, is a prime example. In his attempt to reenact the 1985 Athens-Beirut TWA hijacking incident, director Golan offers an emotional portrait that equates Arabs with Nazi Germany. The film shows the hijackers singling out and persecuting Jewish passengers. Among the wary passengers, a Jewish woman confronts one of the threatening hijackers in a scene that invokes a sense of stark contrast between Arab aggression and Jewish innocence. That a woman stands up to the terrorists seems to be a gendered token to the bravery of Jewish women as well (figure 5). Rather than capturing the real negotiation process—which, in reality, ended with the release of the hostages—the film presents a dramatic rescue by Major Scott McCoy (Chuck Norris) and his American Delta Force, reaffirming the necessity of a military response to Arab terrorism. The film also imagines the Arab presence in the United States as a source of instability and violence: one of the terrorists, the audience learns, plans to blow up the White House with help from Arabs in the United States.

In her critique of the Israeli filmmaking industry, Ella Shohat offers a penetrating reading of the Israeli nationalist narrative, which, she argues, draws on Eurocentric Orientalist geographies of East and West in its representation of Arabs and Arab Jews.[42] As products of Israeli cinema, the Golan-Globus films highlighted this narrative by foregrounding American vulnerability (as a proxy for Israel) and advocating war as the ultimate response. Films like *Sahara* (1983), *The Ambassador* (1984), *Hell Squad* (1985), *Invasion USA* (1985), *Appointment with Death* (1988), and many others presented an Israeli vision of Arabs and Muslims, especially those living in the United States, as imminent US enemies.[43] The damaging portrayal continued beyond the Golan-Globus network in such films as *Riding the Edge* (1989), *Blink of an Eye* (1992), *Cover-Up* (1991), *Into the Sun* (1991), and others.[44]

Terrorism-related plots in the above-highlighted films were "not accidental, but propaganda disguised as entertainment."[45] The Israeli government extended direct support to *Iron Eagle* (1986), *Iron Eagle II* (1988), and *Terror in Beverley Hills* (1989). Mossad contributed to the production of *Rosebud* (1975), *The Little Drummer Girl* (1984), *Death before Dishonor* (1987), *Frantic* (1988), and *Navy SEALs* (1990). Other films received help in indirect ways, either through filming in Israel or casting Israeli actors. Overall, the films reveal a pattern of Israeli influence on the images being presented to the American audience through the silver screen. Israeli and Israeli-friendly portrayals contributed to the development of an American filmmaking code when it came to Arabness in the United States at the time. This one-dimensional code was exacerbated by such loaded incidents as the Iran hostage crisis (1979–81), US intervention in Lebanon (1981–83), the Iran-Iraq War (1980–88), the bombing of Libya (1986), and the World Trade Center bombing (1993).

Through its films, Hollywood effectively denied Arab American characters access to their American cultural identity by insisting on presenting US-based Arab characters as primarily alien and invested in advancing Arab politics away from the Israel-US alliance. Filmed in Israel, the Columbia Pictures film *Wrong Is Right* (1982), for instance, depicts an "Eye of Gaza" terror group bent on obliterating Tel Aviv and Jerusalem with atomic bombs. The US-based Arab activists, presented as unnamed Arab students wearing thobes and keffiyehs, use anti-Israeli grievances to justify a series of suicidal bombings across the United States. The bombings strike New York City, Texas, Chicago, Detroit, and Washington, DC. The film renders absent the humanity and rationality of Arabs in the United States, reducing them to ticking bombs of explosive emotionality touting slogans like "Jews own television," "Death to America," and "Death to Israel." The film offers brief criticism of the US controversial foreign policy in the Middle East when a reporter inquires about the deterioration of America's image in the region, but overwhelmingly, the visual treatment of Arab Americans is dismissive.

Well beyond Israeli influence, other Hollywood films similarly popularized conflated associations of Arabness and Islam with fear. For instance, the well-known horror film *The Exorcist* (1973), which is based on the 1971 novel by the Arab American William Blatty, establishes a connection between an excavated statue of an Assyrian demon in Iraq with the possession of an American girl in Washington, DC. The adaptation does not capture the essence of the author's transnational sensibility in dramatizing the interconnectedness of humanity, but rather reduces the author's idea into a shivering portrayal of Islam as a source of fear itself. The film's opening scene of an Islamic call for prayer, for instance, is not mentioned in the book, but adds a filmic effect with a sensibility that invites the audience to conceive difference as a site of fear.

And Hollywood's associations of Arabs and Muslims with fear were diverse and spanned a few genres. In the comedy *Blazing Saddles* (1974), pioneers prepare to defend themselves against Arabs and Nazis.[46] Harlem's Laura Lewis (Diana Sands) joins a mission to rescue a politician held captive in Lebanon in the action drama *Honeybaby, Honeybaby* (1974).[47] James Bond (Sean Connery) deals with an Arab nuclear terrorist Fatima (Barbara Carrera) in the 007 franchise spy film *Never Say Never Again* (1983).

Notably, the nationality of the Arab terrorists in such films varies widely. They could be Libyans in films like *Broadcast News* (1987), *The American President* (1995), and *G.I. Jane* (1997) or Palestinians in films such as *Frantic* (1988), *Ministry of Vengeance* (1989), and *Navy SEALs*

(1990). They could also be Moroccans as in *Beyond Justice* (1992), Syrians as in *Freedom Strike* (1998), Iraqis as in *Three Kings* (1999), or Yemenis as in *Rules of Engagement* (2000). While there is already a broad sense of indifference to country of origin marked by "they are all the same" type of imagery, featuring specific nationalities in such films was often based on which Middle Eastern country was featured a lot in the news at the time.

Hollywood's representations essentially mainstreamed a public fear of Arabs and Arab Americans.[48] The depiction of Arabs in the United States as terrorists is persistent. The 1980s accelerated the pace of stereotyping, if not the exact content. A Palestinian American terrorist wreaks havoc in Italy in Edward Dmytryk's *The Human Factor* (1975). William Friedkin's *To Live and Die in LA* (1985) perceives a Muslim threat of assassination against the US president. Robert Zemeckis's *Back to the Future* (1985) imagines the threat in the form of a moving van full of Libyans searching for nuclear weapons. William Riead's *Scorpion* (1986) informs the audience of Palestinians targeting civilians, diplomats, servicemen, and military leaders. Gary Sherman's *Wanted: Dead or Alive* (1986) implicates UCLA Arab students in a movie theater explosion that kills at least two hundred civilians, including children, and a plot to unleash poison gas on Los Angeles. In John Kincade's *Terminal Entry* (1986), there are 250 US-based Arab fighters seeking martyrdom who plan to "eliminate all key political and military figures." Arabs in cohort with Russian and Latin American terrorists pose danger when stealing US military equipment in Steve Carver's *Bulletproof* (1988). And in Peter Maris's *Terror Squad* (1988), Libyan terrorists hold American high schoolers hostage in Indiana after failing to infiltrate a nuclear power plant and cause paranoia with machine guns and grenades that target police vehicles.

During the 1990s Hollywood filmmakers stepped up their depiction of the Arab presence in the United States as a threat to US national security. Lewis Teague's *Navy SEALs* (1990) portrays the complicity of a Lebanese American journalist with terrorist groups overseas. In Alan Pakula's political thriller *The Pelican Brief* (1993), an Arab succeeds in killing Supreme Court justices, prompting the US president to blame the terror on immigration officials allowing "foreign terrorists" in the country "again." A former Special Forces soldier in Rick Jacobson's *Bloodfist VI* (1995) saves 375 million from the threat unleashed by a New York–based terrorist group called "Party of Allah," which gains control of a nuclear plant in Nebraska. James Cameron's *True Lies* (1994) features a "Crimson Jihad" group in possession of six nuclear weapons set to cause havoc on US soil. Peter Segal's *Naked Gun 33 1/3: The Final Insult* (1994) reveals an Arab plot to blow up the sixty-sixth annual Academy Awards. Stuart Baird's *Executive Decision* (1996) dramatizes the threat in an airplane-hijacking scene with 406 passengers onboard, including a US senator. A Palestinian with a suicide note that reads "I fly into the arms of Allah" kills the US secretary of defense in protest of an arms sale to Israel in Brian De Palma's conspiracy thriller *Snake Eyes* (1998). And last but not least, Edward Zwick's *The Siege* (1998) imagines New York City under terrorist attacks on civilians and presents a troubling portrayal of its Arab American characters (chapter 3).

Many of these films, across several film genres, portray Arabs in the United States as proxies of Arab foreign interests and anxieties. Such productions promote limited understanding of terrorism and also reveal a systematic lack of interest in imagining Arab Americans as cultural citizens of the United States who are entitled to their ethnic difference. Alternatively, the industry's mainstream imagery conceives this ethnic difference through racialized lenses that not only cast Arabs in the United States as undesirable aliens but dismiss the very idea of Arab Americanness. To put it simply, Hollywood's films of the 1970s, 1980s, and even the 1990s foregrounded homeland security as a key narrative that questioned the American cultural citizenship of their US-based Arab characters and ignored the nuances around Arab and Arab American diversity, complexity, and humanity.

A Foreign Policy Issue

Whereas the Munich massacre fueled American filmmakers' imagination about Arabness as a threat to US national security, another factor—the energy crisis—contributed to defining Arabness as a foreign policy issue during the 1970s. Following Arab countries' humiliating defeat in the brief Arab-Israeli War of 1967, there was pan-Arab support for Egyptian and Syrian use of force to regain parts of the Sinai Peninsula and Golan Heights during the war in October 1973 (also known as the Yom Kippur War or Ramadan War). In response to Nixon's military support of Israel, the Organization of Arab Petroleum Exporting Countries (OAPEC), led by Saudi Arabia, decided to cut oil production and restrict petroleum exports to the United States.[49] The oil embargo (1973–74) was the Arab states' response to US political investment in promoting Israeli interests as a major Cold War ally in the Middle East—a US foreign policy position that John Mearsheimer and Stephen Walt trace back to President Kennedy's administration.[50] More importantly, the embargo created an energy crisis in the United States with immediate repercussions in the American street, ranging from panic about fuel shortages to skyrocketing prices and sensational media coverage. With oil prices per barrel rising from $2.90 to $11.65 between September and December of 1973, the embargo triggered market instability and opened doors for more price hikes by the Organization of the Petroleum Exporting Countries (OPEC).[51] Many Americans saw Arabs as the major source of their gas pump anxieties, which were further exacerbated by the investment of Arab petrodollars in the US economy.

This context provided Hollywood with the impetus to project Arabs as money-oriented, oil-rich, and extravagant people whose wealth represented the threat of rebranding, if not disrupting, American values of liberty and democracy. Perhaps the most sympathetic portrayal of oil-rich Arabs during the 1970s was Richard Sarafian's *The Next Man* (1976), which was edited and renamed for television as *Arab Conspiracy*. The film glorifies the character of a pro-peace, Israeli-friendly Saudi state minister, Khalil Abdul-Muhsen (Sean Connery). "I decided to take this role because it's an unusual one," Connery stated. "I play an Arab statesman who tries to bring peace to the Mideast by some startling proposals. It's an intelligent film about what's happening now, and it has plenty of excitement."[52] The good Arab is likable and well-groomed with an articulate and proper accent, a visual mark of distinction from what Jack Shaheen has dubbed Hollywood's "reel" Arabs of the time.[53]

The Americanized Arab minister offers a novel, if unrealistic, approach to settling the Arab-Israeli conflict. He addresses the United Nations with a proposal for a "new global, social, [and] political contract" that grants Israel admission into OPEC as a nonproducing member. He is forceful in pursuing the resolution, as shown in this excerpt from his second UN speech:

> Saudi Arabia is determined to back Israeli acceptance with all the power at its command. . . . To those who would work with us towards peace, we embrace you. To those who would keep Arabs and Israelis enemies, we defy you. To those who would keep us apart, we shall overcome you."

The reactions to the proposal are polarized, with many invoking rigid "us-them" binaries, thus portraying the dissenting voices of Kuwaiti, Syrian, Iraqi, Libyan, and Egyptian delegates, as well as US-based Arab protestors outside the UN compound, as uncompromising and violent. Those who reject Abdul-Muhsen's idea appear irrational, impulsive, and anti-Western. There are protests, with banners such as "Arabia for the Arabians" and "No Deals, Khalil." The film ultimately culminates with a bombing and the assassination of the minister.

Prior to his assassination, Abdul-Muhsen speaks directly with angry US-based Arab youth activists at a rally, possibly based on a true New York sit-in of the Organization of Arab Students in 1968 calling on Arab delegations not to negotiate with Israel.[54] Upon seeing a passionate protester yelling out his opposition, Abdul-Muhsen steps out of his car and convinces the police officer to stop arresting the activist. The minister acknowledges the protestor's concerns about Israeli aggressions and hugs him as a token of recognition for Palestinian rights. He also affirms that peaceful resolution requires time and asks that the protestor trust him. The point of the encounter, however, is not so much to address the protester's concerns as it is to instruct the audience to identify with the Saudi minister and believe in his resolution to broker an Arab-Israeli peace the American way. In a

6. Howard Beale urges Americans to express their fear of Arabs in *Network* (1976). © Metro-Goldwyn-Mayer.

subsequent scene, the camera shows protestors passing bombs, signaling that violence is the Arab response to the minister's calls for peace.

Portraying Arabs in the United States through the lenses of oil and geopolitics was taken to a different level in Sidney Lumet's highly acclaimed satirical film *Network* (1976).[55] The film is iconic for its critique of US television as a manipulative tool responsible for producing a generation that "cannot think, cannot feel, and which has learned everything it knows about life from Saturday morning cartoons."[56] Howard Beale (Peter Finch), the anchor of a Union Broadcasting System (UBS) television network, invokes the public's sense of patriotism in an effort to block "the Arabs" who are planning to buy the channel. Beale takes advantage of his media podium to educate his followers about how the Arabs' presumed monopoly of neoliberal politics will transform American culture. His angry face, high-pitched tone, and hand gestures communicate his patriotic sincerity (figure 6). In an iconic moment of active citizen empowerment in US popular culture, Beale instructs each one of his viewers to get up off his or her couch and yell out the window, "I am mad as hell and I'm not gonna take this anymore."[57]

Beale's call for public performance resonates with a mythic fear of Arabness. Meant in the Barthesian sense of mythology, a myth solidifies not because of its relevance to "truth" but rather its circulation without critical contestation.[58] Fear of Arabs' oil wealth during the 1970s was partially shaped by Americans' frustration with OAPEC's disruptive embargo and OPEC's frequent price hikes at the time. In this context, Beale's anger represented a moment of anxiety in Hollywood that advocated the portrayal of Arabness in the United States as a foreign policy issue. *Network* made this representation strategy possible through Beale's passionate televised speech, filled with warnings about a looming danger that far outweighed the grim reality of the economy; specifically, the danger of Arabs "buying up America":

> We all know that the Arabs control $16 billion in this country. They own a chunk of Fifth Avenue, twenty downtown pieces of Boston, a part of the port of New Orleans, [and] an industrial park in Salt Lake City. They own big chunks of the Atlanta Hilton, the Arizona Land and Cattle Company, the Security National Bank in California. . . . They control ARAMCO, so that puts them in EXXON, Texaco, and Mobil Oil. They're all over: New Jersey, Louisville, and St. Louis, Missouri. And that's only what we know about them; there's a hell of a lot more we don't know about because all of those Arab petrodollars are washed through Switzerland and Canada and the biggest banks in the country. . . . Right now the Arabs have screwed us out of enough American dollars to come right back and with our own money buy General Motors, IBM, IT&T, AT&T, DuPont, US Steel, and twenty other companies. Hell! They already own half of England! So, listen to me, the Arabs are simply buying us.

Beale's tirade refers to the estimated Arab investment of $29 billion, most in the form of bank deposits and financial securities; there were some nonvital investments in the real estate market and donations to higher education.[59] The rhetorical nature of his speech does not acknowledge that Arab investments at the time fell short compared to Western investments and that Arabs were never allowed to acquire entities essential to US national security.[60]

Beale attracts ratings-based media attention because of his uncompromising personality. He uses explosive rhetoric as a tool to manipulate his audience. He incites fear of Arabs as the embodiment of an alien, if not contradictory, culture to America. He even advocates an aggressive public rejection of Arab presence. Dubbed the "mad prophet of the airwaves," Beale asks his captivated audience to flood the White House with a million telegrams stating, "I don't want banks selling my country to the Arabs." His supporters send six million telegrams and force Arabs away from the UBS channel. "The people spoke," Beale announces triumphantly to his audience, "the people won. It was a radiant eruption of democracy." In his reading of the relationship between Beale and his audience, Craig Hight applauds the film's ability to challenge the audience to associate themselves with Beale's television viewers depicted in the film.[61] This relationship, I stress, is made possible by the manipulation of both Beale's followers and *Network*'s audience and cultivation of their fear and misunderstanding of Arabs. The film advances strict binaries of Arabness and Americanness in ways that annihilate the possibility of imagining such an identity as Arab American.

Public fear of Arabness during the 1970s was reinforced by institutional anxieties regarding Arabs' petrodollar influence on American life. In the sting operation dubbed "Operation Abscam" that started in late 1977 and became public in early 1980, for instance, the FBI interrogated a score of politicians—including seven congressional representatives—on suspicion of soliciting support from a staged "Abdul Enterprises," hence the operation's name.[62] In pursuit of their targets, FBI agents dressed like Hollywood's stereotypical rich Arabs and videotaped them accepting bribes. David Russell's film *American Hustle* (2013) dramatizes this operation, resurrecting a similar caricatured image of the Arab threat. The operation unveiled an institutional effort to produce a threatening image of Arabs in the United States. Despite official apologies from the White House to the disgruntled Arab states, the whole operation underscored deep-seated fear of petrodollars' impact on US politics. Yaqub explains the rationale behind this petrodollar-mania:

> Some feared that Arab states would use their growing economic power to disrupt US support for Israel. . . . Some worried that repugnant regimes in Tripoli, Baghdad, Riyadh, and elsewhere would succeed in purchasing a sanitized image in the US. Some, of a more populist bent, saw Arab petrodollars as an instrument of American corporate aggrandizement. And some (though this sentiment was seldom voiced openly) no doubt recoiled from the specter of swarthy foreigners acquiring assets and enjoying luxuries that few Americans could afford. Underlying all of these concerns was a sense that Arab economic power threatened the independence and dignity of the United States or its people.[63]

The same institutional anxiety seemed to prompt the Department of Energy at the time to issue such bumper stickers as "The Faster You Drive, The Richer They Get," and "Driving 75 is Sheik; Driving 55 is Chic."[64]

Images of oil-rich Arabs as a foreign source of corruption in American politics, society, and culture developed throughout the 1970s across a range of genres. James Bond (Roger Moore) in *The Man with the Golden Gun* (1974) confirms that oil sheiks are plotting "to keep solar energy off market." A Sheik Amani receives a bribe to buy the products of "International Electronics" in *St. Ives* (1976). The US president uses the Statue of Liberty as "collateral" for an "Arab loan" in *Attack of the Killer Tomatoes* (1978). Arabs are busy bribing the president of Taft Aerospace with cash in briefcases in *Fun with Dick and Jane* (1977). In *California Suite* (1978) the audience learns that New York is full of Arabs but "it's not Mecca; it just smells like it." In *Gas Pump Girls* (1979) June (Kirsten Baker) and her friends save her uncle's run-down gas station with some alluring tricks, including dressing as if in an Oriental harem, and convince the Arab supplier of Pyramids Petroleum Products not to use his money and power to "play with everyone's life." And, with America without gas, oil, or cash in *Americathon* (1979), the president considers selling the White House to "Hebrabs," a merger of Arabs and Jews.

Arab wealth as the antithesis of US culture continued as a prevalent theme in many Hollywood productions throughout the 1980s. Alan J. Pakula's political thriller *Rollover* (1981) is a serious film with an alarming and sinister message about Arab danger. The film's plot unfolds against a backdrop of anxiety that the US financial system is on the verge of collapse, partly destabilized by oil prices and concerns about Arab money in banks. A media host in the film asks a financial expert whether there has been a time when the concentration of wealth is in the hands of one group. A mystery bank account 21214 is tied to the mysterious murder of Lee Winters's husband. Played by Jane Fonda, the widow brokers a deal with Arab investors and discovers that the mysterious account belongs to Arabs who secretly move money into gold as a security against any loss caused by the dollar collapsing. As she becomes entangled in a web of secrecy and conspiracy, the film shows Arab wealth as a corrupting force in the US financial industry. The film's messaging extended off-screen too; during interviews about the film, Fonda said, "If we aren't afraid of Arabs, we'd better examine our heads. They have strategic power over us. They are unstable, they are fundamentalists, tyrants, anti-woman, anti–free press. That we have to depend on them is monstrous."[65]

The fear of Arabness continued in Herbert Ross's *Protocol* (1984). In this film, an Arab emir allows the United States to establish a military base in his unnamed strategic country, but only if he can marry a waitress-turned-celebrity named Sunny (Goldie Hawn), who saves him from an assassination attempt during his stay in the United States. The US State Department convinces Sunny to travel to the Middle East as a diplomat, but upon her arrival, she is welcomed as a queen. She is shocked to learn she has been essentially traded to the emir as his spouse. Her character symbolizes America's purity and innocence while the State Department officers are revealed to be corrupted by emirs who scheme to dictate US foreign policy. In addition to organizing an Arab American protest march about the film, the executive director of the American-Arab Anti-Discrimination Committee communicated a timely concern to its filmmakers before its release:

"We do not suggest that Arabs should not be used nor that they cannot be funny, only that you do not perpetuate the negative and hurtful images employed in depicting our community." Despite promises from the film producer to portray the emir as "a true hero," the final cut of *Protocol* presented him as a caricature of Americans' conception of Arabness at the time.[66]

The trauma of the 1970s oil crisis solidified a popular culture reference to a collective memory of Arabs as foreign disruptors of US national politics. In *The Formula* (1980) Arabs are portrayed as the enemy of the US economy as they attempt to deny the viability of a synthetic product that would eliminate the need for oil. In *Wrong Is Right* (1982) a Texan senator incites rage among his supporters against "the Ayrabs" for raising the oil price "four times in two years" in a region that screams "Death of America." Sunny's vulnerability in *Protocol* symbolizes Americans' susceptibility to Arabs' presumed evil plans. And *Power* (1986) presents Arabs as oil-rich conspirators who use their money to undermine America's prosperity. This film's Arabs—codified in an oil company named "Ameriabia"—hire a public relations expert, Arnold Billing (Denzel Washington), to support the election of a politician committed to the US retrogress in solar energy. The plot centers around the US fight for independence from oil as its primary source of energy. It depicts Arabs as shadowy characters with an agenda to control US politics. The rejection of Arab interference becomes a metaphoric expression of an American rescue narrative. This reductive narrative demonstrates how the oil crisis factor contributed to paranoia about Arab nations well beyond the 1970s.

In the transition from Hollywood's earlier images of Arabs as desert-dwelling, camel-riding sheiks to a post-1970s pattern of portraying the Arab presence in the United States as a threat to American life, there were also moments of derisive humor that exaggerated the polarity between American and Arabic cultural identities. The US-based Arab characters in this trope were imagined as incapable of conversing with American codes and values. Comedies like *The Happy Hooker Goes to Washington* (1977), *Cheech and Chong's Next Movie* (1980), *Underground Aces* (1981), and many others feature polarized, caricatured images of

Arabs in America and dislocate them from any affiliation with American culture.[67] Similarly, plots referencing the inherent danger of Arab wealth flourished in the 1990s, with films such as *Hollywood Hot Tubs 2* (1990), *Father of the Bride Part II* (1995), and *Under Siege 2* (1995).

The fact that such films narrowly imagined the presence of Arabs in the United States as shadowy characters at the periphery of American society solidified a process of cultural Otherness that denied Arab Americans their entitlement to American cultural citizenship. The films relied mostly on the premise of foreignness as the primary code in representing Arabs in the United States. They often mixed Orientalist-inspired dress with Western clothing for comic relief; featured characters who impulsively rushed to anger and rich Arab men with fantasies of romancing blonde-haired women; and advanced a hidden agenda to subjugate Americans to their whims.[68] In these films it is Arabs' foreignness—once seen as so exotic and distant—that now poses a dire threat to America and ensures that Arabs within the United States could not be seen as cultural citizens. This pattern of representation emerged partly as a nationalist effort to make sense of the transnational impact of the oil crisis on Americans' cultural memory. It was through this national trauma that American filmmakers and audiences interacted with and entertained understandings of their nation and fellow citizens.

Conclusion

Hollywood's representations of Arab Americans—or their lack thereof—restrict the boundaries of American cultural citizenship. The representation patterns initiated in the 1970s rejected the complexity of Arab American realities, instead refracting them through and constraining them within the marketable lenses of fear and insecurity. Such portrayals relied on reductive codes that minimized US and Arab as well as Israeli and Arab transnational geopolitics into a simplified nationalist narrative of protecting home, land, and security. This framework portrayed Arabs in the United States as the cultural Other, creating a precedent in the industry that has fostered later decades of anti-Arab as well as Islamophobic imagery. While

Arab American characters were scarce and invisible in the years preceding the 1970s, they continued to be invisible during this decade and beyond in an industry that has limited its representations of Arab Americans to the realms of national security and foreign policy. Even though the 1970s was a crucial decade that witnessed a sudden interest in capturing US-based Arab experiences, this growth in Hollywood soon proved problematic. In post-9/11 United States, chapter 3 will show, Arab Americans have continued to evoke fear and hate despite signs of evolution in the industry's portrayal trajectories.

As this chapter explores, the vilification of Arabs and Arab Americans is not a post-9/11 unique construct. Long before 2001, both government institutions and entertainment circles had already indicted the Arab presence in the United States as a threat to homeland security or a source of foreign anxiety. Coercive measures enacted by the Nixon administration, along with continued FBI surveillance in subsequent US administrations, presumed animosity between Arabs and Americans, as if Arab Americans were illegitimate children of conflicting partners. And filmmakers blurred images of Arabs and Arab Americans as foreign threats in entertaining plots that glorified American patriotism through endings that restored normalcy and led the audience to breathe a sigh of relief at the end of their film-viewing experiences. Thus legal citizenship has not always protected Arab Americans, and Hollywood assumed the role of hindering Arab Americans' acceptance as American cultural citizens.

Importantly, anti-Arab discrimination during the 1970s did not pass without any opposition. The label "Arab American" itself was embraced as a post-1967 tool of political activism. The Organization of Arab Students increased campus activism across the United States immediately after 1967. The American-Arab University Graduates was founded the same year. Arab American activism at the time worked through alliances with white leftists, African Americans, and third-worldists in the United States and beyond, united through anti-status-quo politics.[69] Hollywood's offensive portrayals spurred Arab American concerns about politicizing and stigmatizing the community. Jack Shaheen and his spouse started compiling a guide to the industry's forms of vilification, which eventually resulted in Shaheen's comprehensive surveys. Edward Said's seminal work *Orientalism* (1978) offered a scholarly analysis of the discursive metanarratives shaping those representations. And other organizations like the National Association of Arab Americans, the American-Arab Anti-Discrimination Committee, and Arab American Institute joined later to protest the cultural vilification of Arabs and Arab Americans as anti-Western and terrorists.[70]

Not surprisingly, Hollywood filmmakers were not interested in exploring how Arab Americans fell victim to violence as well. Arab American activists endured violations of their civil liberties, as in the well-known case of the FBI's monitoring of Abdeen Jabara and the assassination of the West-Coast regional director of the American-Arab Anti-Discrimination Committee, Alex Odeh, in 1985.[71] Nabeel Abraham identifies three main sources of anti-Arab sentiment during the 1970s and 1980s: xenophobic nativism, jingoistic racism, and ideologically motivated violence. While the first two sources were by-products of "hyper ethnocentrism" in US racialized discourse, the last source was informed by a US-Israeli alignment of narrative against Arabs. The Jewish Defense League and other Jewish extremist groups aggressively enforced this alignment as part of a widened Arab-Israeli conflict. "Their actions were ideologically motivated and premeditated," Abraham confirms, "not merely spontaneous outbursts stemming from anger, fear, or ignorance."[72] But Hollywood filmmakers were not interested in exploring this messy reality; they chose instead to stage and perpetuate hegemonic norms of what it meant to belong in America. Parallel to this nationalist framework is another nationalist framework in Egyptian filmmaking, which challenges Hollywood's negative stereotypes, but nonetheless produces a different form of polarization regarding Arab Americans. Chapter 2 will explore this paradox.

2

Images of Arab Americans in Egyptian Cinema

AS chapter 1 shows, Hollywood's imagination of the Arab presence in the United States since the 1970s has developed as a foreign policy concern in such films as *Network* (1976), *The Next Man* (1976), *Rollover* (1981), and *Power* (1986), or as a national security threat, as in *Black Sunday* (1977), *Wrong Is Right* (1982), *Terror in Beverly Hills* (1989), *True Lies* (1994), and *The Siege* (1998). And as chapter 3 will show, even in post-9/11 portrayals of characters that could be conceived as Arab Americans in films like *The Recruit* (2003), *Five Fingers* (2006), and *Traitor* (2008), positive images are contingent on characters' demonstration of patriotism and still lead the audience to question their allegiance and suspect their involvement in terrorism. These representations function within a reductive tradition in Hollywood that normalizes what it means to be American in ways that alienate Arab and Muslim Americans and present them as perpetually alien.

When it comes to subverting Hollywood in the Arab world, the most important media culture to examine is that of Egypt, home to the largest, most popular, and most prolific Arabic film industry.[1] But how do filmmakers in the Egyptian cinema subvert the US film industry, especially in their imagery of Arab Americans? This chapter explores how Egyptian cinema unsettles US filmic representations of Arab Americans by examining the ways that Egyptian filmmakers counter Hollywood's Orientalist binaries and produce alternative imaginations of Arab Americans. Since the 1990s, I argue, the Egyptian cinema has demonstrated a growing interest in deploying characters and metaphors that define Arab Americans through Egyptian conceptions of class, gender, and generation. In stark contrast to Hollywood, Egyptian cinema also enacts a complicated form of critique of the United States that imagines an alternative narration of Arab American subjectivity. Importantly, Egyptian films depict Arab Americans in ways that transcend US foreign policy in the Middle East, exploring themes such as the false promises of the American dream and nostalgia as a prerogative for an alternative dream. In this sense, Egyptian cinema's subversion of Hollywood is a testimony to the "uneven forces of cultural representation involved in the contest for political and social authority within the modern world order," to echo Homi Bhabha's description of postcolonial literature.[2]

Despite this challenging representational framework, Egyptian cinema continues to depict Arab American subjectivity in reductive ways that reproduce a sense of Arab American Otherness. These portrayals may be different from Hollywood's, but they are still similar in their failure to capture the interstitial nature of Arab American cultural citizenship. In their critique of the United States, the filmmakers I discuss prioritize Egyptian nationalist perspectives, even in their use of allegories that may readily connect with other Arab and Muslim critiques. This prioritizing is not because the filmmakers are necessarily Egyptian per se; this chapter includes works by a Sudanese director and an Egyptian American director. It is rather the Egyptian film industry's hegemonic conditions that emphasize the primacy of Egyptian-based narratives.

"Whether in the United States or the Arab world," Lina Khatib argues, "cinema functions within nationalist projects that narrate the American and the Arab nations, while also using their portrayal of Others in order to construct and strengthen their own identities."[3] With this in mind, the nationalist characteristic of the Egyptian film industry limits possible sites of identity narration and confines the filmic imaginations of Arab Americans within the parameters of Egyptian identity. Moreover, these filmmakers are primarily speaking to an Egyptian audience despite the broad nature of their market and the wide circulation of Egyptian films in the Arab world and among

Arab diasporas. Accordingly, Arab American characters are mostly presented in the industry as first and foremost Egyptian. Film scholar Viola Shafik recognizes an Egyptian nationalist pattern in some of the surveyed films in this chapter that constructs foreignness in familiar terms; she argues that the characters representing Egyptian diasporas in Egyptian cinema are nationalist attempts to converge Egypt's "inside and outside."[4]

I recognize the vigor of the Egyptian cinema's nationalist narrative and build on Shafik's analysis by suggesting that representations of Egyptian Americans are rooted in Egyptian nationalist anxieties amid growing challenges of globalization, migration, and geopolitics. In the films central to this chapter's analysis—*Si'di fi el-Game'a el-Amrīkyya* (An Upper Egyptian in the American University, 1998), *el-Ākhar* (The Other, 1999), *Hallo Amrīka* (Hello America, 2000), *Tayeh fi Amrīka* (Lost in America, 2002), *Gawaz Safar Amrikany* (An American Passport, 2003), *Iskindiriyya . . . New York* (Alexandria . . . New York, 2004), and *Assal Eswed* (Bittersweet, also known as Molasses, 2010)—Egyptian Americans are presented in a state of transition: primarily as first-generation immigrants in the United States whose state of in-betweenness forces them to negotiate their identity and belonging. The films utilize a binary portrayal framework that compels such characters to identify either as American or Egyptian, denigrating the former and celebrating the latter. These binaries help solidify Egyptian critiques of what is perceived as America's corrupting materialism, interventionist foreign policy, and alienating culture. Consequently, the multinational and multigenerational Arab American community, with its array of national and transnational modes of cultural citizenship, is problematically reduced to recycled images of Egyptian immigrants seeking or rejecting the United States. This remains true even though Egyptian films still complicate this binary through multiple narratives of materialism, power, and nostalgia, presented primarily within national allegories of class, gender, and generation.[5]

While the so-called American dream means different things, including social mobility, homeownership, religio-political liberty, individual fulfillment, and material prosperity,[6] Egyptian filmmakers have both defined the American dream in terms of material prosperity and expressed a sense of disillusionment in the American dream as unrealizable and unrewarding, urging their audience to seek out their own dreams in Egypt. Films as early as *Amrīka Shika Bika* (America Abracadabra, 1993), *Agda' Nas* (The Toughest People, 1993), *Arḍ el-Aḥlam* (The Land of Dreams, 1993), and *Ziyarat el-Sayed el-Ra'īs* (Visit of the President, 1994), and as late as *el-Doniya Maklouba* (Reversed World, 2015) and *Talq Sena'i* (Induced Labor, 2018), exhibit nationalist critiques of the public fascination with the United States. As this chapter shows, Egyptian cinema not only articulates a sense of disillusionment in the American dream but also imagines and advances an alternative nationalist vision, one that leaves essentially no space for Egyptian Americans as such.[7] It is worth noting that this simultaneous critique and construction of alternatives to the American dream not only is limited to portrayals of Egyptian Americans' experiences in the United States but also is deeply critical of the Egyptian elite's promotion of consumerism and neoliberal economics as a global fulfillment of the American dream in Egypt.

In an analysis of plots, characters, and cultural contexts, the films surveyed in this chapter may seem promising in offering an important postcolonial challenge to US hegemony, but they employ binaries that deny the possibility of conceiving Egyptian Americans in transnational terms—a consistent portrayal problem, whether the surveyed characters represent Egyptian Americans or are conceived as broad representations of Arab Americans. Although Egyptian cinema pushes back against Hollywood's imagination of Arabs and Arab Americans, it does so within another polarizing frame of Othering that sacrifices Arab Americans along the US and Arab sociocultural and geopolitical divide. This limiting postcoloniality fails to decolonize Hollywood's imperial binary model of representation and adds another layer of cultural Otherness to the imagination of Arab Americans, rendering them doubly alienated in both American and Egyptian cinemas.

Are Egyptian Films Anti-American?

The difference between Hollywood and Egyptian cinema should not be understated. The power dynamics of the respective host countries and the disparity in production and circulation of their products differ. While Hollywood filmmakers enjoy production and distribution support, Egyptian filmmakers must grapple with licensing bureaucracy, state censorship, limited competition, celebrity wage hikes, copyright piracy, and dwindling support from production companies that are heavily competing for profitable films and television series. Consequently, any reading of Egyptian cinema should take its socioeconomic and political context into account, especially before interpreting Egyptian films as "anti-American." The issue is not whether the films express anti-American sentiments, because they certainly produce one-dimensional, often reductive and negative, images of America and Egyptian Americans. Rather the term "anti-American" inadequately captures the coded messages of these films. Indeed, I avoid using the term "anti-American" given its history in US foreign relations of serving a narrative of American exceptionalism that silences postcolonial contestations of US power.[8] The term itself often conflates healthy criticism of the United States with reductive and prejudicial caricatures of American culture and people.[9]

Using the term "anti-American" flattens a complicated reality. Although sensational critiques of the United States in Egyptian cinema often echo narratives that could easily be identified as anti-American, it is important to contextualize such works as ambivalent postcolonial contestations of the US influence in the region. The apparent incongruence of Egyptians' simultaneous criticism of the United States and admiration for the country's prosperity—a "love-hate" relationship that Andrew Hammond diagnoses as "schizophrenic"—speaks to this postcolonial ambivalence.[10] For instance, the radical Egyptian Islamist Sayyid Qutb presents a staunch critique of America as worthless "in the scale of human values" while also acknowledging his admiration for America as the "far-flung world that occupies in the mind's eye more space than it really does on this earth."[11] Many Egyptians offer their critique but simultaneously express a desire to live in the United States, where hard work, social mobility, and justice are relatively cherished. Some Egyptian corporations have even capitalized on this equivocal Egyptianizing of the American dream via consumerist trends that rely on US commodities, pop culture products, and shopping malls.[12] So it should not be surprising that Egyptian films are ambivalent in pairing flattened portrayals of America and American culture as hollow, false, unfulfilling, materialistic, and immoral with a complicated sense of appreciation for American prosperity.

Ziyarat el-Sayed el-Ra'īs, for instance, explores the vanity of searching for the global promises of the American dream, which Egyptian films usually present as a "mirage," to borrow Egyptian film critic Khalid el-Sargany's term.[13] The film provides this critique through a politicized account of Egyptian responses to President Richard Nixon's visit to Egypt in 1974.[14] In the film, people learn of a planned visit of the American president to their remote Egyptian village. Before the visit, the villagers receive a few truckloads of food, presented as part of a US food-assistance program for Egypt. This enhances rumors that their village, like many poor communities in Egypt, will be the beneficiary of an even more generous US gift. Rumors pass as facts among the villagers while they fantasize about the expected gift, which it is thought will be carried in boats across waters separating Egypt and the United States. Not only do these boats carry food for Egyptians, they also bring electric equipment like fans, televisions, washers, carpet cleaners, and refrigerators. The villagers are enthusiastic about the gift's symbolic promise of American prosperity. This prompts them to create a welcoming environment for their guest. They decorate their streets with US flags, their stores with English signs, and their bodies with American T-shirts and jeans. Moreover, they also begin to develop plans to improve their impoverished conditions. They even designate a full day to rehearse speeches, songs, and slogans to be used in their welcome procession. In short, the routine life of the community is suspended, usurped by the prospect of realizing a globally mediated version of the American dream. But, to community members' dismay, the train carrying the president and their imagined ticket to prosperity does not stop; instead, it passes by the village, crushing their hopes and aspirations. *Ziyarat el-Sayed el-Ra'īs* critiques the unfulfilled promises of US neoliberalism and its role in intensifying inequality between the Global North and South populations. The film offers a powerful portrayal of disillusionment in the material allure of the American dream while also acknowledging that, at the heart of the villager's disappointment, lies a deep sense of desire for and admiration of what the United States represents.

Although films like *Ziyarat el-Sayed el-Ra'īs* can be read as vilifying the United States, I suggest that the deeper sense of betrayal is with those Egyptians who are seen as buying uncritically into the American promise of prosperity. Many of the villagers in the film appear more invested in escaping their dire economic conditions through their uncritical celebrations of the US support rather than struggling to improve their own lives on their own terms. Thus, the surveyed films in this chapter are driven less by a hatred of the United States than by a sense of insecurity, loss, and anxiety regarding Egypt's relative appeal as a place to live in and build a future.

In Khairy Beshara's widely circulated film *Amrīka Shika Bika*, the United States is described as a *shika bika*, a nonsensical but rhythmic term that roughly translates into English as "abracadabra," connoting a sense of magic built on illusions. The film presents America as an illusion in the sense that it is a contradictory, confused, and confusing power that is at odds with its own values and principles; the film's poster depicts the Statue of Liberty as villainous and predatory (figure 7). The film presents a critique of the globalized American dream through the story of eight Egyptians, ranging from eight to fifty years old, who are seeking to migrate to the United States. These migrants are fleeing a wave of privatization in Egypt and the government's revision of social programs to favor the ruling elite, both of which have led to deteriorating economic conditions. Although many of them occupy a range of professions—mechanic, physician, tailor, banker, dancer, bodybuilder, and farmer—the characters find themselves increasingly marginalized as the chasm between elite and working class grows wider. They are promised US visas in Romania by a

7. The Statue of Liberty appears villainous and predatory. She is paired in the film's poster with the swindler Mr. Gaber, who dupes the Egyptian migrants in *Amrīka Shika Bika* (1993). © el-Rania Film.

Mr. Gaber (Samy el-Adl), who convinces them of his connections to an American embassy employee there. In their desperation to realize their dreams, the various migrants sell relatives' jewelry, borrow money from friends, and take loans to cover travel expenses.

Once in Romania, the Egyptian dreamers consume American products like Marlboro cigarettes, drink Pepsi and Coca-Cola, and wear blue jeans as part of their perceived journey to happiness, but they are later shocked to learn that Gaber has swindled them. Having lost their money, they experience various forms of hardship, not to mention the emotional turmoil caused by separating from their home. Eventually, the Egyptian government arranges for their travel back to Egypt, where they get hold of Gaber and throw his belongings, mostly American products, into the street. The film foregrounds this moment as their realization that the American dream is a tool to market US products at the cost of local economies and lived realities. The film concludes with a sober tone of pride in Egypt as the only place where Egyptians can truly attain their dreams. The film's title song registers its critique of the American dream: "America is *shika bika*," the song goes. "It plays you hard and turns you upside down."

Even though *Ziyarat el-Sayed el-Ra'īs* and *Amrīka Shika Bika* do not present specific portrayals of Egyptian Americans as the surveyed films in this chapter do, the two films add depth to my critique of the industry's one-dimensional portrayals of America as the defense mechanism of nationalists who are critical of those who seek to migrate and abandon their homeland. To further illustrate my argument in relation to Egyptian Americans, consider Youssef Chahine's *el-Ākhar*. The film's introductory scene features the Palestinian American scholar Edward Said discussing issues of identity and belonging with Adam, the Egyptian American protagonist, and Boujdad, an Algerian American character. Said appears critical of Adam's and Boujdad's perceptions of the irreconcilability of Arabness and Americanness in their identities:

> ADAM: You are an American national and your origin is Palestinian. Where do you belong?

SAID: I hope we stop thinking this way! They [Americans] invented computers, and we [Arabs] invented writing. Forget who contributes what! The Pharaohs' civilization, for example, is just like Beethoven's music. They both belong to all humanity.

BOUJDAD: But do Americans think like this?

SAID: I hope one day we all stop saying "I" and "you" and start using "we" instead!

Throughout the film, however, director Chahine dismisses Said's sobering reflections on polarization and the possibility of imagining Arab Americans on transnational grounds as utopian. The plot reveals a stark contrast between Arab innocence and American aggression. The main character, Adam, is torn between his connection to the United States and to Egypt, but he eventually chooses Egypt and declares the American dream an illusion. Chahine thus presents Egyptian and American as opposed cultural identities, challenging the possibility of imagining Egyptian Americans in transnational terms. Chahine relies on a representational formula of binaries that celebrates Egyptian American characters like Adam for choosing to live in Egypt and realize their own dreams there but denigrates those who choose to embrace the United States in search of their own American dreams.

The label "anti-American" fails to capture these nuanced criticisms and will thus be avoided in my analysis. Instead, I critique the sensational portrayals of the United States and Egyptian Americans in Egyptian cinema while acknowledging the existing power dynamics in US and Egyptian relations and the complexity of Egyptian-based postcolonial narratives. Crucially, the polarized portrayals in Egyptian cinema are driven not by innate hatred or ignorance of America but by the desire to mount an effective local response to empire. The following sections examine the manifestations of the Egyptian cinema's nationalist projections of classed, gendered, and generational binaries of Arab Americans, presented primarily through Egyptian American characters confined within the parameters of the American dream and its Egyptian alternative.

Awlad El-Balad versus *Khawagāt*

Class-based imagery in Egyptian cinema often revolves around the issue of authenticity, which itself builds on an important site of Egyptian collective identity, namely *awlad el-balad* (sons of the country). The notion of *awlad el-balad* concerns one's social conduct, particularly hospitality, generosity, solidarity, chivalry, indigeneity, and national pride. In Egyptian collective memory, the term *awlad el-balad* has been used to connote such positive values and is mostly associated with people of lower socioeconomic class in a class-based system that sets them apart from *khawagāt* (Western foreigners).[15] Egyptian popular culture perpetuates the ascription of *awlad el-balad* to the working class as a critique of the elite, who are usually portrayed as either *khawagāt* or Westernized and therefore as lacking the multilayered virtues suggested by *awlad el-balad*. Since the 1990s, Egyptian films have incorporated this class-based cultural critique in their portrayal of Egyptian Americans as either selfless, community-oriented *awlad el-balad* or selfish, dollar-worshipping *khawagāt*.

El-Ākhar's polarized view of Egyptian American characters plays out through the conflict between an Egyptian American father and his son. Importantly, the film director, Chahine, sets the story in Egypt, so that when the characters collide, the film speaks to the disruptive impact of American-style globalization on Egypt. Consequently, the disparity between Egypt's wealthy and dissolving middle class is mapped allegorically onto a conflict between *awlad el-balad* and *khawagāt*, represented respectively by the son, Adam (Hani Salama) and the father, Khalil (Mahmoud Hemida).

Khalil arrives in Egypt with a group of businesspeople hoping to carry out a proposed interfaith project at Mount Sinai.[16] However, his ignorance of and intermittent disregard for both Egyptian culture and the needs of Egypt's lower-class citizens in particular soon become apparent. At a resort he owns, he lays off half of his employees to restructure the business, declaring, "I am a businessman, not a philanthropist!" Khalil's character embodies the Western-friendly elite of

Egypt, who embrace the American principles of the free market at the cost of the well-being of the working-class community. As Chahine himself puts it, the film's critique emphasizes the one-sided nature of globalization, which allows Western money to invest in the Arab world in the name of the "open market" but denies Arabs the same right to "penetrate America."[17]

The director's nationalist message uses materialism and morality to gauge the extent to which his Egyptian American characters are more American or less Egyptian. Khalil's Egyptian American identity is reduced to a search for wealth at all costs, including at great cost to the Egyptian community. His proposed interfaith project is revealed to be a fraudulent moneymaking scheme, and he ultimately sells the public land allocated to the project, crushing the aspirations of the hired architects. The project's interfaith promise gives way to the pursuit of profit, with Khalil standing for the illusory character of the globalized American dream. Crucially, it is not an American who misleads the Egyptians but an Egyptian American who has forsaken his Egyptian background and is subsequently depicted as a selfish father and emasculated husband.

Unlike his father, Adam becomes disillusioned with American materialism. A UCLA doctoral student, he is in Egypt for dissertation fieldwork on terrorism. Adam falls in love with an Egyptian girl named Hanan (Hanan Tork) and the *awlad el-balad* code of her lower class. He rejects his family's upper-class status as an iteration of the illusory American dream and opts to live with the working-class community instead, in an effort to identify with his Egyptian roots. In one of his family's desperate attempts to influence his decision, he appears dancing with his arranged date, the daughter of the US ambassador in Egypt, but expresses his disdain for the American dream and dismisses her as a potential life partner. For her part, the ambassador's daughter rejects him as well in a symbolic reference to the impossibility of reconciliation between Americans and Egyptians. As Adam begins to feel increasingly disconnected from American culture, he develops an affinity for Egypt's culture instead. This newfound identification with his homeland is captured when he rushes to donate blood for the victims of a terrorist attack and declares: "My father is Egyptian, and I am Egyptian. I will live and die in this Egyptian land!"

Gender plays a central role in Chahine's class-based configurations of identity. In *el-Ākhar*, Adam is torn between his love for his American mother, Margaret (Nabila Ebeid), and his Egyptian love, Hanan. The two female characters of Margaret and Hanan, according to Lina Khatib, stand as gendered representations of the United States and Egypt:

> *The Other* represents the imperialist United States as a devouring mother. A wealthy American businesswoman indulging in a world of fraud, Margaret serves as a classical villain: her unholy alliance with Islamic fundamentalist terrorists, and her selfishness [and] immorality . . . detach us from any identification with her character, and highlight her contrast with Egyptian purity and simplicity as seen in the character Hanan, Margaret's Egyptian daughter-in-law.[18]

The stark contrast between the two women, who represent Adam's American and Egyptian identities, further bewilders him, as he already wrestles with the question of his cultural citizenship. On the one hand, Margaret is a self-centered mother who vehemently rejects her son's marriage and even suggests at one point that Adam's father is not Khalil but an American man named Max. In an effort to win her son back, as she sees it, from Hanan, Margaret enlists the help of Hanan's brother, the newly radicalized Sheik Fathallah (Ahmed Wafik). Fathallah kidnaps Hanan in return for a promised visa to the United States. Unlike Margaret's possessive love, Hanan's love for Adam is unconditional. Hanan is portrayed as innocent, simple, and welcoming. Her Arabic name roughly translates as "tenderness." Her low-income background allows the audience to identify with her as an appropriate representation of Egypt, particularly in contrast to Margaret's wealth, which is associated with the Egyptian elite, often perceived to be American puppets. Hanan rejects her brother's extremist inclinations as deviant and urges Adam to develop a critical attitude toward his parents' shady business corruption. Thus, Adam's marriage

8. Adam's marriage to Hanan is a gendered symbolic gesture to the Egyptian American character's embrace of Egypt's innocence and purity in *el-Ākhar* (The Other, 1999). © Misr International Films.

to Hanan is a symbolic gesture of the Egyptian American character's embrace of Egypt's gendered innocence and purity. The fact that their wedding ceremony features a change from Western classical music to Egyptian traditional music, and the contrast between the couple's Western clothing and the authentically rural clothing of their lower-income Egyptian guests, point to Adam's in-betweenness and his eventual embrace of his Egyptian roots (figure 8).

Adam's disillusionment with his mother's love contributes to his growing detachment from his American background. He first appears hesitant in supporting Hanan's journalistic curiosity, which leads her to uncover details that expose his parents' fake nonprofit scheme. Hanan's desire to discredit Adam's parents represents Egypt's search for independence from foreign influences. When Adam learns about Hanan's published exposé of his parents, he slaps her, but she derisively covers herself from head to toe in black, suggesting that silencing her is equivalent to reducing her to a submissive commodity. Revealing his still-entrenched belief in the US entitlement to penetrate the Other's body, Adam rapes Hanan in an attempt to reassert his masculinity, a symbolic association of violence with Americanness. But as his attachment to Egyptian culture grows, he learns to develop a critical attitude toward the masculinist reiterations of US hegemony. Later, when Margaret denigrates Hanan's Egyptian background as one weakened for thousands of years by colonial occupation by the Hyksos, the Romans, the English, and the French, Adam adds angrily, "And now the Americans!" The film ends with a damning critique of Margaret and US imperialism as Adam and Hanan are brutally killed when caught in the crossfire between Hanan's terrorist brother and Egyptian police. Recalling that it was Margaret who hired Hanan's brother, the audience is left with the message that the United States is a disruptive power with no mercy, even for its own Egyptian American citizens.

Chahine's use of classed, gendered, and generational binaries to critique the American dream and define his Egyptian American characters is central to Egyptian filmmaking. Nader Galal similarly uses such binaries in his portrayal of the Egyptian immigrant characters in *Hallo Amrīka*.[19] Despite the genre difference between *el-Ākhar*, a melodrama, and *Hallo Amrīka*, a comedy, the two films present similarly polarized portrayals of Egyptian American characters. Similar to Chahine's greedy American patriarch, Khalil, Galal's Egyptian immigrant character Noufal (Osama Abbas) has compromised his Egyptian codes of chivalry and generosity during his twenty-year stay in New York. The director begins the film with a phone call that establishes the stark contrast between Noufal's spacious house in New York and his Egyptian cousin's home in an overcrowded and impoverished Egyptian neighborhood. The intercutting images create an extreme opposition between "affluent bourgeois Westernization" and "lower-class Egyptian solidarity."[20] Noufal is presented for the audience as a by-product of Western materialism, and his cousin Bekhit (played by iconic actor Adel Imam) appears as the embodiment of Egyptian *awlad el-balad* authenticity.

After years of no communication, Noufal calls Bekhit to ask for assistance. Noufal wants to sell his land in Egypt, thereby completely disconnecting from the country. Bekhit agrees to help, and with Noufal's support, he subsequently fulfills his deep desire to migrate to the United States. In Noufal's house, Bekhit refuses to accept a commission for selling Noufal's land, citing the *awlad el-balad* code that demands that relatives help one another for no monetary return. When Bekhit turns down a check amounting to 1 percent of the estate's value, Noufal thinks that Bekhit wants more and offers him 2 percent instead. Bekhit continues to refuse and reproaches his cousin: "Shame on you, Noufal! I would not take a penny for my help. Has America changed you, man?" Noufal is appreciative of Bekhit's attitude but soon demonstrates his lack of commitment to the code when Bekhit requests a loan to help him settle in the United States. Noufal wastes no time ignoring the code and offering Bekhit and his fiancée, Adila (Sherine), $200 a week for performing housework duties that include cooking, cleaning, caring for the dog, washing the car, and gardening.

The film suggests that Noufal has been morally corrupted by his blonde American wife, Katy (Enas Mekky), who cannot comprehend the *awlad el-balad* code. She is the one who forces Noufal to refuse to support Bekhit and Adila. It is Katy, too, who raises their children in ways that seem contradictory to Egypt's moral codes. Katy's parenting style appears foreign to the Egyptian audience. She adopts double standards toward her children. She gets furious when she sees Bekhit kiss her son Sam (short for Sami) because she considers same-sex kissing inappropriate, even platonic affection among relatives. Yet she does not see a problem encouraging her teenage daughter Madonna (her nickname for Madiha) to sleep with her boyfriend; indeed, Katy even appears to grieve that her daughter is still a virgin, which runs completely counter to Arab codes of conduct. Next, Katy turns her attention to Adila, encouraging her to dress in a sexually provocative way in the name of women's empowerment, and to carry a gun for protection, pointing to the irrelevance of male protection. Although these scenes are meant to offer comedic relief, together they offer a polarized image of Americans and Arabs that allows no room for any Egyptian American space or identity as such.

The film presents Noufal as an Egyptian immigrant who chooses to reject the collective spirit and moral codes of his Egyptian background in return for America's hollow promise of material success. This is illustrated most vividly when Bekhit is almost hit by a car. Although Bekhit is not hurt, Noufal convinces him to file a hit-and-run accident report to claim millions of dollars in compensation. Noufal's enthusiasm for the scheme, however, is contingent on receiving 25 percent of the compensation amount. When the plan is first hatched, Noufal and Katy suddenly become friendly and hospitable to Bekhit and Adila, but when the plan seems to fall through, the hosts quickly kick their guests out of their house. Throughout the film, Noufal fails to come to terms with his Egyptian *awlad el-balad* nonmaterial values and constantly aligns himself with American materialist-consumerist tendencies instead.

In sharp contrast to his father, Noufal's Egyptian American son, Sam (Ayman Mohammed), tries to reconnect the family with their Arabic and Islamic heritage. Sam decides to learn Arabic and accompany Bekhit to the mosque for Friday prayers. He learns such Arabic words as *shahamah* (chivalry) and *nakhwa* (generosity) and practices them in his life. When Bekhit is unable to work because he gets sick, Noufal withholds his weekly allowance, but Sam promises to work in Bekhit's place. He will secure the income for Bekhit, but only on the condition that his father does not learn of his actions. When Bekhit criticizes Noufal's seeming indifference toward his daughter's engaging in premarital sex, Sam agrees but also points out the conflict between Bekhit's perceptions of the United States and his own actions. "If you think America is a devil," Sam asks, "then, why did you come to America?" Unable to respond, Bekhit smiles and says, "You're the only one in this family who still has some Egyptian left in him!" Honesty thus validates Sam's sense of his Egyptian cultural background. While his father is drawn to American materialism at the cost of his Egyptian code of honor, Sam is drawn to the promise of the morally defined relationships embraced by his visiting Arab relatives and his ancestors.

The articulations of difference in *el-Ākhar* and *Hallo Amrīka* center on the issue of respect (or lack thereof) for the *awlad el-balad* code of honor. The films exemplify a polarizing dynamic in Egyptian cinema that presents binary images of Egyptian Americans as either Egyptian community contributors or American dollar worshippers. This narrative ascribes positive and negative values alongside fixed and rigid spatial identity formations. Using Egyptian nationalist constructions of class, gender, and generation adds depth to this polarity but still does not produce thought-provoking portrayals that subvert Hollywood's imagery in disruptive terms.

Seeking an Alternative Dream

Inasmuch as Egyptian filmmakers' imagination of Egyptian immigrants and Egyptian Americans reflects a sense of disillusionment with the American dream, this imagination simultaneously searches for an alternative Egyptian dream. Although there is no clear articulation in the surveyed films of what this dream could look like, there is an explicit message deterring migrants from leaving their homeland in favor of staying and creating the parameters of what could one day be "the Egyptian dream." This alternative dream, the films suggest, may not necessarily contradict the American dream, but it will be one made in Egypt, one in which immigrating in search of social mobility, individual success, and even personal ambition is considered a selfish measure divorced from a commitment to one's own Egyptian community.

As early as 1954, Egyptian film director Ahmed Kamel Morsi offered a sense of this alternative dream in *Amricany min Ṭanṭa* (An American from Tanta) through the coming-home story of Egyptian immigrant Mahrous (Soliman Bey Nag) and his family. Having failed to realize the American dream, Mahrous returns to Egypt where he schemes against a poor civil servant, Ibrahim Afendi (Hussein Riyaḍ). Through a fake promise of employment, Mahrous gains access to Afendi's savings, but when Afendi learns of the deception and confronts Mahrous, the latter pledges to work, along with his family, to pay back the debt. In the film, the scheme's illusionary promise stands in for the unfulfilled promise of the American dream for Egyptian migrants, while it is only in Egypt that Mahrous and his family ultimately realize their aspirations.

Hani Sabri's 2015 film *el-Doniya Maklouba* (Reversed World) underscores a similar nationalist narrative. Despite its poor filming techniques and cheap comedic thrills, the film's creative script invites the audience to learn about Jack (Bassem Samra), an American seeking immigration to Egypt to realize his "Egyptian Dream." America, in the film, has become a third world country, where a third of its population lives in poverty. It is a country where corruption, unemployment, violence, and crushed aspirations are on full display. Egypt, on the other hand, has developed its economy and become the Great Republic of Egypt, an international power with interventionist foreign policies in the West. Jack, like many of his American fellows, has dedicated his life to escaping his impoverished conditions and, after many visa rejections, finally resorts to travel via a dangerous smuggling operation. Armed with a degree in Arabic language from New York University and a fascination for a seven-thousand-year-old civilization, Jack defies death and arrives in Egypt, ready to explore the country's historical sites and tourist attractions. Jack's successful realization of his dream to be in Egypt stands in sharp contrast to the more frequently depicted failure of other characters in Egyptian films for whom travel to the United States is either unrealizable or meaningless. In this sense, the film is testimony to the nationalist narrative that underwrites Egyptian filmmaking and imagines Egypt as a place worthy of hopes and dreams.

Indeed, this nationalist message has been at the center of Egyptian filmmakers' imagination of Egyptian immigrants since the 1990s and is evoked particularly strongly by their use of nostalgia. The characters in the surveyed films find hope in Egypt only when they claim it as their home and as the place where they can realize their dreams. The films mobilize the concept of *el-ghorba* (alienation and foreignness) in making sense of this nostalgic sentimentality. The Arabic meaning of *el-ghorba* carries a double-layered sense of alienation and foreignness, triggered by the departure from one's homeland and a nostalgic desire to reconnect with it. *El-ghorba*, in this sense, serves as a conceptual tool underwriting the Egyptian films' images of Egyptian immigrants as caught between a sense of Otherness, should they leave Egypt's borders, and of nostalgia for their homeland. Egyptian filmmakers have taken an active role in promoting this idea of *el-ghorba* by locating characters at the crossroads of an alienating American culture and a welcoming Egyptian homeland.

The above-mentioned *Amrīka Shika Bika* relies on nostalgia to accelerate its migrating group's growing disillusionment with the American dream. The sudden death of the eldest member of the group creates a deep sense of anxiety for the group about meanings of migration, alienation, and nostalgia for their lives. Protagonist el-Mansi (played by actor and singer Mohamed Fouad), whose name roughly translates as "the forgotten," reminds his fellow dreamers that they will perish in foreign lands if they fail to return to their home. In one of the film's viral songs, el-Mansi asks rhetorical questions that capture the essence of the film's message: "What does home mean? Does it mean a land, borders, a place, or a state of longing?" The solidarity that emerges within the diverse traveling group, meant to symbolize Egyptians of different classes, professions, and religions, serves as a nationalist call for Egyptians to realize their dreams at home.

In *Arḍ el-Aḥlam* (The Land of Dreams), nostalgia disrupts the travel plans of the leading character, Nargis (Faten Hamama), to the United States to realize the American dream for her children. Throughout the film, Nargis is emotionally consumed by her fear of leaving her relatives, neighbors, and friends. While bidding her mother farewell at a nursing home, she bitterly cries, "Damn America that turned us to this!" Nargis is already nostalgic about leaving the familiar for the foreign. She looks at an old tree, reflects on her life, and wonders whether she should leave the place that has become part of her soul. The foreignness of American culture reveals itself to be a challenge as she continues listening to tapes of English conversations for beginners. "I don't know English," she complains, "and there, everything is in English: people, television, and neighbors!" Her struggle outweighs the lure of migration and reveals the value of staying at home. She eventually decides not to emigrate. Nargis's children are aware of their mother's struggle, and they learn to see the value of their homeland and their mother's decision.

While the main characters in *Amrīka Shika Bika* and *Arḍ el-Aḥlam* experience disillusionment with the American dream without even making it to the United States, the main characters in *Hallo Amrīka* and *el-Ākhar* arrive at the same conclusion after living within US borders. After winning $10 million in settlement money, *Hallo Amrīka*'s Bekhit and Adila still fail to find peace, as they are chased by their hosts, lawyers, and many others who seek only their fortune. The film ends with a scene in which Bekhit and Adila throw all the money behind them to force those chasing them to slow down and collect it. As the latter scramble to pick up the money in the street, the World Trade Center is shown looming in the background, suggesting the United States as a site of constant search for financial growth and materialism, divorced from *awlad el-balad* values. Similarly, at the end of *el-Ākhar*, Adam gives up his American identity and dies holding hands with Hanan, whose gendered representation as Egypt adds more depth to the film's ending and meaning to Adam's rejection of the corruption that his American mother and Egyptian American father represent.

Chahine's 2004 film *Iskindiriyya . . . New York* captures the sense of *el-ghorba* through the story of Yehya (Mahmoud Hemida), an Egyptian film student in the United States who eventually becomes well known after fifty years of working as a film director.[21] Director Chahine dedicates a prequel film *Iskindiriyya . . . Lih?* (Alexandria . . . Why?, 1979) to capture young Yehya's struggle to realize his passion and desire to travel to the United States. The final scene of this prequel shows Yehya in a ship of immigrants awed by the Statue of Liberty on their arrival in New York. In this film Chahine hints at the hardships awaiting the shipborne young migrant, Yehya, by replacing the Statue of Liberty shot with an alternative image that personifies the statue as a woman with missing teeth and smeared makeup who vulgarly laughs and winks (figure 9). This personification is a visual rendering of the director's critique of the existing contradiction between the American dream and the country's harsh reality for Arab immigrants. In

9. Director Youssef Chahine's personification of the Statue of Liberty underlines his critique of the contradiction between the American dream and the country's harsh reality for Arab immigrants in *Iskindiriyya . . . Lih?* (Alexandria . . . Why?, 1979). © Misr International Films.

Iskindiriyya . . . New York, Yehya's fascination with American culture leads to a profound sense of disappointment and regret, shaped by his experience of anti-Arab racism. As an aspiring young student pursuing a degree in acting in California during the 1940s, Yehya encounters the stereotype of Arabs as backward and uncivilized. A fellow student wonders whether he lives in a tent and rides camels. He is also escorted out of the Columbia Pictures studios for being an Arab. Yehya's experience with anti-Arab racism throughout his stay in the United States underscores the film's consistent portrayals of American culture as unwelcoming, if not alienating.

Yehya struggles to complete his studies and almost collapses when financial hardship forces him to return to Egypt two months before graduation. In a touching scene, he passionately embraces his American lover, Ginger (Yosra El Lozy), as his despair reaches its

10. Yehya holds American love Ginger as his American dream almost collapses in *Iskindiriyya . . . New York* (Alexandria . . . New York, 2004). © Misr International Films.

limits (figure 10). Luckily, however, he manages to complete his studies. After doing so, he then decides to go back to Egypt, where he becomes a dedicated and acclaimed director. Despite Yehya's international acclaim, US film distributors do not accept his work for forty years because of his Arab perspective. In 2000 Yehya is finally recognized at a New York film festival celebrating his work, which comes at a time when his frustration with the United States' anti-Arab foreign policy has also reached a critical turn. There, he again meets Ginger, who informs him that her twenty-five-year-old son, the well-known ballet dancer Iskandar (Ahmad Yahya), is in fact Yehya's. Iskandar soon rejects his father, however, because he is not ready to acknowledge any Arab ancestry, partly because of the anti-Arab stigma in the US entertainment industry. Yehya erupts in tears because his love for America is deeply wounded. The United States rejects his Arabness twice: first when he was a student seeking inclusion in a racist environment and again when his son expresses shame because of Yehya's Arab heritage. The film concludes with Yehya wandering around the "city of foreigners" while the musical refrain "New York kills any sense of longing" plays in the background, a symbol of America's tendency to destroy family ties.[22]

Iskandar is presented as a heartless and insensitive individual whose Americanness manifests through his rejection of the world beyond US borders. When he declares that Arabs do not exist on the map, his mother informs him that the world does not end at the United States' shorelines. His limited understanding of the Arab world recycles Hollywood's Orientalist imagery; as he complains to his mother, "You want me to have a father coming from a land where they live in tents and ride camels, where people are backward and ignorant!" In a subsequent conversation with Yehya, Iskandar boasts of his pride in belonging to the United States—"the most powerful nation in the world"—and denigrates his father as belonging to a still-developing part of the globe. His dignity injured, Yehya dismisses his son's rejection as arrogance and cruelty, traits he comes to equate with the United States' reckless global character. Chahine uses the same actor to play young Yehya and Iskandar in *Iskindiriyya . . . New York*, which is important because it stages a stark contrast between the two individuals in terms of their relationship to family and home. The young Yehya's return to Egypt is glorified as a model of the Egyptian immigrants who never lose connection with their homeland. His career success in Egypt suggests Chahine's version of an Egyptian dream, a dream modeled on Chahine's own career. Iskandar, in contrast, represents the director's denigrated image of Egyptian Americans who may appear to be successful in realizing their material ambitions of the American dream but ought to be viewed as failures in retaining their Egyptianness.

Ibrahim Zaki's TV film *Gawaz Safar Amrikany* (An American Passport) presents an image of an Egyptian American who, unlike Iskandar, can transcend stereotypes and claim Egypt as her home. The work features Gina (nickname for Galila, played by Lebanese actress Madlin Tabar), who is visiting Egypt after twenty years of living in California. She has come to bury her father, who never stopped loving his country of origin. Gina is snobbish, angry, and disrespectful. She represents everything negative that Egyptians might think of Americans. Throughout the film, she undergoes a process of disillusionment as she uncovers more about the very country that she seeks to forget. She eventually decides to stay in Egypt and gives up her plans to sell her father's business. Her love for an American, John, shifts to an Egyptian named Mahmoud. She rejects the US media–fed linkage of Arabs with terrorism as she learns more about the complexity of injustice and resistance. The film, though didactic and naively nationalistic, conveys an important message at the core of the Egyptian filmmaking industry—that one's home is like one's fingerprints, something that one cannot change.

The same nationalist message is illustrated through the character of Masri el-Arabi (Ahmed Helmy) in Khaled Marei's *Assal Eswed* (Bittersweet); the rough translation of the character's name is "Egyptian the Arab." Masri is an Egyptian American who left Egypt as a child and lived in the United States for twenty years. He travels back to Egypt to capture photos of the place he vaguely remembers as his ancestors' land in order to enrich a photography exhibit that he plans to stage in New York. During his stay, Masri encounters a range of attitudes as he negotiates his own identity. Initially, he chooses not to carry his US passport, preferring to show his Egyptian one to demonstrate his connection with Egypt. He ridicules the idea of showing his US passport and being treated as a foreigner in his country of origin. But he soon realizes what it means to lose the special treatment accorded to Americans. He experiences a delay at the airport, a cancellation of his hotel reservation, subjection to extra bureaucratic procedures at a car rental company, a low standard of service at the Pyramids, and intimidation at a police station.

Worn out by the ill treatment his Egyptian passport elicits, Masri disposes of it as soon as he receives his US passport. The US passport opens doors to privileges denied to Egyptians (figure 11). With the new passport in hand, he is treated exceptionally well by the same people who previously abused him. They recognize his American status and respect him accordingly. Masri's celebration is short-lived, however. Boasting his American status soon invites trouble, when he is beaten at

11. Masri is ecstatic upon receiving his US passport in *Assal Eswed* (Bittersweet, 2010). © United Brothers Cinema.

a rally protesting US foreign policy. His belongings, including the US passport, are dispersed and lost. With no proof of either Egyptian or American nationality, Masri is forced to look for his childhood neighborhood. There, he interacts with his childhood friends and neighbors and is reminded of the *awlad el-balad* code of generosity, hospitality, and community support. Masri's struggle, then, becomes whether to leave for the United States or stay in the community he has come to consider family.

The interaction between Masri and an old neighbor, Hilal (Youssef Dawood), introduces the premise of an alternative Egyptian dream. "I don't understand how people emigrate," Hilal declares, expressing his disdain of migration. "They waste their lives abroad, and then wish to be buried in this land as if this country is merely a cemetery!" He asks Masri, "Do you plan to get buried here or abroad?" His emphasis on burial expresses a popular Egyptian sentiment that keeps emigrants attached to their original homeland, even if it fails to deter them from emigrating. The idea appears again toward the end of the film when Masri asks an old sailor whether he wants to leave his country. The sailor responds that he wants to die there. Masri's follow-up question, "But, when you die, you will not feel it?" is met with the sailor's appeal to the metaphysical as he affirms, "My spirit will be here!"

As an Egyptian American, Masri is conflicted about leaving or staying in Egypt. He feels that his life has already been shaped in the United States, and the socioeconomic circumstances in Egypt are dire. But Hilal draws a different portrait for Masri to consider:

> Son! I always say, "Thank you God!" Do you want me to say it the American way so you can understand?! . . . If I look at circumstances the way you do, I will see a lot of bad things and I may become a non-believer. If you only search seriously in these tough circumstances, you will definitely find many good things. This point, however, needs someone who can feel! . . . It may be true, as you say, there are a lot of good things in America, but those things are easy to get one day. Meanwhile, we have things that are hard to get; otherwise, I would have the one standing in front of me [Masri] feeling and sensing!

This emotional call for perseverance and enduring hardships is what underpins the alternative vision to the American dream in these Egyptian films. It takes Masri some time before he realizes the emotional dimension of his experience in Egypt, particularly the power of the *awlad el-balad* code in energizing individuals around their community. He decides to stay. *Assal Eswed* reveals the role played by nationalism in defining cultural citizenship in a globalized but fractured world. Masri's experience with the two passports (and no passport at one point) speaks to that role. His disillusionment with the American dream is a result not so much of despair about America—as depicted in many other Egyptian films—but rather hope in and nostalgia for the Egyptian homeland as the only site where one's dreams can truly be realized.

Regardless of their different approaches, Egyptian filmmakers use *el-ghorba* as an important tool to construct an alternative sense of longing to that of the American dream. They develop this dynamic by imagining the Egyptian diasporic experience in the United States as one of struggle against an alienating culture and by reawakening their protagonists' emotional connection to Egypt. This representation strategy polarizes the Egyptian American image. Egyptian Americans like Iskandar who choose to distance themselves from their Arab roots are imagined to embrace American culture and repudiate anything Arab, whereas Egyptian Americans like Galila and Masri attain self-realization only once they identify themselves with their original home country and choose to live there. Ultimately, these films suggest that the American dream offers only alienation for Arabs, who must return home in order to become whole.

An Identity for Filmmaking or Filmmakers?

Egyptian directors Youssef Chahine, Nader Galal, Khairy Beshara, Daoud Abdel Sayed, Munir Rady, Ibrahim Zaki, and Khaled Marei have all contributed in various ways to the Egyptian cinema's binary framework of conceiving Otherness, which oftentimes comes at the cost of failing to articulate the nuanced experience of Arab Americans. Even non-Egyptian filmmakers working in Egyptian cinema, such as the Sudanese director Saeed Hamed, and Egyptian American directors like Rafy Gerges, still abide by the industry's parameters. Hamed, for instance, does not shy away from the cinema's binaries in his film *Si'di fi el-Game'a el-Amrīkyya* (An Upper Egyptian in the American University).[23] The film offers a staunch critique of the banality of the American dream through its vilification of the Egyptian American character Sirag (Hany Ramzy), a professor of political science at the American University in Cairo. Sirag is portrayed negatively for disrespecting *awlad el-balad*, as he chooses instead to show support for US foreign policy interventions in the Arab world. Claiming to have embraced the American spirit of democracy and freedom, Sirag insists that there are no differences between students and their instructor and that democracy is an ideal to be celebrated and embraced. But

Sirag's intolerance of any critique of US foreign policy renders his reading of democracy one-dimensional and puts him at odds with his Egyptian community, notably the working-class Egyptian students who challenge his American way of defining democracy and liberty. The university itself is presented as an elitist institution that seeks to re-create a miniature model of America in the heart of Egypt.[24] Prominent among Sirag's challengers is Ahmed (Fathi Abdulwahhab), who invokes the *awlad el-balad* code in a contentious moment with the university's administration:

> Will our study here force us to forget our Arab identity and belonging? We are here on Egyptian land and nobody can restrict our freedom and sweep away our will. If the university's administration prevents us from demonstrating against oppression and terror, thinking that we are dead, then let it be known that we are still alive and that we will resist. If norms of justice are dead, we retain our right through hope and resistance!

Ahmed's words map the university-student relationship onto the broader realm of US-Arab encounters. He rejects Sirag's insistence that students should forget anything they have learned outside the classroom. "This is antidemocracy," he protests. "This means your opinion is the only right opinion, the university's opinion, or America's opinion." Ahmed utilizes the classroom as a stage for activism, highlighting the chasm between American ideals and policies. When Ahmed distributes pictures of civilian victims of the economic sanctions against Iraq following the 1990–91 Gulf War, Sirag seeks to silence Ahmed by reporting him to the university's administration after threatening to fail him in the course.

The contradiction between Sirag's call for freedom and his actions is reminiscent of historian Rashid Khalidi's critique of America's freedom as a euphemism for its need to "invest the world over."[25] Such a profit-driven project of American freedom can be advanced only by silencing local critical voices like Ahmed's. Ahmed's critique of US hypocrisy is illustrated when he leads efforts to commemorate the fiftieth anniversary of the Israeli occupation of Palestine. At a student sit-in at the university, an Israeli flag is shown being burned—for the first time in an Egyptian film—while Ahmed delivers a stirring speech condemning Israeli aggressions and calling out America's double standard. "America stands behind all this and protects it," he declares, "while leaving us, Arabs, to its fatal weaponry, and ignores Israel's behavior and its discriminatory practices." Sirag, meanwhile, sides with the university's administration and ignores issues of concern to his Egyptian students.

Khalaf (Mohamed Henedi), the film's protagonist, embraces Ahmed's reasoning after some hesitation. A local farmer whose dedication to education has earned him admission to the prestigious American University in Cairo, Khalaf experiences a series of personal and political confrontations and emerges disillusioned with America. "When I joined the American University," Khalaf says in his graduation speech, "I was very impressed with America." "Three years later, after this admiration has gone," he continues, "I've found that inside me there are meanings and a tradition more important than what has impressed me." Khalaf argues that Arabs do not hate America but reject American aggression, ridicule, and efforts to make Arabs feel inferior. "We hate bullying and imposing opinion by force," he states. "We hate those who say we are backward or that we are less than them." Khalaf's disillusionment is shaped by the activism on campus and emerges as a response to Sirag's sense of entitlement and superiority at the cost of his own people. Throughout the film, characters question Sirag's allegiance to his Egyptian homeland. "If one day," Ahmed asks him, "you were to hold a distinguished position at the United Nations or the International Monetary Fund, which country will you be loyal to? Egypt or America?"

Crucially, Hamed repeatedly portrays Sirag as emasculated and effeminate. His masculinity is challenged throughout the film by Khalaf, who also seeks to attract Sirag's girlfriend, Abla (Ghada Adel). Sirag's failure to express his manhood comes to the fore when he loses a swimming challenge against Khalaf. In the staged contest, Khalaf's friends sneak behind Sirag and easily intimidate him into removing his underwear, leaving him to battle a sense of embarrassment that scars his masculinity. Further stressing the gendered nature of Sirag's weakness, Khalaf and his buddies celebrate their symbolic triumph by addressing him by the feminine name "Susu" as they reproach him for being Americanized. "If you stepped on your origin," they sing, "what would be left for you, Susu?" Sirag's masculinity is also challenged by his students, whose protests against the US support of Israeli aggression are depicted as manly and heroic. Perhaps the ultimate measure of Sirag's effeminacy is Abla's decision to break up with him toward the end of the film. He is eventually forced to resign and return to the United States. Unlike the character of Adam in *el-Ākhar*, who is glorified as a martyr for defending the ever-resilient Egyptian homeland, Sirag is rejected as an impotent embodiment of the surrender to US power and dominance.

Like Hamed, the Egyptian American director Gerges chooses to work within the Egyptian cinema's framework and offers simplified, unnuanced depictions of Egyptian immigrant characters. *Tayeh fi Amrīka* (Lost in America) was written, produced, and directed by Gerges himself and contrasts Americanized Egyptians with those who choose to cling to their roots, thereby reproducing binaries central to mainstream Egyptian filmmaking. The film opens on an airplane with a scene featuring two Egyptians from different economic backgrounds. The working-class Sherif (Khaled Nabawy) aspires to realize his American dream with only $200 in his pocket, while the entrepreneur Adel (Muhammad Lutfi) is en route to meet his Egyptian American cousin, Nour (Hala Sheha), whom he is arranged to marry. At the airport, Nour and her mother, Nahla (Iman), wait for Adel, but he is held by US Customs and Border Protection officers who mistake his dried *mulukhiyya* (a type of mallow leaf used in Arabic cuisine) for marijuana and force him to stay the night while they wait for a translator. Unable to afford taxi and lodging costs, Sherif also decides to spend the night at the airport, but when he overhears that Nour and Nahla do not know what Adel looks like, he decides to impersonate Adel and is welcomed accordingly.

Later that night at Nahla and Nour's spacious villa, Sherif eavesdrops on a conversation between the two women that reveals the real motives underlying the marriage. Nahla and Nour are Egyptian Americans at odds with each other, with the former representing what it means to be American and the latter representing what it means to be Egyptian. Nahla is an Americanized Egyptian whose obsession with material possessions and desire to maintain a wealthy lifestyle preclude any concern for her daughter's actual well-being; she is intent on forcing her daughter to go through with the arranged marriage. Nour is an innocent daughter caught between her desire to lead a happy life and her mother's insistence on sustaining her lifestyle. Sherif decides to stay and enjoy his temporary affluence. He is served by an English butler and has easy access to fancy food, name-brand clothing, and nice cars. He also dates the beautiful Nour and falls in love with her. The temporary nature of this American dream haunts him, however, and reminds him of sea waves, which start big and promising but collapse and vanish at the shore. Such is the promise of materialism embodied by Nahla, who plots to convince her would-be son-in-law to sell his properties and business in Egypt and settle down in the United States. Even at the wedding, Nahla is focused on securing her material well-being. She invites a close friend to discuss business proposals with Sherif, still impersonating Adel, and insists she is motivated only by concern for her daughter. Her friend, however, clearly knows otherwise and nods sarcastically.

Despite being Egyptian American himself, Gerges employs a recurring trope of Egyptian filmmaking by contrasting American and Egyptian cultures as stark opposites and, moreover, portraying those cultures in specifically gendered and generational terms. He pits those guilty of embracing American materialism, like Nahla, against those who choose love over profit, like Nour. Nahla is a dollar worshipper and thus symbolic of America's corrupting materialism, while the romantic Nour represents Egypt's idealism. Nahla's wrangling of the marriage-for-business deal is presented as evidence of America's materialism. Nour reluctantly accepts Nahla's arrangement but eventually deviates from her mother's plans when she uncovers Sherif's identity. She rejects Adel's wealth and opts to continue her romantic relationship with Sherif.

Meanwhile, the real Adel is hospitalized after being accidentally shot by a gang member and meets the Lebanese American nurse Iman (Rajia Baroudi). Inserting this character in *Tayeh fi Amrīka* represents a major departure from the other surveyed films, as she not only provides relief from the suffocating images of materialism in the lives of Nahla and Sherif but also moves beyond the usual imagination of Arab Americans as primarily Egyptian. Iman first connects with Adel by enthusiastically communicating with him in Arabic. Next, she references classic Arabic music and films. Knowing that Adel is lost and is unable to contact his family in California, she hospitably invites him to stay at her modest apartment. Iman further demonstrates her Arab honor code by orienting Adel to life in America. In addition to sharing his sorrows, she tries to bring happiness to his life by purchasing airline tickets to allow him to return to Egypt. Her Lebanese background underscores a pan-Arab message that, regardless of differences across national cultures, Arabs still share common cultural codes and a heritage that ought to be maintained in the United States. Although the director's development of this character stresses a level of awareness of Arab American complexities, the film's overall development of its characters remains rooted in the old binaries.

The national or transnational background of the filmmakers, therefore, does not seem to have an impact on the binary representations of Arab Americans in Egyptian cinema. What defines these binaries, in other words, is not the identity of the filmmaker but the nationalist imperatives behind Egyptian cinema's narrative norms. So, not all Egyptian and Egyptian American filmmakers necessarily employ this portrayal framework, but those who work in Egyptian cinema most likely do. The film *AmericanEast* (2008)—analyzed further in chapter 5—is an example of how different films produced outside Egyptian cinema can be. Although its Egyptian American director, Hesham Issawi, has directed several films in Egypt, his *AmericanEast* departs from Egyptian cinema's codes because it is a US production, but not a Hollywood mainstream one. The film is in English, not Arabic, and features a great many Middle Eastern American actors, as it is both filmed and staged in Los Angeles. *AmericanEast* presents a critique of Hollywood's casting practices and challenges constructions of Arab Americans in Hollywood. It allows Sayed Badreya—an Egyptian American actor who has been typecast for decades in Hollywood in "terrorist" roles—to play the lead role of an Egyptian immigrant, Mustafa, and in so doing, affords him a level of agency as an actor that he has otherwise been denied in Hollywood. The character struggles to realize his American dream amid the institutional discrimination and anti-Arab public backlash that followed the 9/11 attacks. As an Egyptian American widower, Mustafa's challenge is to balance the various dictations of his Arabic identity and the daily demands of life in Los Angeles. He finds himself challenged by familial, cultural, and political demands that overwhelm his American dream to pay off his debts and become a successful businessperson. He is forced to navigate post-9/11 paranoia wherein FBI agents are increasingly invested in interrogating ties between his Islamic background and terrorism. He also finds himself entangled by obligations to raise his Americanized family—two children and a sister—according to Egyptian traditions. Equally challenging are managing his Habibi café and running his one-taxi company. Throughout the film, the camera captures the personal struggles of the many Middle Eastern immigrants inhabiting Mustafa's home and businesses in a layered narrative. The Egyptian American director's portrayals of identity in this film are, therefore, distinct, primarily because it is produced outside Egyptian cinema.

The representation framework of Egyptian cinema is not determined by the identity of its filmmakers. The industry is not exclusively limited to Egyptian directors; it could also welcome other directors—such as the Sudanese filmmaker Hamed and the Egyptian American Gerges—so long as they are invested in the cinema's binaries, which function to enhance geopolitical and sociocultural differences between the United States and Egypt, and also polarize representations of Egyptian Americans accordingly. Filmmakers working in Egyptian cinema portray Egyptian immigrants only as Americans or Egyptians, although this binary is coded in various ways: as generational, as in the contrast between Khalil and Adam in *el-Ākhar*; as informed by class, with the *khawagāt* or Westernized elite against the *awlad el-balad* ethics, as in the contrast between Khalil's crooked business elite and Adam's new working-class family; or as gendered, with emasculated Arab American characters like Khalil and Sirag and women coded as American immoral or Egyptian innocent, as in the contrast between Nahla and Nour in *Tayeh fi Amrīka*. These differences are presented as natural as opposed to political, thus making Egyptian Americans' choice to be either American or Egyptian seem inevitable instead of constructed—indeed, constructed in large part through film.

Conclusion

The Egyptian filmmaking industry has actively resisted the perceived US cultural imperial project represented by Hollywood. The dominant cinema in the Arab world has spearheaded efforts to portray postcolonial independence and reclaim a sense of representational agency. The cinema's output has promoted Egyptian critiques of the United States through allegorical references commonly deployed by Arabists and Islamists and provided its audience in the Arab-speaking world with materials to push back against US cultural hegemony. As illustrated in this chapter, Egyptian cinematic tropes enact a complicated form of critique that correlates the nationalist imperatives of the Egyptian nation-state with certain political, social, cultural, and economic territories in the Egyptian popular imagination of the United States. Egyptian films articulate a sense of disillusionment with the American dream and with globalization itself as a Western-driven process. They portray the United States as a land that alienates Egyptian Americans and construct alternative dreams based on nostalgia and belonging, to deter more people from emigrating.[26]

These cinematic forms of subversion fail, however, to move beyond merely reversing Hollywood's one-dimensional binary constructions. The industry's writers, directors, and producers, regardless of their identity, operate within a highly polarizing frame of reference that glorifies everything Arabic and denigrates anything American. The result is a form of Othering that simplifies understandings of Arab Americans along the US and Egyptian sociocultural and geopolitical divide. In giving voice to critiques of US hegemony, Egyptian films leave no space for Arab Americans beyond the rigid distinctions drawn between Egyptian and American cultures. The films and their directors articulate a spatial morality that abstractly contrasts materialism, power, and nostalgia with the categories of cultural citizenship defined through nation, class, gender, and generation. Egyptian American images, then, become a tool to mediate Egyptian grievances about globalization, migration, and geopolitics. Portraying Noufal, Khalil, and Nahla as dollar worshippers in *Hallo Amrīka*, *el-Ākhar*, and *Tayeh fi Amrīka*, respectively, and their children Sam, Adam, and Nour as value-conscious individuals, speaks of a representation strategy that demands Egyptian Americans proclaim their cultural allegiance as either American or Arab. The same representation formula is used to denounce Egyptian American characters like Sirag in *Si'di fi el-Game'a el-Amrīkyya* and Iskandar in *Iskindiriyya . . . New York* as aberrations, while celebrating other characters like Adam in *el-Ākhar*, Galila in *Gawaz Safar Amrikany*, and Masri in *Assal Eswed* as the quintessential manifestation of the Egyptian identity.

Such binary constructions in Egyptian filmmaking not only limit the possibility of more complex understandings of the United States among audiences in the Arab world but also render Arab Americans alienated by both Hollywood and Egyptian cinemas. Noufal, Sam, Bekhit, Adila, Adam, Khalil, Sirag, Iskandar, Galila, and Masri are oversimplified articulations of a very complicated Arab American identity that defies reduction along the lines of spatial morality. In short, although Egyptian cinema offers images that challenge Hollywood's own strictly nationalist framework, the former's representation framework fails to recognize the empowering potential for Arab American cultural citizenship in a transnational context.

3

Challenging Hollywood's Terrorism Syndrome

THE FIRST TWO CHAPTERS of this book illustrate how Hollywood and Egyptian motion pictures have long held images of Arabs in the United States hostage to nationalist politics of representation. For decades, the two film industries have produced sensational imagery encoding a simplistic repertoire of East-West binaries venerating the "Self" and vilifying the "Other." Hollywood filmmakers have both relied upon and reinforced a nationalist and racialized rhetoric that has generated often-blurred stereotypes of Arabs and Arab Americans, presented primarily through the lenses of national security and foreign policy. Meanwhile, Egyptian cinema has offered images of Arab Americans as glorified Egyptians or denigrated Americans, advanced through a nationalist critique of the United States that activates class-based, gendered, and generational binaries. In this context, constructions of the Arab American image since the 1970s in Hollywood and since the 1990s in Egyptian cinema have promoted a limited sense of cultural citizenship, rendering Arab Americans doubly alienated in both American and Egyptian collective imaginations.

Sunaina Maira critiques American scholarship on cultural citizenship as failing to engage adequately with the issue of migrant belonging and minority exclusion; specifically, she points to a lack of attention to the transnational context within which migrant communities circulate.[1] Despite the growing visibility of Arab Americans in scholarly and literary production as well as civil society and entertainment circles, both US and Egyptian film industries tend to dismiss the transnational configurations of the label "Arab American." Cinematic representations of Arabness continue to portray Arab Americans through either the lens of "terrorism" in the case of Hollywood or "resistance" in the case of Egypt. Meanwhile, articulations of Americanness in both contexts question Arab Americans' patriotism and allegiance.

Such representation patterns fail to recognize Arab Americans' agency. Instead, they mediate a "mortal" sense of identity, to borrow the Lebanese French thinker Amin Maalouf's characterization of nationalist constructions of diasporic identities. Reducing identity to one single affiliation, he argues, invites "partial" and "intolerant" considerations of migrants that render them torn between their "country of origin and country of adoption."[2] Both Hollywood and Egyptian films recycle US and Arab sociocultural and geopolitical encounters through their reductive, sometimes even dismissive, portrayals of Arab Americans. They reveal a deep disinterest in, if not outright rejection of, the interstitial space that Arab Americans occupy and the hybrid subjectivities they inhabit. Meant in Homi Bhabha's sense, hybridity defies hegemonic calls for purity and operates in a third space that disrupts dominant nationalist imperatives. "The process of cultural hybridity," Bhabha maintains, "gives rise to something different, something new and unrecognizable, a new area of negotiation of meaning and representation."[3]

In this chapter, I depart from the hegemonic emphasis on polarization in the first two chapters and search for emerging representation strategies in Hollywood that engage with this sense of hybridity. I first survey US films produced in the post-9/11 context that demonstrate a growing consciousness of and interest in Arab Americans' cultural citizenship. This survey is conscious of the post-9/11 confluence of anti-Arab racism and Islamophobia in the United States, coded through what Leti Volpp refers to as the "citizen-terrorist" trope, which draws from Orientalist and racialized profiling of Arabs, Muslims, and those mistaken as such, as potential terrorist suspects, thus disqualifying them as cultural citizens.[4] At the same time, I point out the ways in which even filmmaking efforts to frame Arab and Muslim Americans as citizens rather than terrorist suspects often require performances of patriotism and endorsement of the underpinning logic of the US so-called "war on terror." For instance, the audience learns to suspect the Arab and Muslim American characters in *The Recruit* (2003), *Five Fingers* (2006), and *The Sentinel* (2006) but the endings honor the characters as patriotic Americans because of their government duties in the CIA, the FBI, and the Secret Service.

Following this survey, I then focus on the character of Samir Horn (Don Cheadle) in Jeffrey Nachmanoff's *Traitor* (2008), specifically considering the intersection of his Arab, Black, Muslim, and American identities in the context of the US "war on terror." Battling foreign and homegrown terrorism in the United States, Samir proclaims a multilayered sense of cultural citizenship, responding to the US dictates of patriotism while preserving a diasporic critique of empire.[5] I argue Samir's experience reconciles, albeit in limited and sometimes unproductive ways, the urgency to critique Hollywood's nationalist tradition in alienating Arab Americans with the possibility of incorporating considerations of the Arab American community's transnational map of cultural citizenship, reconciling both not necessarily as mutually exclusive sites of identity formation.

The Limits of Post-9/11 Visibility

That the interplay of racial profiling, patriotism, and terrorism constitutes a major theme in Hollywood's post-9/11 films should not come as a surprise. In the immediate aftermath of 9/11, the rhetoric of nationalism normalized a seemingly endless state of emergency, casting any criticism of the government as unpatriotic or offensive to the grief-stricken nation. "Americans are now being asked not to be critical," W. J. T. Mitchell complained, "not to question the judgment of our leadership."[6] The United States, stressed Judith Butler, missed the opportunity to "redefine itself as part of a global community when, instead, it heightened nationalist discourse, extended surveillance mechanisms, suspended constitutional rights, and developed forms of explicit and implicit censorship."[7] Americans were reduced to what Lauren Berlant termed "infantile citizens" whose curiosity to understand the causes of terrorism and the appropriate measures undertaken to counter it was met with oversimplistic references to the terrorists' cultural identity as a driving force behind the attacks.[8] In his congressional speech following the 9/11 tragedy, President George W. Bush issued a sensational and polarizing response to the equally reductive question: "Why do they hate us?" He pondered:

> They hate what they see right here in this chamber: a democratically elected government. Their leaders are self-appointed. They hate our freedoms: our freedom of religion, our freedom of speech, our freedom to vote and assemble and disagree with each other. . . . These terrorists kill not merely to end lives, but to disrupt and end a way of life. With every atrocity, they hope that America grows fearful, retreating from the world and forsaking our friends. They stand against us because we stand in their way.[9]

Bush's speech and the policies it served to legitimate were charged with Bernard Lewis's Orientalist polarizations and Samuel Huntington's "clash of civilizations" rhetoric.[10] References and analogies to Pearl Harbor at the time further invoked memories of World War II and justified a renewed Cold War security culture in the government's declared "war on terror."

Citing a rising threat of homegrown terrorism, the Bush administration unleashed a spate of racialized strategies. "Preventive detention" was used to round up twelve hundred noncitizens of Arab and Muslim background. Not yet citizens, these individuals had no rights to contact their families or seek legal representatives and were sometimes subjected to physical and verbal abuse while in custody.[11] The subsequent "special interest" designation opened the door for more arbitrary detentions. Thousands of Arab and Muslim visitors arriving in the United States since 2000 were held and interviewed by the Department of Justice, while the FBI conducted at least two hundred thousand interviews by 2005.[12] The "Absconder Apprehension Initiative" prioritized the removal proceedings of Arabs and Muslims in a deportation list that reached 314,000. And a "Special Registration" program required Arab and Muslim nonimmigrants to register with the Department of Homeland Security, further branding them suspected "enemies within."[13]

Arab and Muslim Americans, along with anybody who could be profiled as such, were targeted as potential threats and mapped into a racialized narrative that questioned their patriotism. The PATRIOT Act (2001) granted US law enforcement agencies the authority to intrude into the daily lives of Arab and Muslim Americans.[14] Law enforcement officers have been allowed to search their telephone and email records without court orders. They have also undertaken "sneak and peek" searches of homes and businesses without warrants or even the owner's or occupant's permission or knowledge. The Transportation Security Administration and US Customs and Border Protection have employed racially informed procedures to single out Arab and Muslim immigrants for further investigation. All of these strategies are an extension of a "war on terror" campaign that has legitimized renditioning suspects and subjecting prisoners of war, or purported "enemy combatants," to inhumane treatment in violation of the Geneva Convention accords.[15]

The Los Angeles Police Department attempted to map Arab and Muslim communities as part of their efforts to identify ways to quarantine the threat of homegrown terrorism.[16] In New York, there were attempts to grant firefighters the right to inspect and search any apartment or housing unit occupied by suspects. A community facility in Irving, Illinois, was renamed the "Irving Mosque" for a drill involving thirty government agencies including the Illinois Law Enforcement Alarm System. Storming the "mosque" with an armored vehicle, the officers participating in the mock exercise rescued a hostage tied to explosive devices and killed the Muslim terrorist, who happened to carry an Arab name.[17] The National Defense Act signed by President Barack Obama on the eve of 2012 empowered law enforcement agencies with the authority to arrest American citizens suspected of any terrorism-related connections.

Many Americans may not have been aware of the full extent of the post-9/11 backlash, yet their tacit approval has been continually courted through a culture industry that ensures Arab and Muslim Americans remain inextricably associated with terror. "The constructed narratives of terrorism in popular culture," explains Karin Gwinn Wilkins, "suggest the ways in which dominant ideologies are structuring our interpretations of global conditions in which events occur, our senses of fear and blame for conflict, as well as our desire for heroic conquest as resolution."[18] Even when coping with grief, appeals to multicultural America as a ground of national unity have been slow to celebrate Arabs and Muslims as part of the American cultural mosaic.[19] Liberal television shows like *Real Time with Bill Maher* as well as conservative long-running programs like *The O'Reilly Factor*, *The Glenn Beck Program*, *Just In with Laura Ingraham*, and *Hannity's America*—along with radio talk shows like *The Rush Limbaugh Show* and *The Savage Nation*—are just some of many media productions that have traded in various forms of anti-Arab racism and Islamophobia. Fiction writers have also used their imaginative power to depict Arab and Muslim Americans as a source of danger for the United States. John Updike's *Terrorist* (2004) and Robert Ferrigno's *Prayers for the Assassin* (2006) offer portrayals of Islam as a threat to US national security. President Obama, during his only presidential visit to a US-based mosque, noted the culture industry's skewed representation and commented, "Our television shows should have some Muslim characters that are unrelated to national security."[20]

Associating Arabs and Muslims in the United States with terrorism has spiked in parallel with a rising sense of public fear and anxiety, resulting in an alarming increase in the reported cases of violence, harassment, threat, and attack.[21] Fighting terrorism has become, in fact, a contemporary phase of institutionalized racism in the history of Arab and Muslim immigration experiences. Post-9/11 civil liberty reports by the American-Arab Anti-Discrimination Committee show a dramatic increase in anti-Arab racially driven attacks in the United States.[22] The Council of American-Islamic Relations has issued annual civil rights reports since 1995 that reflect a similar pattern of violence.[23] Targeted in their place of work, in their place of worship, and in the downtowns and suburbs of their cities and towns, Americans perceived by others as "Middle Eastern" have experienced an unenviable form of post-9/11 visibility. Instances such as the Oak Creek shooting (2012) and the Chapel Hill shooting (2015), in which nonwhite Americans perceived to be Muslim and Arab were killed, are only some in a long list of violent examples.

To be sure, there has been slow growth of public disillusionment in the conflation of Arab and Muslim Americans with terrorism and a rising sense of activist dedication in Arab and Muslim American communities. Some changes in Hollywood's representation of Arab and Muslim Americans appear promising to researchers and activists interested in challenging the industry's narrow imagination of Americanness. But the shifts remain small and, in some cases, serve only to offer the same racialized imagery but in increasingly subtle forms. Filmmakers continue to deny Arab and Muslim American communities the right to define their sense of belonging beyond certain nationalist boundaries of what constitutes an American sense of cultural citizenship. The following section reviews post-9/11 trends in filmic representation and highlights the dominance of the citizen-terrorist trope, even in those films attempting to offer a more critical perspective.

Film in a Climate of Fear

Edward Zwick's *The Siege* (1998) represents one of the earliest examples of Hollywood filmmakers' deployment of racial tokenism in portraying Arab American characters. By racial tokenism, I refer to the practice of casting minority actors as tokens of American multiculturalism but effectively using them to perpetuate white narratives. Operating within the "thriller" genre, *The Siege* depicts New York City as under threat from a terrorist cell composed of Arab and Muslim immigrants. The film follows passionate and dedicated FBI agent Anthony Hubbard (Denzel Washington), CIA agent Sharon Bridger (Annette Bening), and Major General William Devereaux (Bruce Willis), a military officer. Despite favoring different approaches to fighting terrorism (foreign and homegrown), the three figures—representing three different arms of the US government—search in their own ways to preserve national security.

The film deserves credit for foreshadowing the post-9/11 nationalist response, which saw dramatically increased executive powers trump Americans' civil liberties, promote the presumed effectiveness of torture techniques, and solidify racial profiling in the name of fighting terrorism. *The Siege* also raises concerns about the use of CIA covert operations in advancing US foreign policy objectives. The technology and resources available to the terrorists, the audience is informed, have been provided by the CIA undercover agent, Bridger, as part of a plan aimed to empower Iraqis for unidentified reasons. This could be read as a tacit critique of the US role in supporting the Mujahedeen, who hailed from the Arab and Muslim worlds to wage "jihad" against the Soviet aggressions in Afghanistan during the 1980s.[24] Ultimately, however, the film suggests that homegrown terrorism is a phenomenon exclusively advanced by Arabs and Muslims in the United States who seek to secure their demands by targeting crowds of civilian Americans in public buses, movie theaters, elementary schools, and multicultural gatherings. Arabic and Islamic identity markers are conflated, with Islamic practices such as ablution, praying, wearing traditional clothing, and growing beards presented as signs of extremism. The terrorists' cultural and religious affiliations are portrayed as inherently opposed to and incompatible with the United States' cultural norms. Accordingly, military officers racially profile Arabs in the United States, including characters that could be perceived as Arab and Muslim Americans, and round them up in barbed-wire enclosures for further investigation—images that recall the internment of Japanese Americans during World War II (figure 12).

True to its tokenism, however, *The Siege* then offsets this imagery by also presenting an Arab American who demonstrates both American patriotism and pride in his Middle Eastern cultural heritage. FBI agent Frank Haddad (Tony Shalhoub) embraces an inclusive multicultural notion of America and works to protect its security while also preserving his ethnic and religious identities. The film's conclusion celebrates the triumph of multiculturalism as America's promise to citizens like Haddad and his family. Americans of various creeds and

12. US-based Arabs and Muslims rounded up in military-installed cages in *The Siege* (1998). © Twentieth Century Fox.

ethnic backgrounds rush out into the streets to reject military control, demand an immediate restoration of proper law enforcement agencies, and decry the sense of humiliation directed against Americans of Arab and Muslim backgrounds.

Haddad's role in the film advances the rhetoric of what Steven Salaita calls "imperative patriotism," which he defines as the assumption or demand that "dissent in matters of governance and foreign affairs is unpatriotic and therefore unsavory."[25] Most post-9/11 positive portrayals of Arab and Muslim Americans have been imbued with this sense of patriotism and its strict boundaries for citizenship, belonging, and national interest.[26] *The Siege* invites the audience to empathize with the Arab American community, but only to the extent prescribed by national security politics. Haddad's status as an Arab American hero is linked to his ten-year tenure as an FBI agent and granted in return for projecting other Arabs and Muslims in the United States as terrorists. Protesting the racial profiling and incarceration of his own son as a suspect, Haddad questions his own cultural citizenship. He decides to side with his Arab and Arab American communities by giving up his FBI badge and stating, "I am one of them. I'm no longer your sand nigger." The moment of disruption is resolved, however, when Haddad and his partner, Agent Hubbard, kill the bad Arab-in-America terrorist, thus restoring the terms of US multiculturalism and civility.

The Siege serves as a precedent to a post-9/11 pattern of depicting Arab and Muslim Americans through what Evelyn Alsultany refers to as "simplified complex" representations. Primarily examining the post-9/11 television industry, Alsultany describes this representation trend as, at first glance, a seemingly positive one that adopts strategies to "offset the stereotype of the Arab/Muslim terrorist" in order to create the impression of complexity.[27] The identified strategies include but are not limited to scattered references to Arab and Muslim American patriotic characters, sympathetic portrayals of post-9/11 Arab and Muslim victims, humanizing depictions of terrorists, and approving projections of US multiculturalism. Such strategies, nonetheless, provide "reassurance that racial sensitivity is the norm in US society while simultaneously perpetuating the dominant perception of Arabs and Muslims as threats to US national security."[28] Tracing the US film industry's deployment of such simplified complex representations reveals works that appease liberal filmmakers' commitment to multiculturalism while accommodating marketable terrorism-related plots.[29] Though improvements over the industry's pre-9/11 dismissive portrayals of Arab Americans' cultural citizenship (see chapter 1), these films do little more than distance their makers from charges of racism and discrimination. The result is a paradox: superficially nuanced portrayals that resubject the Arab and Muslim American image to the industry's racialized binary codes.

Post-9/11 films are replete with simplified complex representation strategies. Unlike earlier portrayals that did not clearly articulate the cultural citizenship of Hollywood's Arab and Muslim American characters but rather strictly presented them as aliens seeking to terrorize Americans or foreign disruptors of US politics, the simplified complex mode articulates Arab and Muslim Americans' cultural citizenship in the context of their victimization by and/or renunciation of terrorism, which shapes images through the good Muslim/bad Muslim as well as citizen-terrorist binaries. In this context, post-9/11 Arab and Muslim American characters have a limited form of cultural citizenship that is contingent on their demonstration of loyalty and even self-sacrifice, but not without leading the audience to suspect the characters' potential for treason. Examples abound especially in psychological thrillers, with characters such as Layla Moore (Bridget Moynahan) in *The Recruit* (2003), Dark Eyes (Saïd Taghmaoui) in *Five Fingers* (2006), Aziz Hassad (Raoul Bhaneja) in *The Sentinel* (2006), and Rina Humphries (Lora Kojovic) in *Unthinkable* (2010), to name but a few.

Roger Donaldson's *The Recruit* (2003) is a spy thriller that narrates the story of a corrupt CIA senior agent, Walter Burke (Al Pacino), who recruits young Americans to the CIA but pits them against each other to steal valued CIA security software. Burke assigns the recruit James Clayton (Colin Farrell) to spy on his fellow Arab American agent Layla Moore, or as later revealed, Layla Nasari, born to an Algerian mother and a French father. James and Layla fall in love, but at the same time, the audience is led to believe that Layla is a traitor. Burke informs James that Layla is a "sleeper" and tasks him with tracking her and learning about her terrorist "handlers." For much of the film, the audience identifies with James in his patriotic mission and grows ever more suspicious of Layla's behavior. The film concludes with a twist, which reveals Layla as herself on a CIA-endorsed mission that ultimately shows Burke to be the real traitor. Once a suspected terrorist because of her Arab background, Layla is thus redeemed by the film's end as an American patriot.

Characters like Layla constitute part of a post-9/11 representation trend in which filmmakers demonstrate their commitment to American multiculturalism by apparently exposing and critiquing, but not without capitalizing on, the audience's presumed tendency to suspect Arab and Muslim Americans. Plot twists like that in *The Recruit* serve as a kind of "aha" moment meant to reverse the audience's feelings toward a character presented until then as untrustworthy. The result, however, I argue, relies not only on contrasting good Muslims with bad Muslims and citizens with traitors, but on blurring these categories and drawing the audience's attention to the difficulty in discerning between them. Despite redeeming the Arab and Muslim American characters at the end, such portrayals reinforce precisely the perceptions they supposedly mean to unsettle—namely, that Arab and

Muslim Americans could easily become radicalized and betray their own society.

Lawrence Malkin's *Five Fingers* (2006) similarly and deliberately confuses its audience in its portrayal of terrorism and patriotism. Initially, the story seems to be about the kidnapping of Dutch pianist and banker Martijn (Ryan Phillippe) and Gavin (Colm Meaney), his English tour guide in Morocco. The three kidnappers, Ahmet (Laurence Fishburne), Aicha (Gina Torres), and Dark Eyes (Saïd Taghmaoui) appear to be "Muslim terrorists" dressed in traditional Moroccan clothing. They shoot Gavin and torture Martijn to reveal the true purpose of his visit to Morocco. Martijn slowly and painfully loses five of his fingers, while also hearing the Islamic call to prayers. The grim, dark torture scenes are cross-cut with romantic, airy flashbacks to Martijn's romance with his Moroccan girlfriend in Holland, which invite the audience to empathize with Martijn as a symbol of white purity and innocence. He is, after all, in Morocco to establish a food program to nourish children. By the film's end, however, this image is reversed when the audience learns that Martijn is in fact part of a terrorist network to poison consumers of fast food chains through a biological weapon developed by a retired chemist. Ahmet, Aicha, and Dark Eyes are revealed to be CIA agents, and the torture scene is in a New York City warehouse. Gavin, Martijn's tour guide, is also revealed to be a part of the team. When their mission is complete, Ahmed and Aicha are shown leaving the warehouse, with the Statue of Liberty in the background.

The film is disturbing not only for its torture scenes, but also for the character of Dark Eyes. Of the three supposed Muslim terrorist characters, Dark Eyes is the most silent and deadly. Throughout the film, he is shown video-recording the interrogations, intimidating Martijn, and eventually killing him. He only speaks once, and it is in the form of an angry curse in Arabic directed at Martijn. At the end of the film, Ahmet and Aicha remove their "Islamic" clothes and go for a drink, but Dark Eyes does neither. He does not even have a name. The character was perhaps added to give the film greater authenticity. He is played by an actor of Moroccan origin, unlike Ahmet, played by the well-known African American actor Laurence Fishburne, or Aicha, played by Cuban American actress Gina Torres. Although the three characters suggest diversity within the CIA, the film does not provide Dark Eyes the same agency as the others. Though visible throughout the film, his presence remains tokenistic. And once revealed to be a CIA agent, he is apparently redeemed as a patriotic American, but his character is not normalized in the same way as the others.

In Clark Johnson's *The Sentinel* (2006), the Secret Service character of Aziz Hassad is marginal as well. The thriller centers around a "mole" within the Secret Service who leaks information to a group that plans to assassinate the US president. Secret Service agent Pete Garrison (Michael Douglas) investigates but is eventually framed as the main suspect. He escapes arrest and embarks on a solo mission to clear his name and reveal the true culprit. Hassad's character does not occupy much screen time. As positive as the idea of including a Muslim American character in the Secret Service may sound, his presence is marginal. He is merely a Muslim American character that appears a few times throughout the film among other agents. His character, however, seems important enough to invite the audience to suspect him as a potential traitor. The screen shows his face multiple times when taking the polygraph test along with his fellow agents. Words in Arabic float across the screen next to other foreign languages in a visual effect that associates terrorism with foreigners. There is even a mention of al-Qaeda as a possible source of the threat. Injecting Hassad's character does not present a heroic Muslim American model, but rather simply uses his presence to raise viewers' suspicion. Toward the end of the film, he is shown exchanging fire with the terrorists in defense of the president. There is no clear reference to whether he is killed in action, and his presence in the Secret Service is no longer visible at the end. His absence underscores his irrelevance to the overall film.

And finally, Gregor Jordan's *Unthinkable* (2010) presents audiences with a particularly brutal version of the classic "ticking time bomb" scenario. Special interrogator Henry Humphries (Samuel Jackson) must torture the Muslim American terrorist Yusuf Atta Mohamed (Michael Sheen) in order to locate several nuclear bombs planted in various US cities. In an undisclosed location, and with FBI investigative support, Henry butchers Yusuf, cutting off his fingers and genitalia, pulling his teeth, and electrocuting him, but to no avail. He fails to force Yusuf to confess the bomb locations, even after slaughtering Yusuf's Muslim American wife in front of him. Only when Henry moves to torture Yusuf's young children does the latter reveal some of the locations, though he stops cooperating once his children are removed from the scene. In justifying Henry's actions, the film offers a bloody ending as some of the bombs explode, suggesting that it should have been reasonable to torture Yusuf's children to save others. The film essentially legitimizes torture as the only effective method to fight "Muslim" terrorism.

Unthinkable racializes its characters in ways that only appear to play "against type" but further strip Arab and Muslim Americans of cultural citizenship and agency. Making the character of Yusuf a white convert named Steven Younger suggests some level of sensitivity to racial profiling, but it comes, I argue, at the cost of still denigrating the idea of being a Muslim American. In order to exonerate Henry from being critiqued as Islamophobic, the film features his devout Muslim wife, Rina (Lora Kojovic). Originally from Bosnia, Rina helped Henry in Afghanistan by tending to his tortured prisoners and helping them recover from the inflicted wounds. Importantly, however, she "does not go to a mosque," as an FBI agent mentions at the beginning of the film. And she does not wear traditional Muslim clothing like Yusuf's wife and children. Rina is presented as a patriotic Muslim American, but her character is marginal, included only to legitimate Henry's actions. Indeed, both Henry and Rina, an African American and a Muslim American, respectively, bring diversity to a plot otherwise dominated by white characters. But their Americanness hinges on their willingness to prioritize patriotism and subject their Muslim American prisoner to horrific torture. The film thus deploys its "positive" portrayal of some nonwhite characters to service a film narrative that denigrates Muslim Americans more broadly. And what makes this portrayal even more dismissive is the fact that most of the characters are not even played by either Arab or Muslim American actors.

In these films, good Arab and Muslim American characters emerge in relation to their government service, the pinnacle of patriotism; but as such, their American citizenship is stressed only to the extent prescribed by national security politics. There are other films that dramatize this representation pattern beyond government service. Joseph Castelo's *The War Within* (2005), for instance, depicts a conflict between the patriotic family of the "good" Muslim American, Sayeed Choudhury (Firdous Bamji), and the "bad" Muslim-in-America, Hassan (Ayad Akhtar). Hassan, affiliated with a radical terrorist cell in New Jersey, intends to terrorize New York City, but encounters mounting opposition from Sayeed. "I am not saying things are perfect here," argues Sayeed, "[But] look around you in this restaurant: Jews, Muslims, [and] Christians are eating comfortably, safely, [and] peacefully. What's wrong with that?" Hassan reads Sayeed's continued efforts to dissuade him as unsophisticated and futile. In a prerecorded message he explains, "My friends! By the time you read this, I'll be gone. You are Americans now and America has been good to you. It's become your home. The country you love. I know you cannot understand why I have done what I will do—what I have to do—but ignorance is not innocence." The film ends with Sayeed detained as a terrorist suspect, an outcome presented as ironic, thus implicitly critiquing the practice of racial profiling.

Such critique of racial profiling is not necessarily new: *Escape from L.A.* (1996) is one of the earliest pre-9/11 films to use this imagery. The film features a Muslim American woman, Taslima (Valeria Golino), being rounded up along with other "undesirable and unfit" citizens and put on a post-apocalyptic Los Angeles Island. "I was a Muslim in South Dakota," Taslima grieves. "All of a sudden, they made it a crime." In *Escape from L.A.*, it is Taslima's cultural difference that makes her "undesirable." What makes post-9/11 filmmaking distinct is its portrayal of Arab and Muslim Americans as victims of a racial profiling process specifically informed by Hollywood's citizen-terrorist representation pattern, which seems to suggest that unless characters are portrayed as patriotic supporters of the United States' antiterrorism campaign, their default portrayals are ones of suspected terrorism or treason.

The shocking nature of the 9/11 attacks, combined with the government's politicized responses, fueled powerful fears of Arab and Muslim Americans as dangerous. In this context, the industry's citizen-terrorist portrayals function as a mechanism to absolve (at least to some extent) the characters conducting racial profiling, or even committing violence against Arab and Muslim suspects by showing them as motivated by legitimate fear of another 9/11. Thus, when filmmakers produce discriminatory images of Arab and Muslim Americans, or even limited critiques of racial profiling, there is an implicit message that when Americans discriminate, their reasons are understandable. This is traceable in post-9/11 comedies like *Malibu's Most Wanted* (2003), *Soul Plane* (2004), and *American Dreamz* (2006) as well as serious films like *Land of Plenty* (2004), *Crash* (2004), *Pretty Persuasion* (2005), *Flightplan* (2005), *Crank* (2006), *Sorry, Haters* (2006), *Fatwa* (2006), *Rendition* (2007), *Towelhead* (2007), *The Visitor* (2007), *Source Code* (2011), and *Non-Stop* (2014).[30] Even films like *Waterborne* (2005), *Inside Man* (2006), and *The Gold Bracelet* (2006), which critique the profiling of Sikh Americans in a phobia that renders Hinduism, Islam, and Sikhism "theologically, morally, and socially illegitimate,"[31] pay tribute to the reasonable basis of post-9/11 fear.[32]

What are we to make of this pattern of critiquing racial profiling in post-9/11 films? The problem, I argue, is that such critiques fail to challenge the public backlash against Arab and Muslim American communities. Instead, these film narratives serve only to echo political correctness or calls for multicultural sensitivity. Jeff Renfroe's *Civic Duty* (2006), for instance, criticizes the damaging effects of public racial profiling while maintaining a paradoxical advocacy of its necessity. The film's protagonist, Terry Allen (Peter Krause), grows suspicious of his Middle Eastern neighbor, Gabe Hassan (Khaled Abol Naga), based on nothing more than Gabe's dark complexion, minimalist lifestyle, and connections to his brown-colored community. After failed attempts to secure the FBI's attention, Terry decides to invade Gabe's house and solicit forced confessions at gunpoint. Dismayed by

Terry's racist attitude, Terry's wife reports him to the authorities, who eventually incarcerate him and set Gabe free. Despite its seemingly sympathetic portrayal of the Arab American character, the film concludes by revealing Gabe's association with a terrorist group, retroactively validating Terry's actions.

The trend is a subtle and seemingly contradictory one. Blatantly negative depictions of Arabs and Muslims in the United States as pure evil have not so much disappeared as become paired with other images that also humanize those same communities, albeit through restrictive tropes only. It is important to note, however, that this is true only with regard to representing Arab and Muslim Americans; films promoting negative portrayals of Arabs and Muslims in general are still rampant—for example, *Rules of Engagement* (2000), *Black Hawk Down* (2002), *Team America: World Police* (2004), *The Kingdom* (2007), *Zero Dark Thirty* (2012), *American Sniper* (2014), and *Beirut* (2018). Even in films that do not directly involve Arabs or Muslims, there is a consistent reliance, especially in apocalyptic scenarios, to make references to the 9/11 tragedy—for example, *The Day after Tomorrow* (2004), *War of the Worlds* (2005), *28 Weeks Later* (2007), and *I Am Legend* (2007).[33] In some films, such as *The Cavern* (2005), *The Cave* (2005), *The Descent* (2005), *The Descent: Part 2* (2009), and *Catacombs* (2007), there are references to caves and rugged hideouts in attempts to invite the audience to associate fear with supposed elements of Arabic and Islamic cultures, such as scorched desert, rugged mountains, ominous music, etc.[34]

Overall, Hollywood's post-9/11 portrayals of Arab Americans show signs of change from earlier decades of outright demonization to conditioned acceptance. This transition is, as I argued above, seriously limited and limiting. Post-9/11 films might project Arab Americans with some nuance but remain reductive in their imaginations of identity beyond the constraints of nationalism. The films actively reject the possibility of envisioning the transnational contours that complicate understandings of Arab Americans' identity and cultural citizenship. This rejection is clearly stated through portrayals of Arab Americans as capable of only one form of allegiance and affiliation. In other words, one is either completely and patriotically American or secretly and treacherously loyal to another country. Arab Americans can try to claim a transnational identity all they want, but these films suggest that, ultimately, one must choose a side. In this context, Hollywood's filmmakers primarily adopt a national sense of rejection of complexity in their narrations of Arab Americans that leaves no space for disruptions of perceptions. The following section analyzes a film that wrestles with this cinematic structure and attempts to offer a different sense of conceiving Arab Americans' cultural citizenship, even while operating within the existing limitations of Hollywood's post-9/11 representations.

Beyond the Citizen-Terrorist Paradox

Jeffrey Nachmanoff's 2008 film *Traitor* provides a rare reading of an Arab-Black-Muslim American character's struggle with identity and cultural citizenship beyond the post-9/11 citizen-terrorist paradox. The character of Samir (Don Cheadle) is revealed in unexpected ways, keeping the audience in a state of suspense and uncertainty. At the beginning of the film, Samir is presented as a stereotypical radical whose anger and frustration at the unwelcomed interventions of the West, the United States in particular, in the lives of Arabs and Muslims lead him to embrace violence and chaos as disruptive political means. Held at a Yemeni prison on terrorism charges, he befriends the radical Omar (Saïd Taghmaoui), who later introduces him to Fareed (Alyy Khan), the leading figure of an international terrorist cell, al-Nathir (Warning). Samir is initiated into al-Nathir when he bombs the US embassy in France. The subsequent scenes show intercutting images of the FBI's frenzied investigation of Samir's background and his mother's and girlfriend's rejection of the presumption that Samir is a citizen-turned-terrorist.

The plot twists, however, when the audience learns that Samir is, in fact, a spy seeking to infiltrate al-Nathir and thwart planned attacks on the United States. The US intelligence agency with which he works has chosen to keep his mission "off the books." The story becomes more intricate when his intelligence contractor, Carter (Jeff Daniels), is killed. Unaware of his mission, the FBI, represented by the

13. Samir retires in search of spiritual peace in *Traitor* (2008). © Overture Films.

typical good cop/bad cop agents Roy Clayton (Guy Pearce) and Max Archer (Neal McDonough), respectively, identifies Samir as a high-value target. Samir is plunged into a nail-biting game of hide-and-seek with US authorities while he continues his mission against terrorism. Toward the film's end, his undercover identity is finally revealed, transforming him into a hero with a clean record. He turns down an offer to work for the FBI, citing his faith-based disillusionment with both terrorist cells and US counterterrorist agencies for their use of violence and their normalization of narratives that turn human lives into commodities. Having bloodied his hands, both literally and metaphorically, through his duty as a US undercover agent in al-Nathir, Samir decides to retire for worship in search for heavenly forgiveness, inner peace, and spiritual tranquility. A close shot of his prayer among his Muslim community evokes a deep sense of remorse and search for peace (figure 13).

Traitor is a serious, albeit still limited, attempt to challenge the exclusionary readings of American cultural citizenship in post-9/11 Hollywood, at least in relation to Arab and Muslim Americans. Commissioned by Disney to develop the film—which was initially conceived by comedian Steve Martin in 2002—screenplay writer and director Nachmanoff invested time in research and consultation with some Muslim American communities.[35] Subsequently, he became aware of the complexity of identities and experiences of many Arab and Muslim Americans during the "war on terror" era. Nachmanoff thus sought to convey an activist sense of agency in Samir's fight against terrorism.

Perhaps one of the most intriguing things about Samir is the way in which he is shown negotiating multiple identities. He is an American of both Arab and Black Muslim backgrounds, made possible by the union of his Sudanese father, who teaches Samir Arabic in Sudan at the beginning of the film, and his African American mother, who raises him in Chicago after his father's death. Particularly enlightening here is Moustafa Bayoumi's correlation of the broad Arab American and African American experiences codified in the phrases "driving while black" and "flying while Arab" to capture both communities' struggles against institutionalized racism. On the one hand, Samir's ability to communicate and befriend the Arab and Muslim terrorists, Bayoumi argues, speaks to a subgenre in action films that suggests African Americans "know better than whites how to talk to Arabs." On the other hand, the characters in such films remain deeply embedded in the "benevolence of American imperialism," as Bayoumi contends, "For if the face of [the] US belongs to an African-American, how racist could the empire be?"[36]

Insightful as it is, Bayoumi's reading still doesn't capture the full multilayeredness of Samir's identity. Rather than analyzing Samir as being internally conflicted, we can read the character's collapsing of both "Arabness" and "blackness" as disruptive of binaries. Bayoumi is right to suggest that the film "collapses the good Muslim/bad Muslim dichotomy," as indeed could be said of many of the above-surveyed thrillers, especially when the plot keeps the audience uncertain about characters' "real" loyalties.[37] I would suggest, however, that *Traitor* collapses not only the good Muslim/bad Muslim binary, but also the associated yet distinct binaries of Arab/African, national/international, domestic/foreign, and local/empire. Samir occupies and traverses multiple US, Arab, Black, and Muslim spheres, producing a peculiar character who defies singular narration or categorization.

It is this empowering sense of identification that simultaneously reaffirms Samir's response to his duty and his critique of it. Moved by both Islam's message of peace and respect for human lives and US nationalist calls for duty, Samir is inspired to confront al-Nathir extremists and to protect his American homeland. Having witnessed the death of his father in a terrorist car bombing in Sudan, and mourned the deaths of 9/11 victims as an adult raised in the United States, Samir is deeply saddened by the radicals who, as the American Muslim scholar Hamza Yusuf puts it, have hijacked the name of Islam to advance their political grievances.[38] The film's emphasis on the faith-driven motivation of Samir's counterterrorism mission unsettles Islamophobic voices in the United States that project Islam as the antithesis of Western liberalism.[39] Samir's role as a former Special Operations officer with military expertise in explosives and his history of fighting alongside the Mujahedeen in Afghanistan allow him access to al-Nathir. Once he loses contact with his US intelligence contractor, however, he is forced to battle the post-9/11 citizen-terrorist framework that questions his allegiance and reconfigures his Arab, Black, Muslim, and American identities as mutually exclusive.

Nachmanoff's script proved too complicated to meet Disney's sensationalistic format, forcing the director to navigate independent filmmaking.[40] Eventually picked up by Overture Films, with a medium budget of $22 million, Nachmanoff shot the film in five countries—Canada, France, London, Morocco, and the United States. It accumulated gross earnings of about $23.5 million in the United States and over $27.8 million worldwide. Despite featuring high-profile Hollywood actors and a strong start with a gross of about $10 million in the first weekend of its release, the film lost momentum almost immediately afterwards.[41] Various factors were blamed for the film's failure to generate more traffic. Despite some technical criticism of its computer-generated images, many reviewers considered the plot a major drawback. Critical of storytelling that "slips out of complexity into perplexity," one reviewer wondered whether the audience was ready to handle "moral ambiguity and narrative intricacy" in thrillers engaging with terrorism.[42] Yet this was precisely Nachmanoff's experiment: how to produce an "intelligent" thriller that worked within Hollywood's action genre. Put differently, he wanted to determine whether a film could raise critical questions in the area of terrorism while still entertaining the audience. Nachmanoff explained:

> Our ambitions were modest for the film purely as a fun espionage story, but it also has a political edge . . . and those films are hard to sell in America. Audiences seem to want their entertainment to be mindless, where they don't really have to think about anything, or they want them to be really serious. I've always thought it is possible to do both.[43]

Traitor has a rating of 65 percent on the popular review aggregator site rottentomatoes.com and 7/10 on the Internet Movie Database (IMDb). The film's lowest reviews on IMDb focus on what Peter Bradshaw calls Nachmanoff's "fantastically flaccid and perfunctory gestures of friendship toward the Muslim world."[44] One American rater denounced the film as an effort to "erode American patriotism" with an "untrue" portrayal of Muslims as "family oriented, spiritual, thoughtful and worthy of our sympathy."[45] Another American rater declared the film "anti-American propaganda" that attempts to establish "moral equivalence between us and the terrorists."[46] Conversely, one Jordanian viewer, for example, challenged these gestures by protesting the director's failure to offer a more nuanced view of Arabs and Muslims outside the United States.[47] The only "good" Muslim in the film, after all, is an American one. Such angry responses from both Arab and American viewers reveal the resilience of the very polarizations that Samir's character was meant to disrupt.

Samir's agency in *Traitor* draws from Arab and Muslim American struggles in the United States to redefine terrorism beyond racial profiling. The popular myth that "all Muslims are not terrorists but nearly all terrorists are Muslims" continues to circulate within US popular culture. Despite the FBI's reporting emphasis on the role of certain "right- and left-wing extremist groups" and "drug cartels" in addition to so-called "Islamic political terrorists" in homegrown terrorism, mainstream media reporters and pundits have exercised racially defined discretion in assigning the word "terrorism" on the basis of perpetrators' backgrounds.[48] Even in cases exhibiting all the main elements of the FBI's definition of terrorism as a violent act "intended to intimidate or coerce a civilian population, or influence the policy or conduct of a government by mass destruction, assassination, or kidnapping,"[49] if the perpetrators are not perceived to be Arab or Muslim, the term "terrorism" is rarely invoked. Hollywood films reinforce this perception when they continually filter the Arab and Muslim American image through the racialized lens of terrorism. However sympathetic, the mainstream imagery of Arab and Muslim Americans keeps them tethered to, and tainted by, the context of terrorism.

In an attempt to speak to *Traitor*'s tagline, "The truth is complicated," Nachmanoff offsets the industry's racially saturated imagery of homegrown terrorists by refraining from showing the terrorist characters wearing traditional clothing or growing beards. When revealing the identities of the US-based terrorists, the camera focuses on four of them: a black man, a nonscarfed woman, a working Middle Easterner, and a racially ambiguous family man. This emphasis on race, gender, and marital status, which underlines an implicit critique of post-9/11 racial profiling, promises a complicated reading of homegrown terrorism in exchange for a license to portray the four Muslim Americans as ticking bombs waiting to blow up fifty public buses in the United States. The large number of terrorists in this film, which reviewer David Stratton found "disturbing,"[50] capitalizes on the audience's preconceived blurring notions of domestic terror and Arab and Muslim American communities. Thus, Nachmanoff ends up reinforcing the very racialized portrayals that his work seems to criticize. In this sense, *Traitor* fits the above-surveyed post-9/11 Hollywood films.

Despite this limitation, *Traitor* does critique racial profiling as a post-9/11 backlash against Arab and Muslim American communities and reflect the sense of disillusionment at least some portions of the American public feel with regard to the "war on terror." The film offers critical readings of the industry's racially coded anti-Arab and Islamophobic imagery, most explicitly through the character of Agent Clayton (Guy Pearce), who mediates "a way for Westerners to view somebody like Cheadle."[51] Clayton expresses his frustration with Homeland Security's racialized directive to map potential suspects by rounding up "guys who fit the profile." "Homeland Security is a waste of time and resources," he declares at one point. "We'll never find them [the terrorists] this way. There are 1.2 billion Muslims in this world. Only 20 percent of them are Arab. These people could look like anybody." Clayton argues they should more thoroughly investigate individuals already suspected rather than using state apparatus to coerce the Arab and Muslim American population at large. He refuses to ascribe terror as an inherent tendency within Islam and maintains that terrorism is a version of political violence. He rejects the characterization of the terrorists in terms of "failed heterosexuality" (i.e., terrorists end their lives to fulfill their sexual fantasies through the promised seventy-some virgins).[52] In a conversation with his partner, he further cites the KKK's manipulation of the Christian faith as an example that disrupts the popularized conceptions of Islam as an exclusively and inherently violent religion. "Where I grew up," he emphasizes, "the Klan burned crosses in front of people's houses and called it Christianity. [It] seems every religion has more than one face."

Yet even Clayton's seemingly race-sensitive investigation invokes racialized assumptions. When identifying Samir as a potential terrorist suspect, Agent Clayton perceives him as fitting what he describes as the "classic" profile of a terrorist, driven by the "cultural shock" of being caught "between traditional Islam and the West." This shock and subsequent clash of identity, he suggests, is specific to Arab and

Muslim migrants and even citizens. This argument follows Samuel Huntington's flawed logic that Muslims living in the predominantly Judeo-Christian United States experience cultural clash because of their adherence to their Islamic practices.[53] This understanding of Islam as fundamentally incompatible with American civilization saw newfound popularity immediately after 9/11 and seems to have found purchase once more within President Donald Trump's administration. This has provided fertile ground for renewed xenophobia, communicated primarily through conservative media and religious establishments. Rod Parsley, for example, the senior pastor of the World Harvest Church in Columbus, Ohio, described Islam as a historical and permanent enemy of the United States.[54] In one of his fiery sermons, he preached:

> I can't begin to tell you how important it is that we understand the true nature of Islam. That we see it for what it really is. In fact . . . I do not believe that our nation can truly fulfill its divine purpose until we understand our historical conflict with Islam. . . . I know that this statement sounds extreme. But I am not shrinking back from its implications. The fact is that . . . America was founded in part with the intention of seeing this false religion destroyed. And I believe September 11, 2001, was a generational call to arms that we no longer can afford to ignore.[55]

Such polarizing assessments of terrorists' cultural and religious identity as the driving force for their extreme acts of violence both rely upon and validate the "clash of civilizations" theory. The premise that Samir fits a "classic" profile specifies this difference as a ground for unassimilability and later legitimizes his torture by the FBI.[56]

It is important to recognize the degree to which this understanding of Islam has been accepted and perpetuated at the highest levels. Consider, for example, the institutionally commissioned and highly cited report in terrorism studies and security intelligence circles, "Radicalization in the West: The Homegrown Threat" (2007). In this report, senior intelligence analysts at the New York City Police Department (NYPD), Mitchell Silber and Arvin Bhatt, investigate five cases of "homegrown" terrorism to establish a psychological radicalization pattern that accounts for the transformation of a citizen into a traitor. The report subscribes to an approach in the field of terrorism studies committed to psychologizing the terrorist's deviance in terms of personality disorder, political frustration, or failed heterosexuality, and it emphasizes the abnormality and monstrosity of the terrorist through racial tropes that legitimize the state to quarantine and discipline its citizens.[57] The analysts conclude that Muslims residing in the West, particularly in the United States, are radicalized through four stages: "Pre-Radicalization," "Self-Identification," "Indoctrination," and "Jihadization."

According to the authors, the second stage initiates an alarming transition from an ordinary lifestyle to another defined by one's association with the *salafi* (ultraconservative) version of Islam, thereby reducing the multilayered basis of ultraconservatism into a breeding ground for terrorism. They stress that identifying with ultraconservatism serves as a precursor to radicalization, which is often triggered by four factors: "economic" (losing a job, blocked mobility), "social" (alienation, discrimination, racism—real or perceived), "political" (international conflicts involving Muslims), or "personal" (death in the close family.) The process, which can happen within a short period of three months, can be spotted early through symptoms like wearing traditional clothes, growing a beard, or giving up cigarettes, drinking, and gambling.

Such instances of institutional racial profiling have sustained prejudice and discrimination against Arabs and Muslims in the United States and subjected their communities to the citizen-terrorist paradox through erroneous racialized associations of religious identity with terrorism. *Traitor* denounces the identity-based premise of such a trend. Samir's life certainly appears to fall within the parameters of the NYPD's report. He experiences the four triggers identified as precursors of radicalization. He loses a job because of the post-9/11 social unrest against Muslim-looking signs. When an FBI investigator asks why Samir was fired from his job in Chicago, the company's manager states, "When you wear a skullcap and pray to Allah five times a day, people are gonna notice; some of our clients complained." Samir, therefore, experiences a form of social prejudice that results in economic hardship.

Politically, US policies toward the Arab and Muslim worlds outrage Samir, particularly the US military's invasion of Iraq in 2003. At the personal level, the childhood memory of watching his father die in a car explosion continues to haunt him. Experiencing such hardships, however, leads Samir to embrace his religion and turn it into a generative source of American patriotism rather than a ground for treason. If anything, Samir's story stands as testimony against the report's superficial contention that subscribing to an Islamic identity through wearing particular clothes or forsaking certain habits constitutes an early symptom of radicalization. His open expression of his Islamic identity correlates with some of the report's signs of a potential terrorist. He wears the traditional skullcap while praying with others in the mosque. He objects to indulging in behavior that contradicts Islamic teachings. For example, in an encounter with one of al-Nathir's leaders who justifies drinking alcohol to "blend in," he responds by citing a *fatwa* (Islamic ruling by a recognized authority) that Muslims can only do so if death is imminent.

Criticizing the racialized undertones in the US "war on terror" policy, Nachmanoff provides Samir with the agency to contest US claims to innocence and US justification for resorting to violence in fighting terrorism. When interrogated by FBI agents and charged with collaborating with terrorists for selling them explosives, Samir, still undercover, proclaims that he sells to whoever can afford it and notes his interest in considering the US government as a possible client. When the interrogators stress that the United States does not "kill innocent people," he responds, "Oh yeah, they do, genius; people just usually have darker skin." Presenting Samir as a former sergeant in the US Army Special Forces once sent to Pakistan to train the Afghani Mujahedeen serves as a reminder of the contradictions underlying the US deployment of hard power in the Muslim world. Meanwhile, a close shot of Agent Clayton and Samir in the interrogation room, with the threatening and abusive Agent Archer appearing

14. Clayton interrogates Samir as a potential homegrown terrorist in *Traitor* (2008). © Overture Films.

in the background, already reveals an important critique of white-on-black institutionalized violence (figure 14). Nachmanoff further develops his critique of the US racially informed foreign policy by allowing one of al-Nathir's members to pronounce his grievances, albeit in a Hollywood-style Middle Eastern accent:

> We train to kill, but it doesn't mean that we love violence. We use violence only because it has been used against us. The crusaders have invade[d] our land, drop[ped] bombs on our people, stole[n] our natural resources. We are fighting to end the suffering. We are fighting to end the humiliation and murder of our people. The American[s] accuse us of killing innocent civilians, yet they have been spilling the blood of innocent Muslims for decades. Does our blood not count?!

By offering this rarely seen perspective and showing how Samir is forced to navigate the implications of racial profiling, both at the institutional and public levels, *Traitor* invites the audience to identify with his struggle and begin questioning the adequacy of the "clash of civilizations" narrative.

Samir is presented as a heroic ideal for "non-Muslim Black Americans and non-Black American Muslims, especially those who are enthralled by popular notions of Black masculinity infused with Hip-Hop culture, radical politics, and social justice."[58] His Black Muslim character also shows, however, the role faith can play in driving and taming aggressive masculinity. Mourning the eight people killed by his remotely triggered bombing operation in France, Samir tearfully agonizes over his actions and prays to God for forgiveness. He reproaches Carter, the intelligence contractor, for not valuing human life and for legitimating violence in the same way as terrorists. When Agent Clayton recognizes Samir's heroism and tells him he is a free man with a newly clean record, Samir responds: "I'm a free man? This doesn't feel like freedom to me, Clayton. You think because you hit 'delete' on some computer somewhere that that's it, it's over? I made choices about people's lives. And I gotta live with that." His conscious rejection of violence echoes Talal Asad's critique of the moral justification of killing rooted in liberal, conservative, and radical logic alike.[59]

The film certainly does continue to embed its images of Arabs and Muslims within the confines of terrorism, but it also challenges the rigid mapping of Islam and the United States as contradictory sites of identity formations. Instead, it presents Islam as an inspirational source of patriotism in the life of Muslim Americans. Samir's activism reflects the consciousness of an indigenous version of American Islam that interacts with transnational Muslim issues while retaining an interest in responding to domestic conditions of political activism. In a sense, Samir embodies the Muslim American emphasis on the specificity of the American context for the development of their religious and national identity.[60] The relationship between Samir's Muslim community and the state are marked by "suspicion, hyper-surveillance, and political violence from the security apparatus of the public sphere."[61] Samir's Islam, however, is in fact a ground for both his initial participation in the state's antiterrorism campaign and his later decision to leave it—all without compromising his sense of patriotism and belonging to the United States. The director's investment in utilizing "ambivalence," to use Homi Bhabha's sense of the term, in depicting Samir's character foregrounds the interstitial nature of his activism and entertains a multilayered sense of identity that challenges preconceived, US nationalist notions of cultural citizenship.[62]

This is why allegiance emerges as such a critical theme in *Traitor.* The film's plot bewilders its characters and audiences alike with respect to Samir's citizen-traitor status, leading Arabs, Blacks, Muslims, and Americans to similarly question Samir's sense of belonging and loyalty. Throughout the film, Samir's loyalty is questioned, not only by the terrorists and the FBI agents, but also by the different audiences who may identify with him through nationalism (American, Sudanese), ethnicity (American, Arab, African), or religion (devout, secular); at times, he is likely considered a traitor by each one of them. To further complicate this question of allegiance, Samir prefers to describe himself as being "from all over" when questioned about his background.

Portraying Samir in this transnational sense proves empowering and challenging at the same time. It allows him to navigate the national contours shaping his multiple identities while raising questions about his commitment to a particular identity. When the Arab and Muslim European character Omar expresses his confusion (i.e., dreaming in English and not feeling at home speaking his native language), Samir responds, "I don't feel at home anywhere." It is this emphasis on nowhere-ness that points to the disruptive possibilities of imagining Arab Americans in transnational terms. Cheadle describes the type of challenges his character confronts:

> It was interesting to me because the character that I play in the movie, Samir Horn, seemed to be somebody who encapsulated all those questions within his own journey. . . . What is my allegiance to my faith, what's my allegiance to my country? I feel like they're both letting me down in some ways. Who do I believe in? Who do I listen to? Ultimately, who takes responsibility for these things?[63]

The very thought of suspecting Samir as a traitor is made possible by the way his identity struggle challenges existing, rigidly drawn US nationalist boundaries around Arab and Muslim Americans. He is a man of faith who sincerely believes that Islam refers to an absolute submission to Allah. He is in a romantic relationship with a photojournalist, a secular lifestyle that traditional Islam arguably forbids outside of marriage. He is a US military expert fighting with the Mujahedeen against the atrocities of the Soviets in Afghanistan and with his other fellow Muslim militants against the Serbs' ethnic cleansing of Muslims in Bosnia. He makes explosives and teaches al-Nathir's members how to wear them. He facilitates their networking and even blows up the American Consulate in France himself. To justify his actions while undercover, he cites Martin Luther King Jr.: "If a man hasn't discovered something that he will die for, he isn't fit to live." His violence is dictated by his mission to undermine the terrorist group, and he retains a deep conviction that the terrorists are the worst enemies of not just the United States, but of Islam itself.

This multilayered biography, one reviewer notes, "demands that we entertain the possibility that Samir is a bad guy, and also that he retain[s] our sympathy when our doubts about him are most acute."[64] Ultimately, the film suggests the futility of understanding Samir's allegiance through certain clear-cut identity categories (i.e., Arab, Black, Muslim, or American). His allegiance is rather defined through multiple identities forged in a transnational context, thus unsettling the very title and premise of the film and raising a novel question: Who are the traitors in a transnational world—and what exactly are they betraying?

Struggling with his personal encounter with his father's death and believing in the Islamic teachings about the sanctity of life, Samir debates both members of the al-Nathir organization and the US intelligence and law enforcement agents at various points throughout the film. He criticizes both for legitimizing killing to achieve a specified goal, be it shaking a US empire for the extremists or stopping the "bad guys" for the US security apparatus. Arguing with Omar, he insists that the Mujahedeen's tactics in fighting the Soviets in Afghanistan are not translatable to waging full-scale wars against civilians. He questions the true meaning of "jihad" in Islam—that is, that war, even if driven by defense impulses, constitutes the lesser jihad while the greater jihad lies in overcoming worldly temptations and leading a virtuous lifestyle. When branded a traitor by the terrorist group, he counters that the real traitor is the one betraying Islam's message of love and peace through violence.

The citizen-terrorist paradox in *Traitor* projects Samir's identity at the crossroads of the imperatives of US patriotism and Islamic morality. It unveils a necessary dimension of Arab and Muslim American cultural citizenship that simultaneously contests terrorism and maintains a critique of violence in fighting it. Samir identifies himself as an American Muslim whose faith guides his patriotic duty to protect his fellow Americans. When reminded by the intelligence contractor to remember where his loyalty lies, Samir states, "I answer to God," to indicate that his actions are prompted by a religious, not necessarily a nationalist, duty to defeat terrorists. His morality is informed by a religious code that stipulates, "If you kill an innocent person, it's as if you've killed all mankind!" Even when reminded by Agent Clayton that Islam similarly stipulates in the same verse, "If you save a life, it's like you've saved all mankind," he chooses to sustain his mournful stance toward the innocent victims of his mission.[65] Having seen, as his mother puts it, "enough deaths to understand the value of life," he turns down the offer to work with the FBI. The film ends with Samir praying in a mosque among his fellow worshippers.

Despite recycling Hollywood's post-9/11 codes of patriotism and racial profiling, *Traitor* still displays a serious attempt to move beyond the citizen-terrorist paradox. The emergence of Samir as a hero with a complex sense of belonging presents the possibility of imagining post-9/11 Arab and Muslim American cultural citizenship in postnationalist terms that advocate ethnicity, religion, and one's Americanness as mutually inclusive sites of peace and violence.

Conclusion

Hollywood's post-9/11 portrayals may seem to depart from earlier one-dimensional representations of Arabs and Muslims in the United States, but, as this chapter demonstrates, these portrayals merely resort to blurring the lines between citizenship and terrorism in ways that reinforce cultural Otherness. Films like *The Recruit*, *Five Fingers*, *The Sentinel*, *Unthinkable*, and even *Traitor* present heroic imagery of Arab and Muslim American patriotism, but this imagery already imagines such characters as defenders of US national security. What sets *Traitor* apart, however, is its demand for more subtlety in narrating identity. In *Traitor*, Samir Horn (Don Cheadle) personifies the congruence of Arab, Black, Muslim, and American identities in the "war on terror" context. In battling foreign and homegrown terrorism in the United States, he exhibits a complex sense of identity characterized by his religious consciousness and patriotic duty; both inform his fight against terrorism and his critique of the damaging effects of the "war on terror."

Traitor builds on the possibilities established through Nachmanoff's seminuanced portrayal of the character of Samir. As highlighted above, Samir personifies post-9/11 Arab and Muslim American anxieties around the citizen-terrorist paradox. This paradox reduces Arab and Muslim minority status into an exclusionary site of cultural citizenship, and filters questions of belonging through US racialized and nationalistic rhetoric. Nachmanoff's staged construction of this paradox, though disruptive in its mode of imagination, is still embedded within Hollywood's one-dimensional depictions of Arabness and Islam. The possibility of Samir's diasporic agency is contingent on the vilification of all the other Arab and Muslim characters in the film. Another limitation in Nachmanoff's transnational framework is its lack of a proper contextualization of US, Arab, and Muslim geopolitics. A nuanced reading of Samir's diasporic activism necessitates a serious consideration of the Arab and Muslim American transnational engagement with the "war on terror" issue, beyond institutionally sanctioned missions to save civility and innocence in the United

States. It requires a look into the Arab and Muslim American constant negotiation for identity in the context of US interventions in the geopolitics of the Arab and Muslim worlds in the name of fighting terrorism.

While *Traitor* may not necessarily be considered the poster-child film of the idealized narration of Arab Americanness, it certainly opens the doors to thinking creatively beyond Hollywood's traditional Orientalist and racialized engagement with Arabness and Islam. It offers the opportunity to consider certain ways to challenge the industry's hegemonic portrayals. Chapters 4 and 5 navigate other sites—Egyptian and Arab American filmmaking, respectively—and search for similar disruptive post-9/11 filmic measures that attempt to move beyond the national constraints of cinema surveyed in chapters 1 and 2.

4

Disrupting Egyptian Depictions of Arab Americans

AS DEMONSTRATED in the first three chapters of this book, the Arab American image in US and Egyptian motion pictures has been hostage for decades to nationalist politics of representation. The two film industries have offered sensational images of Arab Americans that conform to a commercially coded repertoire of East-West binaries. This chapter continues the effort started in chapter 3 to depart from such hegemonic emphasis on polarization by shifting from the filmmaking experience of American director Jeffrey Nachmanoff in *Traitor* (2008) to that of Egyptian Adel Adeeb's *Laylat el-Baby Doll* (The Baby Doll Night, 2008). Despite the limiting nature of their relevant film industries, the two films, I argue, register a post-9/11 disruptive consciousness of Arab American in-betweenness and propose new ways to imagine Arab American subjectivity on the silver screen. While the Arab and Muslim American image in *Traitor*, as discussed in chapter 3, wrestles with ways to move beyond identity binaries and citizen-terrorist constructs, the image in *Laylat el-Baby Doll* engages with the notion of diasporic activism. Both types of images, I contend, offer critical interventions, even though in limited ways, in visualizing Arab American cultural citizenship at the crossroads of US and Arab encounters.

Laylat el-Baby Doll stands out as a unique contribution to Egyptian cinema both in form and content; notably, it also boasts the highest budget in the cinema's history at the time of E£40 million (roughly $8 million then). It is a feature film that interweaves elements of docudrama and facts on screen via direct conversation, didactic tone, and dramatization of several historical moments that range from the Holocaust to the Palestinian-Israeli conflict, 9/11, and the US invasion of Iraq. Its production company, "Good News," owned by the director's brother Imad el-Din Adeeb, has helmed a number of big-budget films.[1] In *Laylat el-Baby Doll*, the producer and the director decided to honor the recent death of their father, Abdel Hai Adib, by releasing a film that features his screenplay. The film received much publicity, partly thanks to the third brother, Amr Adeeb, who hosted the popular television show *al-Qahira el-Youm* (Cairo Today), and partly because it features fifteen celebrities from Egypt, Syria, Lebanon, and Tunisia. The film, however, failed to attract an audience in Egyptian movie theaters; it stopped screening after only two and a half months and made only an estimated E£7.25 million.[2] With an Egyptian moviegoing public increasingly interested in comedy and less drawn to serious drama at the time, the film had several disadvantages from the outset—including, but not limited to, its depressing content, the timing of its release, an emphasis on scripted conversations, the inclusion of unpopular American and Israeli perspectives, weak acting, its 150-minute length, a heavy dose of politics, and backlash to the film's huge budget and the estimated E£13 million devoted to marketing.

The film's content is also difficult to interpret or categorize politically. It lacks an explicit anti-imperial vision challenging Western hegemony, choosing, rather, to advocate peace while critically engaging with several divergent perspectives, all of which leave the audience—whether Arabs, Muslims, Israelis, or Americans—uneasy. The multiplicity of voices and perspectives in the film generated backlash from Egyptian film critics like Tariq el-Shinawi, Adel Abbas, Nader Adli, and Ashraf Bayoumi, who considered it disorienting and insufficiently developed.[3] This criticism, however, does not acknowledge the weight of the film's intricate narratives and the filmmaker's challenging task—that is, to dramatize a plot heavily dominated by decades of US and Arab geopolitics, and the resulting state of confusion and complexity, in a one-night setting.

Laylat el-Baby Doll advances a multilayered narrative that follows the parallel stories of six characters, representing American, Arab, and Arab diasporic perspectives. The events of the two-and-a half-hour-long film take place on New Year's Eve of 2007, in a storyline filled with many intense flashbacks to painful memories of Arab, Muslim, Jewish, and American collective traumas. The main storyline is driven by a terrorist threat to blow up the Cairo-based Plaza Hotel. The primary target of the threat is a visiting delegation led by two Americans representing two ends of the US political spectrum: Sarah (Layla Olwi) and Peter (Gamil Ratib). Sarah, the head of a civil society organization named American Organization for World Peace and Friendship, is a liberal Democrat on a mission to advocate the rejection of terrorism and promote peace and cooperation between Arabs and Americans. Peter, a retired, decorated marine commander turned businessman, is a conservative Republican whose right-wing leanings inform his support for the US deployment of hard power in the Middle East. A second pair of characters, Awadain (Nour el-Sherif) and Shokry (Gamal Souliman), represent divergent trajectories of Arab-based extremism. Awadain, an electrical engineer who once championed Arab causes, is now a terrorist targeting American tourists in Egypt and planning to blow up the Plaza. Shokry, a Syrian experiencing an identity crisis in the ever-changing Arab world, shares Awadain's grievances but eventually distances himself from the latter's newfound commitment to violence.

These four characters are positioned sometimes in conversation, sometimes in confrontation, with each other and with two other Arab diasporic characters: Layla Khoury (Ghada Abdulrazeq) and Hossam al-Ashry (Mahmoud Abdel Aziz). Layla, Awadain's girlfriend and lifetime love, is an Arab American of a Jewish background whose opposition to Israeli aggressions against Palestinians prompts her to forsake her journalistic duty in the occupied territories and embrace an activist stance that, ultimately, claims her life. The central character in the film, Hossam, is an Arab Muslim who lives in the United States, where he runs a travel agency and commutes to Egypt as part of his agency's organized tours for American visitors. He reconciles polarized US and Arab rhetoric by voicing concerns for US national security without compromising his criticism of the government's so-called "war on terror." The transnational space that Layla and Hossam occupy allows forms of diasporic activism that reflect, shape, and intervene in the polarizing US and Arab narratives of Sarah, Peter, Shokry, and Awadain. The significance of this portrayal lies in the film's lack of emphasis on these characters' Americanness but captures their experiences as disjunctures at the crossroads of US and Arab geopolitics and diasporic agency.

My analysis of *Laylat el-Baby Doll* in this chapter draws from Nadine Naber's conception of a broad "spatiotemporal context" in which Arab diasporas in the United States are not necessarily disconnected from the Arab world, especially when dealing with issues of US institutionalized violence, racism, and Islamophobia. "Of course, Arab and Muslim diasporas in the United States may not experience military violence in the same ways or to the same degree as the people in the countries targeted by the bombs or the bulldozers," Naber contends, "but Arab and Muslim diasporic life is constituted by racism and imperial military violence all the same."[4] The two characters of Layla and Hossam in *Laylat el-Baby Doll* symbolize two modes of diasporic activism that reflects a US imperial continuum in the lives of Arab diasporas regardless of where they reside. To make sense of the two characters' contexts of struggle, I build on Arjun Appadurai's term "diasporic public spheres," which refers to deterritorialized channels of bodies and ideas effected by globalization, or the "new order of instability in the production of modern subjectivities," as he describes it.[5]

My conception of diasporic public spheres differs from Appadurai's, however, in that I do not share his faith in the demise of the nation-state in the face of a rising postnational global order.[6] Instead, I locate the Arab diasporic experience as caught in the disjuncture between the sustained relevance of nationalism in today's globalized context and the proliferation of hybrid identities within diasporic communities as they navigate the contemporary transnational flow of commodities, ideas, technologies, corporations, and people. Hearing and understanding US-based Arab diasporic voices, I argue, requires continual resistance against the alienating contestations of both US racialized and Egyptian nationalist narratives. Hence, I read Layla's and Hossam's diasporic public spheres as spaces in which the two characters navigate competing voices and perspectives that define and mediate their respective identities. Exploring the particularity of these disjunctures, especially in the realm of US and Arab cultural imaginations, reveals how cultural citizenship, especially for immigrants and nonwhite Americans, as Sunaina Maira argues, cannot only be defined through the "political, social, and economic dimensions of citizenship" within the national narrative of the United States—and that of Egypt, I should add—but could also encompass one's "social realm of belonging," which sometimes stretches transnationally as this chapter illustrates.[7]

Thus, this chapter offers a close reading of the diasporic public spheres of the Arab diasporic characters in *Laylat el-Baby Doll* to highlight some possible configurations that could help in complicating existing national imaginations of Arab Americans in Hollywood and Egyptian cinemas. This film was chosen because of its unique cinematic contribution to visualizing US and Arab interconnectedness in the lives of US-based Arab diasporas and its departure from the Egyptian mainstream reductive representations, analyzed in chapter 2. In this film, Layla's and Hossam's diasporic public spheres are defined by echoes of US power in the Middle East and Arab anti-imperial responses. Simply put, my reading of these spheres in this chapter emphasizes the dynamic nature of Arab diasporic activism in today's globalized but heavily nationalistic environment.

Fatal Mode of Diasporic Activism

Homi Bhabha notes, "It is in the emergence of the interstices—the overlap and displacement of domains of difference—that the intersubjective and collective experiences of nationness, community interest, or cultural value are negotiated."[8] *Laylat el-Baby Doll* captures the essence of this observation through its structured portrayal of the idea of diasporic activism and how it is understood, articulated, and enacted in relation to US, Arab, Muslim, and even Israeli narratives and perspectives. This section analyzes three fatal modes of activism that the Arab American Layla and Arab characters Awadain and Shokry embody as they struggle against the ramifications of US and Arab as well as Israeli and Arab geopolitics. Although the primary emphasis in this section is on Layla's diasporic activism, it is critical to discuss both Awadain and Shokry as part of Layla's diasporic public spheres that shape her identity and performance. Adeeb's narration style emphasizes this interconnectedness, which, I argue, is central to make sense of the deterritorialized nature of post-9/11 imperial hegemony and resistance. The forms of activism that these characters embrace lead, ultimately, to their deaths—a cynical end that suggests the futility of their endeavors. Their deaths, however, also speak to broader Arab-based grievances related to US and Israeli aggressions; they are all traumatized victims of the US invasion of Iraq in 2003 and continued Israeli atrocities in Palestine. Using flashbacks, their stories are portrayed as transcending the boundaries of time and space; they are allegorical testaments to resilience, loss, and power.

Layla represents a diasporic identity that is not only missing from US popular constructions of Arab Americans and Jewish Americans, but also underexplored in both Israeli and Arab popular cultures. Born and raised in the Egyptian neighborhoods of Faggalla and Shoubra, Layla belongs to a community of Jews, ranging from 700,000 to 850,000, who lived across the Middle East and North Africa prior to the establishment of Israel in 1948, and who developed a unique sense of Jewish Arabness or Arab Jewishness. Arab Jews share a rich cultural heritage that takes pride in Jewish identity but frames it "not in opposition to Arab culture, to which they belonged quite organically," as Israeli writer Amnon Raz-Krakotzkin puts it.[9] In fact, Lital Levy observes that the term "Arab Jew" was "reclaimed by scholars such as Ella Shohat, Sami Shalom Chetrit, and Yehouda Shenhav as part of a political project of intervention into the normative terms of Zionist discourse."[10] As a child, Layla wrestles with the clashing nationalist narratives of Arabism and Zionism that became increasingly polarized in the aftermath of the Arab-Israeli War (1967). The audience is provided with a glimpse of this tension through a flashback to the growing animosity against Arab Jews in Egypt following the 1967 war and the effect of this animosity on Layla's social life. Awadain, the neighborhood Arab Muslim kid, is warned not to play with Layla anymore after his older brother is killed in the war. She is eventually forced to leave Egypt as part of wider relocation and displacement programs sanctioned by Israeli and Arab governments and orchestrated by Western powers.[11] The camera's blurred imaging of her departure suggests a critical reflection on how the Egyptian Jewish community's experience of being uprooted is fading from, but is still part of, the Egyptian collective memory.[12]

Reflecting on the disruptive nature of the Arab Jew displacement, Ella Shohat maintains that Arab Jews arriving in Israel were positioned in "a new linguistic and discursive environment, at once geopolitical (the Israeli-Arab conflict), legal (Israeli citizenship), and cultural (East versus West)."[13] For contemporary Arab Jews opting to migrate to the United States like Layla, the film suggests, the disruptive experience is not dissimilar but more complicated. Even though the film does not provide details about Layla's connections to the United States beyond her disclosure that she has an American passport, Layla's experience reveals how American citizenship potentially allows Jews like her to connect with their original Arab homelands in ways that Israeli citizenship does not.

Layla refuses to reject her Arab background in two ways. First, she develops a romantic relationship with her childhood friend Awadain. In one flashback, Awadain and Layla accidently reunite in a hotel lobby in Iraq, where they both stay as part of their media missions to cover the US invasion. The camera moves slowly to capture the emotional reunion through close-up shots that signify both loss and power. Their connection embodies their sense of loss for each other. Awadain represents the opportunity for Layla to cling to her Egyptian past. And Layla represents hope for Awadain to lead a family life with his love, a future that he will soon be deprived of, contributing to his transformation into a terrorist. Meanwhile, their connection embodies a sense of loss for each other not only as individuals but also as representative of the lost unity among Egyptian communities of Islamic and Jewish backgrounds. To reclaim this sense of unity, Awadain and Layla challenge the societal taboo that forbids their romantic relationship. In fact, they decide to marry but delay the wedding until Layla's return from a reporting assignment in the Palestinian territories. Their reunion certainly disrupts norms and constraints that have challenged Layla's ability to reclaim her connection to an Egyptian Jewish heritage fractured by chauvinism, at once Arabist, Islamist, or Zionist.

Second, Layla further demonstrates her connection with her Egyptian heritage by articulating a pro-Arab critique of Israeli aggressions. She does not hesitate to support a protest organized by an international group opposing Israel's controversial wall construction project (also known as the Israeli-West Bank Barrier), which inhibits Palestinians' mobility and hinders their ability to declare an independent state. During her reunion with Awadain, she explains that he should not be surprised by her pro-Palestinian stance and her ability to reconcile the imperatives of her Jewish, American, and Egyptian identities with the human values of peace and justice. This stance constitutes a critical moment of disruption, upending the assumption that all Arab Americans of Jewish background must identify with either Arabness and Islam or Jewishness and Westernness.

Layla's multiple identities (Egyptian, Arab, Jewish, and American) reveal the complexity of Arab diasporic formations. The popular understanding of Arabs in the United States, for instance, does not usually factor in the possibility of a Jewish element, or even a Christian one, for that matter. Two misconceptions have fed this limited understanding. The first relies upon a dichotomized understanding of the Middle East in terms of two broad and fundamentally opposed identities: Arabs and Jews. The second misconception draws from a politicized association of Jewishness with Europeanness, an association further solidified through Israel's close political connections with the West. Drawing from her own personal experience as an Arab-Jewish American, Shohat illustrates how such misconceptions make an identity such as Layla's difficult to understand:

> Americans are often amazed to discover the existentially nauseating or charmingly exotic possibilities of such a syncretic identity. I recall a well-established colleague who despite my elaborate lessons on the history of Arab Jews, still had trouble understanding that I was not a tragic anomaly—for instance, the daughter of an Arab (Palestinian) and Israeli (European Jew). Living in North America makes it even more difficult to communicate that we are Jews and yet entitled to our Middle Eastern difference. And that we are Arabs and yet entitled to our religious difference, like Arab Christians and Arab Muslims. . . . In an American context, we face again a hegemony that allows us to narrate a single Jewish memory, i.e., a European one. For those of us who don't hide our Middle Easternness under one Jewish "we," it becomes tougher and tougher to exist in an American context hostile to the very notion of Easternness.[14]

Layla is similarly confronted with questions of allegiance within a hegemonic conceptual framework that does not recognize the multiplicity of her identity and the interstitiality of her activism. By transgressing US nationalist constructions of Arabness and Jewishness, Layla presents a viable Arab American image that defies existing categorizations of identity and suggests a distinct diasporic mode of belonging.

And yet, ultimately, Layla's mode of diasporic activism is fatal, mainly because of the "tragic anomaly" of her identity. Her death is dramatized in a scene that recalls the gruesome death of young American activist Rachel Corrie, who was crushed by an Israeli armored bulldozer in the Gaza Strip in 2003 when she attempted to disrupt the demolition of a Palestinian doctor's home.[15] In the Gaza town of Rafah, Layla forsakes her role as a journalist and decides to stand up against the might of Israeli Defense Forces. During a peace activist demonstration, Layla stands up to an Israeli tank bent on demolishing the house of a Palestinian family. Her embrace of the symbol of Palestinian struggle, keffiyeh (black and white checkered scarf), underscores an important shift in her role from that of a journalist into an activist (figure 15). In a direct and personal statement, she addresses

15. Layla talks to an Israeli lieutenant moments before her death in *Laylat el-Baby Doll* (2008). © Good News.

one of the Israeli soldiers and appeals to his humanity through a series of rhetorical questions:

> Do you have a wife? A fiancée? Will you be OK someday if a tank like this runs over your children because they are defending their homeland? So, your commander's conscience is absent, where is your conscience? Human being is God's conscience on earth.

Soon after Layla's speech, she turns around, but her scarf is trapped in the tank tread, forcing her to fall under the tank. As the tank runs over her body, the voiceover of another activist describes her death as an intentional Israeli act of barbarism. So, was her death an accident or an atrocity?

The simultaneous projection of the two versions of Layla's death reflects existing controversies surrounding real-life Corrie's death that range from an Israeli version claiming human error to activists' view citing Israeli brutality. The choice to confuse the audience about Layla's death enraged some Egyptian commentators, who critiqued the film as supporting Israel. Equally important, this choice validates the film's interest in transcending singular narrations and in entertaining multiple perspectives of various issues. While this representation strategy may blur Israel's responsibility for Layla's death, it certainly confirms the interstices of Layla's mode of activism.

Regardless of the confusion around Layla's death, the incident itself is critically presented as a moment of triumph for the Israeli project, which considers Layla a casualty deserving no sympathy, even in the United States. This triumph is framed negatively within the film, however, which critiques the United States' pro-Israel stance with yet another subplot drawn from reality. A monologue titled *My Name Is Layla Khoury* is scheduled for performance in New York City, but is canceled when its recounting of Layla's pro-Palestinian activism is determined to be inappropriate. The reference here is to the negative reception of *My Name Is Rachel Corrie* in the United States—a play based on Corrie's diaries, which were edited by Alan Rickman and Katharine Viner—after its initial success in the Royal Court Theater London in 2005. In 2006 the New York Theatre Workshop postponed the play indefinitely due its political content.[16] In the film, a peace activist explicitly condemns the cancelation of *My Name Is Layla Khoury* as an "act of censorship" and notes the irony of its occurrence "in the very nation that claims to be an example of democracy, justice, and freedom!"

Throughout the film, the US-Israeli alliance, manifested through US monetary, military, political, and cultural support, is projected as a geopolitical front for an imperial project that continues to disregard the aspirations and demands of Arabs and Muslims.[17] Upon hearing the news that the United States has refused to vote in favor of a UN resolution condemning Israeli bombardments of Gaza, a frustrated character wonders, "Until when will America continue to challenge the world in this way?!" The popular song "Ya 'Aam 'Arabi Isḥa" (Uncle Arab, Wake Up, 2004) plays in the film as a critical reminder of this sentiment, with lyrics that condemn both the United States and Israel:

> Two sides of the coin: America and Israel
> They turned the world a jungle
> And lit the fuse!
> America and Israel

Are but bullies
And, for many years
They have become terrorists
Two wide hands
Grabbing the whole region
They'll slice it up
And pass it out.[18]

Notably, this is a follow-up song to the earlier, arguably even more popular song "Ana Bakrah Israel" (I Hate Israel, 2000), which also features in the film. A taxi driver transporting Awadain plays the song and dances to its words: "I hate Israel / I'll say it if asked / Even if I get murdered or politically prisoned." The unnamed taxi driver represents the average Egyptian who only seems indifferent to Arab-Israel geopolitics, but is actually deeply embedded in the conflict. Awadain learns that the driver hates Israel because his brother, an Egyptian-recruited soldier serving his country as part of a mandatory program in the Palestinian-Egyptian border, was shot dead while guarding his unit. The driver explains that his deceased brother was the sole provider for a family of seven but was paid a salary of only E£150. He criticizes the Egyptian government for their impoverished conditions and the Israeli government for his brother's death.

By incorporating these songs and the taxi driver's account, the film captures an Arab critique of the US-Israel geopolitical alliance. The film further references the influence of Israeli lobbying in the United States. The American Israel Public Affairs Committee (AIPAC) is depicted in the film as the ultimate lobbying force, spearheaded by neoconservatives' contributions to the electoral campaigns of US presidents and congressional representatives. "The fact that we all know," a journalist in the film notes, "is that for any candidate to win the presidential election in the United States, he has first to appeal to AIPAC and secure its approval. To put it simply, Israel is the one controlling American foreign policy, and not vice versa."[19] The film foregrounds this alliance as unholy, for it has allowed Israel to violate Islamic and Christian religious sites, denied Palestinians the right to establish their own stable state, and contributed to tension in the Middle East through its military deployment, population displacement, and territorial expansion. The alliance, the film suggests, serves as a geopolitical source of tension that sustains Arabs' sense of oppression in the Arab world and in the diaspora.

It is in this context that diasporic activism for a character like Layla reaches a fatal ending. Her calls for peace and coexistence fail the test of transcending the strictly drawn national boundaries carved around her own multiple identities. The US-Israeli alliance does not permit her Jewishness and Americanness to unfold in ways that accommodate her Arab cause. The brutal ending to her life in Israel and the refusal of American cultural producers to commemorate her heroism reveal the influence of geopolitics in the production—and rejection—of an Arab diasporic activism. If geopolitics is about the impact of power dynamics and space-based politics on individuals' perceptions of themselves, then Layla's search for justice is a desperate effort to claim her own unique form of disruptive agency.

Layla's fatal mode of diasporic activism overlaps with two other fatal modes of activism—one driven by revenge, another driven by disillusionment—which are represented by the characters of Awadain and Shokry, respectively. Awadain is an emasculated and helpless Egyptian who resorts to violence as the only means to make sense of his life of despair. He becomes an activist in response to a political environment that punishes those Arabs and Muslims who refuse to conform to US, Israeli, and even Egyptian state militarized imperatives. His transformation from an Arab hero fighting for justice and defending his homeland to a terrorist unleashing devastating explosives that kill random civilians speaks directly to the very nature of the conditions that produce terrorism. He does not become violent simply or instantaneously but goes through an inhumane process that drives him to irrational measures.

Awadain's radicalization starts in Iraq, where he travels as part of a media mission covering the US invasion. He quickly finds himself unable to remain an objective observer, however, as he identifies with the Iraqis' pain and suffering. Even traveling from the airport to his hotel, he is immediately confronted with the lived material consequences of US imperialism in the region. An unnamed Iraqi truck driver picks him up and drives him off the blocked airport road through what turns out to be a battle zone. With the sound of explosions and air strikes in the background, the driver sings in a desperate attempt to preserve some sense of normalcy. Awadain is surprised and unable to comprehend this act; it is his first day in Iraq after all.

As the two travel through a few chaotic, war-torn settings, the driver laments the impact of the conflict and the impossibility of sustaining aspirations and dreams in such conditions. "Death is like a hidden trap everywhere," he remarks. He sings, the audience learns, as a way to cope with the constant sounds of explosion and his paranoia about losing a family member. In a series of rhetorical questions that reveal his pessimism and despair, the driver asks: "Where is livelihood? Where are our children? Where is Iraq? Where are you God?" Recalling his hope that the Americans would bring rescue and reform, the driver reflects bitterly on how he and other Iraqis like him thought it "would start raining dollars," but instead, it "rained bombs" that ruined homes, orphaned children, and fractured the country. Looking at his current conditions, he invokes President Saddam Hussein's name in a moment of nostalgia for the old regime. Expressing no love or hatred of the deposed president, the driver's mention of the name represents simply another desperate attempt to return to normalcy. During Hussein's rule, the driver remembers that at least Iraqis, regardless of their class, did not "sleep hungry" and all belonged to "one Iraqi nation." He continues to compare now versus then:

> Now the cursed Americans are slaughtering Iraqis like chickens, and if that weren't bad enough, the sectarian militias, the armed fighters are coming from other countries to incite more sedition among Iraqis, between Shia and Sunna, to kill each other as if we are not one nation and do not share one religion. There is only bitterness! There is only bitterness!

The driver is not uncritical of Saddam, but he also recognizes that the number of casualties during Saddam's thirty-five-year rule cannot by any measure exceed those who died at the hands of the armed militias and the American forces.

Awadain's encounter with the driver is not really a conversation per se. He remains silent for the most part and only asks questions. Even when the driver begs him for a reaction, Awadain is dumbfounded and states that he cannot comment. Far from implying a lack of engagement, his silence suggests how much he has been impacted by the driver's account. Afterward, Awadain develops an increasingly critical attitude toward the US forces in the country. This shift in attitude, however, soon attracts the attention of Peter, the director of Abu Ghraib prison. Peter invites Awadain to a private meeting in which he interrogates Awadain's connection to "terrorism," a word that Awadain substitutes with "resistance."

Peter's definition of terrorism is directly linked to power and can only conceive of fighters targeting the US military as terrorists—a logic that Awadain challenges in two ways. He first emphasizes that resisting occupation is an internationally recognized right. Then, he rebukes Peter for using a politicized definition of terrorism as a pretext to jail and torture opposition, a return to Saddam Hussein's way of doing business. As tension between the two characters increases, Peter invites Awadain to Abu Ghraib to investigate and learn the truth about the "humane" treatment of prisoners. The tone of authority in Peter's language prompts Awadain to project his own agency and state that he reserves the choice to accept or reject the invitation. This voice is troubling to Peter, who reminds Awadain that he is under Peter's protection in the country. He implicitly threatens Awadain's life by reminding him that he must secure Peter's permission before moving within the country. Peter's embodiment of hardcore nationalism is familiar to Arab audiences as Awadain forcefully draws some parallels:

> I am really surprised. America, the symbol of the free world, has emergency laws, courts martial, preventive detentions, and tapping conversations. What's worse are the restrictions on the media. Welcome to the third world!

In Awadain's eyes, the United States has abandoned its democratic rhetoric to expand instead its hold on power—the very same impulse of nationalist projects being resisted by many Arabs in their countries. Awadain expresses the Arab public frustration that by enforcing such militarized policies, America is not much different from any other country in the third world, where national crises are used to suspend citizens' rights.

Awadain's critical evaluation of the United States' post-9/11 "war on terror" tactics serves as an important reminder of the damaging effects of hypernationalism and points to the contradiction between US rhetoric and its foreign policy militarism. The film further captures this through Awadain's rejection of Peter's logic of necessity—a logic that each US administration since the 1950s has used to justify state-sponsored aggressions in Arab lands. Peter, a dedicated marine, sincerely views his service to his country as noble and is bewildered by the popular post-9/11 question: "Why do they hate us?" Peter's interpretation is superficially similar to the one circulated by President George W. Bush's administration, blurring the lines between identity and violence and encouraging many religious zealots to entertain the clash of civilizations theory. Unable to fathom Iraqis' rising anger, he is enraged by the escalation of violence against US forces in Iraq. "We came with our troops and children to liberate them from their rulers and their extremists' terrorism," he privately confesses to Sarah. "We sacrificed everything we have to heal them." Sarah's response is arguably even more troubling, framing the Iraqis as suffering from illness and noting that "nobody takes medicine against their will." Ultimately, the film humanizes Peter by allowing him to express his nostalgia for his family and home while defending his role in Iraq. He is also an adamant critic of the lack of democracy in the Arab world, which continues to feed his faith in American exceptionalism. His confrontation with Awadain in Iraq symbolizes the broader conflict between US militarism and Arab resistance, and the film uses their conflict to critique their respective power dynamics.

The film sheds lights on the sense of insecurity in the post-war transition, which was mainly a product of the failing policies of the

Coalition Provisional Authority (CPA), a US-led administrative authority installed to govern Iraq at the time. The CPA's measures—eliminating Iraq's social welfare programs, auctioning its sectors to private corporations, releasing its whole army from its duties, and failing to prevent the eruption of identity-based violence and the looting and burning of public establishments and educational institutions—have been perceived as not merely a result of the de-Ba'athification of the country, but rather an intentional and systematic erasure of Iraq's past, designed to create a mini-US model in the Middle East. Awadain's exposure to this authority sows the seeds of his transformation into a dedicated terrorist who cannot differentiate between battle zones and tourist attractions.

He experiences firsthand the disjuncture between rhetoric and practice of the US antiterrorism campaign when his assistant is shot dead and he himself is arbitrarily locked in Abu Ghraib, where he undergoes extreme forms of humiliation and torture. Promises of freedom and democracy collapse in this jail, which ironically accommodated the torture of dissidents prior to the US invasion of 2003. Real-life images of US soldiers inflicting physical and mental pain on the prisoners, exposing them to different humiliating scenarios of forced nudity and disgracing the Holy Qur'an, have circulated globally.[20] The references are thus familiar when Awadain is forced by US soldiers to pose for pictures on top of other prisoners in an orgy of nudity (figure 16). He is intimidated by dogs and forced into uncomfortable, inhumane positions for long hours. When Awadain rejects the sexual seduction of an American female soldier, she removes his genitalia—a symbolic gesture of the United States' stripping of Arab masculinity.

Using emasculation to suggest injured Arab masculinity is a powerful Egyptian filmmaking tool to criticize Arabs' weak resistance to the United States' imperial advances; emasculation in this context symbolizes availability for Western penetration, made possible when Arabs fail to respond to violence committed in their lands. The traumatized men in Egyptian films like Mohamed Amin's *Laylat Soqūt Baghdad* (The Night Baghdad Fell, 2005) exemplify Arab passivity against US interference in the Middle East. *Laylat Soqūt Baghdad* features the story

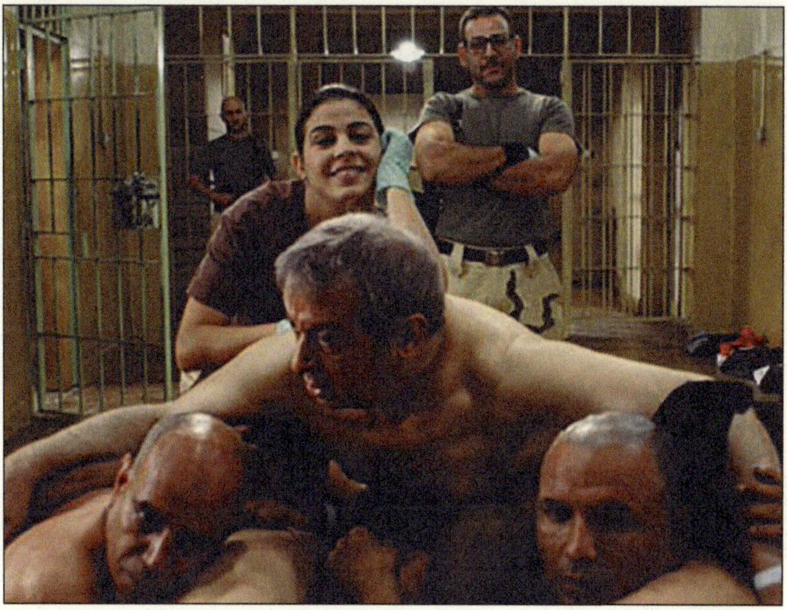

16. Awadain's humiliation spurs his later acts of terrorism in *Laylat el-Baby Doll* (2008). © Good News.

of Tariq (Ahmed Eid), a once bright high school student who is pressured to develop a defensive weapon to deter any future US invasion following that in Iraq. The pressure overwhelms Tariq, who describes the technology gap between the United States and Egypt in terms of light years. He seeks motivation by immersing himself in nationalist music and even derisively hanging a picture of a US marine he names "John" at the back of his toilet lid. In a moment of collapse, he smokes marijuana to escape the anxiety but soon begins to hallucinate that John is getting ready to rape him. Later, in a passionate address to his neighbors, Tariq's paranoid school principal invokes this analogy of invasion and rape by exclaiming that the country's defenses are so weak, they might as well confront any potential US invasion of Egypt with the plea, "Please, Don't F**k me!" Thus, this film, like *Laylat el-Baby Doll*, uses rape as a metaphor for US imperialism in the Middle East.[21] Directors Adel Adeeb and Mohammed Amin, along with Sherif Mandour in *Ma'alish Iḥna Benetbahdhel* (No Problem, We're Getting

Screwed, 2005), present staunch critiques of US imperial coercion through their reenactment of Abu Ghraib prison as a site of rape and a crisis for Arab masculinity.

Tariq's sexual vulnerability in *Laylat Soqūt Baghdad* coincides with rising frustration with his inability to perform heterosexually (i.e., through sexual intercourse with his wife). As the trauma takes its toll on his masculinity, he fantasizes about an erotically dancing US secretary of state, Condoleezza Rice, who rekindles his sexual appetite. Seizing the opportunity, he asks his wife to wear US military clothing, which eventually enables him to come to terms with his sexuality. The formula seems to work with others when the neighborhood women also use US military clothing to lure their inactive husbands to bed. The resuscitation of Arab heterosexuality through US military clothing is contingent on the characters' ability to reclaim their masculinity, held hostage by recurring nightmares of losing masculinity in the infamous Abu Ghraib prison, a site that transforms Awadain's life for good.

Following his experience in Abu Ghraib, Awadain's activism turns into a fatal mode in *Laylat el-Baby Doll.* The audience learns that Awadain's search for vengeance is not merely a result of his injured masculinity, but a desperate backlash for losing his manhood, particularly enhanced both by his emasculation and his loss of Layla. Awadain seeks blind revenge against westerners and "the West" writ large, because he perceives the US-Israeli alliance as a Western front for erasure of Arab heritage, self-determination, and dignity. After taking Peter hostage at knifepoint in Cairo, Awadain screams out his grievances: "What would happen if an American citizen or soldier experiences my pain? Wouldn't you avenge him?" The brief but tense exchange leads nowhere as Peter emphasizes human errors and Awadain's thirst for vengeance is not quenched. Awadain escapes the police after shooting Peter but is eventually surrounded and asked to surrender. He threatens to blow up the hotel and demands to see Peter or President Bush. Insisting that he is not a terrorist but a victim demanding rights in a global order, he refers bitterly to the failure of the International Court of Justice and the United Nations to recognize individuals like him.

Police snipers kill Awadain just before he can detonate the explosive, but not before the audience sees the causal link between the US "war on terror" campaign and his turn to terrorism. Far from differentiating between extremists and moderates, the so-called "war on terror" has blurred the two categories, pushing some toward ever more violent means of expression and creating fertile conditions for suicidal modes of activism.

Like Layla and Awadain, Shokry's journey also sees the character turn to a fatal mode of activism that leads, ultimately, to his death. His soul-searching for a sovereign Arab land is deeply influenced by the tendency of both the Cold War and the "war on terror" to reduce the Arab world to a mere site of clashing narratives. In the early 1970s, Shokry is placed in political confinement because of his pan-Arab views and his participation in antigovernment protests. While imprisoned, he endures hardship because he fails to affiliate with either socialist or Islamist groups, the main blocks of opposition in Egypt at the time. In a comedic scene, Shokry is tossed from one group to the other. Both the Islamists and the socialists ask him whether he is an *akh* (brother) or a *rafiq* (comrade). Naively unaware of the political meanings of the terms, he shares the wrong answer with each group and gets beaten accordingly. In this way, Shokry stands in for the Arab masses who suddenly find themselves caught up in unfamiliar narratives, ones that demand they claim their political affiliation in an increasingly polarized environment. When Awadain comes to Shokry's rescue in jail, the two become friends. Shokry's embrace of Awadain is a token of how Arab masses hailed him as a hero prior to his descent into extremism.

Shokry recollects his life changes after his release from jail. He ventures the streets for three years, searching for a job to no avail. Because of his previous protest against Sadat, he will never be able to get work commensurate with his university degree qualifications. Thus, he ends up working as a taxi driver, transporting both Awadain and Hossam to and fro throughout the film. As he drives them, he is pulled in opposing directions by their ideas—Awadain's inclination to violence in the name of resistance and Hossam's calls for peaceful protest. At the beginning of the film, Shokry is sympathetic to Awadain. "Oppression and helplessness," Shokry remarks, "force someone like Awadain to become like someone depicted in the media." Soon, however, Shokry becomes disillusioned with Awadain, seeing him less and less as a hero and more as a vengeful fanatic blinded by personal grievances. Shokry eventually addresses Awadain: "I am sorry, but I will not be involved in your planned attack against civilians who did you no harm. I can understand your revenge against your oppressor," Shokry continues, "but not against people living around you." Awadain's plans, however, are set in motion and he does not want to back down. He accuses Shokry of treason and shoots him in the back.

Shokry's death symbolizes the sense of betrayal experienced by much of the Arab public in relation to heroes-turned-terrorists like Awadain. His initial support for Awadain's radical form of resistance is rooted in his own struggle to claim a sovereign postcolonial agency. When existing resistance narratives fail to deliver this sense of agency, he is drawn to the charismatic Awadain, whose vehement critique of US hegemony seems clear-sighted. But though Shokry embraces Awadain's challenge of imperialist projects, he cannot subscribe to the polarizing rhetoric that blurs the line between fighting oppression and becoming oppressors. In this way, Shokry is symbolic of Arabs who continue to voice their opposition to US interventionist policies without subscribing to means of violence against civilians. His disillusionment and subsequent rejection of extremism is a metaphor for the dilemma of some contemporary Arabs, trapped between the mechanics and philosophies of resistance and terrorism. As a representative of Arab citizenry, Shokry becomes ever more disenchanted with Awadain's claim to fight for a just and noble cause. That this position costs Shokry his life is a critical reference to the cancerous effects of extremism, accelerated through intolerance and brutality.

Layla, Awadain, and Shokry adopt various forms of activism, but all meet fatal ends. Their collective failure speaks to the state of powerlessness that Arabs experience in the face of US imperialism, whether in the form of unchecked support to Israel or aggressive interventions in neighboring Arab countries. The characters illustrate the filmmaker's cynical yet realistic contemporary understanding of the impact of institutional injustice on individuals like Layla, Awadain, and Shokry, and the communities they represent. Despite the various identities of their aggressors—be they Israeli occupation, US military, Egyptian dictatorship, or terrorists—the deaths of all three characters serve as a reminder of how slippery resistance has become in today's Middle East. That Awadain and Shokry function as part of Layla's diasporic public sphere adds a critical layer to imagine some of the interstices defining an Arab American experience with activism. While there exists in reality various modes of Arab American activism in the spectrum of US and Arab as well as Israeli and Arab geopolitics, the only mode of activism that seems to have any promise, the film suggests, is the neoliberal mode of diasporic activism. This is illustrated through Hossam's proactive engagement with both Arab and American perspectives. The following section explores this specific mode of diasporic activism as an important but benignly disruptive mode of interaction between the United States and the Arab world.

Neoliberal Mode of Diasporic Activism

Parallel to the fatal mode of diasporic activism represented by Layla and her Arab spheres of Awadain and Shokry, *Laylat el-Baby Doll* also portrays a neoliberal mode of diasporic activism through the engagement of the US-based Egyptian character, Hossam, with his own spheres—that is, the various characters that represent American and Arabic perspectives. The film's plot unfolds through intercutting scenes of Hossam's diasporic life, defined by his commitments to work and family; in fact, Hossam functions as the anchor to the film's many different narratives and perspectives. Having lived in the United States for twenty-some years, Hossam owns a travel agency in collaboration with his Egyptian uncle and is struggling to conceive a child with his wife. In the film, he escorts the American peace delegation to Egypt, where he is responsible for arranging their travel logistics and safety. During the visit, Hossam is also desperate to spend one romantic night with his Egypt-based wife, in the hopes of finally conceiving a child. Upon arriving in Egypt for a one-day visit, however, Hossam struggles to balance time between his job and his marital life. The process of realizing his own dreams—both professionally and personally—will not be easy.

Perhaps a limitation imposed by the dominant politics of representation in Egyptian cinema, *Laylat el-Baby Doll* does not clearly specify whether Hossam is an American citizen, an immigrant in the United States, or simply a sojourner. However, in a film replete with nationalist perspectives of geopolitics, the fact that Hossam's character is not anchored in a specific national realm is quite intriguing. The film locates the character in a transnational space that defies narrow conceptions of identity and cultural citizenship. It is not clearly determined whether the film imagines Hossam as an Arab American per se, but what seems clear is how he is forced to navigate treacherous terrains that constantly question whether he is an Arab or an American rather than both. As this section demonstrates, Hossam appears as someone who would rather be in two places at once and is reluctant to choose between the United States and Egypt. Unlike the other characters, who have strong ties to their own lands regardless of where they are, Hossam's belonging is mapped transnationally as his cultural citizenship cannot be confined to one nation-state. He is more than capable of belonging to two spaces even though he can only be physically in one.

This welcomed complication not only opens the door for imagining what it may be like to be part of a US-based Arab diaspora, but also questions whether the United States and Egypt are willing to accommodate this sort of cultural citizenship. The film resolves this challenge by limiting Hossam's diasporic activism to a neoliberal mode, placing emphasis on the role of corporations' profit-driven logic and imperatives in taming government and public narratives. This is most evident in Hossam's immediate contacts, who promote the motto "business equals peace." While Sarah and Peter adamantly differ in their views of their government's use of hard power in its Middle Eastern foreign policy calculations, the film presents the two American characters in agreement as far as their belief in the power of the neoliberal global economy to deliver peace, perhaps in a subtle critique of Thomas Friedman's "Golden Arches" theory of conflict resolution.[22] Sarah blames the Bush administration's post-9/11 "war on terror" hawkish measures for fueling anger among Arabs and Muslims, whereas Peter frames the US exercise of military power as a noble American gesture to help liberate Arab and Muslim populations from the tyranny of their own rulers. His understanding of post-9/11 US and Arab geopolitics is one in which Arabs and Muslims are considered "sick" populations "in need of cure," with Americans representing a benevolent force of healing. In contrast, though she acknowledges Arabs' ailing conditions, Sarah maintains that they cannot be treated against their will. This difference, though seemingly nuanced, captures the way in which some Americans, regardless of their political affiliations, are incapable of transcending their deep-seated cultural bias against Arabs. Fixed in their common characterization of Arabs as diseased, both Sarah and Peter seek to "rescue" the region by establishing trading transactions with Egyptian businesspersons such as Hossam's uncle. The philosophy of opening markets for multinational corporations, Sarah argues, serves as a mediatory space for conflict resolution and tension reduction. Peter, the former head of Abu Ghraib prison in Iraq, is now a CEO of a US corporation. Regardless of his ideological difference, he shares Sarah's philosophy and is in Egypt to fulfill it.

Hossam's uncle is an Egyptian entrepreneur who represents the Egyptian elite, often caricatured in Egyptian cinema as serving US interests at the cost of their own people, both in terms of narrative and economy (see chapter 2). The uncle is at his breaking point when Awadain shoots Peter. He is frantic when talking to Hossam in the hospital and clearly expresses his concern that he may lose his business deals if US authorities escalate the issue. This prompts Hossam to question whether the American delegation in Egypt is there for peace or business. The uncle rejects the premise of the question by prioritizing instead his business considerations; he expresses his willingness to accommodate any regime's demands so long as his business thrives. "If we were living during kingdom days, I would be a royalist," he stresses. "If during socialism days, I would be a socialist; I am now in support of openness to free trade." From his uncle's perspective, Hossam ought to remain silent and refrain from challenging his American guests. Sarah is important to the uncle because her brother heads an influential group in the US Congress. Introducing this political element helps the uncle define his relationship with Sarah as a strategic alliance that transcends their own individuality and becomes representative of their countries. Losing Sarah's business, according to the uncle, effectively means that Egypt will also lose congressional approval of US aid. Hossam's response is critical, however, when he rejects US aid if it comes at the cost of one's dignity. "May God ruin those who forced us," he remarks, "to grow cantaloupe and kiwi instead of growing wheat." Egyptian sovereignty, the audience learns, is in the hands of an elite that puts business and profit over any other issues impacted by US and Arab geopolitics.

Hossam's activism functions within this neoliberal milieu. His resistance is not fatal, like Layla's, but it also fails to achieve more than ambivalence, questioning all the other perspectives surrounding him. He embraces a tone that calls for peace and coexistence with Israel. Mindful of the Egyptian-Israeli peace treaty, he advocates ending bloodshed and devastation. When reminded by a journalist about the Israeli scale of devastation, he pleads for the audience to "forgive and forget." "Time is surely capable of making us forget our pains and agonies," he reflects, "just like life: sun and rain, thunder and lightning, storms and hurricanes, and then sun again!" At the same time, Hossam's call for peace is not without an active awareness of Israeli aggressions, particularly in the occupied territories. He still grieves over the death of his girlfriend, who fell victim to an Israeli military invasion of the Nativity Church in Bethlehem. He sincerely sympathizes with Sarah's personal account of her family's terrifying experience during the Holocaust, but he also draws a link between this and the Holocaust-like experience of Palestinians. "What the Israeli army does nowadays to the Palestinians," he points out, "is a lot worse than what Hitler did to the Jews!" To emphasize his message, the camera cuts to a screen shot of a statement by the Israeli deputy defense minister, Matan Vilnai:

> Millions of Jews were killed in the Holocaust concentration camp. Millions of Christians, Freemasons, Gypsies, and Communists were killed in the Holocaust. Palestinians will bring a Holocaust upon themselves by stepping up cross-border rocket fire from the Gaza Strip.[23]

"Do you know," Hossam goes on to ask rhetorically, "there are millions of mothers in Palestine, Iraq, and Lebanon today, in the beginning of the third millennium, who have the same feelings of fear that your mother had?" When Sarah protests the reference to Hitler, he maintains that "oppression, injustice, tyranny, and dictatorship remain despite the change of perpetrators' names." Another screenshot displays, "According to UNRWA, the number of Palestinian refugees in the Near East registered since 1948 is around 5 million."

Hossam contests Americans' expectations that Arabs and Muslims should embrace peace without reflecting on the role of the US government in escalating the tension. Sarah's passionate efforts to convince Arabs and Muslims to end their "anti-American boiling state of anger," as she puts it, exhibit an inherent critique of US foreign policy. "How can I talk about equality," she states, "while I behave in a racist way with my black colleague, refuse to talk to a student because he is a Muslim, or refuse to participate in a competition just because there is a Jewish student." Hossam reiterates the US responsibility to enforce peace through sponsoring Arab-Israeli negotiations, suspending its military operations in Iraq, adopting a more engaging foreign policy approach, and loosening its restrictive policies against Arab and Muslim Americans. He emphasizes the hypocrisy of US foreign policy:

> Like millions of people in the world, I was dreaming of American democracy—America that liberated the world from Hitler's Nazism and Mussolini's fascism. . . . But unfortunately, President Bush went beyond Hitler and Mussolini by expressing his own will. He destroyed Afghanistan, bombed Iraq, which allowed terrorism to spread around the globe. . . . You spent three trillion dollars. Imagine if this money was spent to develop the region, improving health care, education, and creating projects. Surely, this was going to be the biggest war against terrorism!

Hossam shares his personal experience of the backlash against Middle Eastern–looking Americans in the immediate aftermath of 9/11. He recounts how someone confronted him in a New York bar about his Muslim identity, and seeking revenge against Muslims in general, attacked him with a knife. When talking to Sarah, Hossam thus insists that the United States adopt laws that ban hatred against Arabs and Muslims.

Hossam's diasporic activism and interstitial sense of agency engage with the polarizing narratives dominant in both the United States and the Arab world. Hossam reflects a sense of Arab diasporic consciousness that is critical of US empire both through its domestic racial profiling and Middle East foreign policy. In addition to his engagements with Sarah and his uncle, Hossam continues to communicate a critical tone with Peter, Shokry, and Awadain. His encounter with Peter reflects an Arab diasporic anxiety around the polarizing rhetoric emerging in the US "war on terror" context. In a conversation structured to dismantle stereotypes that have dominated US and Arab cultural politics since 9/11, the two characters set out their respective arguments. When Peter protests the Arab sensational readings of George W. Bush, Dick Cheney, and Condoleezza Rice as the embodiment of American society, Hossam challenges the stereotypical reading of Osama bin Laden as the embodiment of the Arab and Muslim worlds. In his attempt to justify US interventionist foreign policy, Peter expresses anguish over the loss of "3,500" civilians during the 9/11 attacks. Hossam, in turn, criticizes the consequences of US foreign policy, pointing to the death and injury of "one million" Palestinians since the inception of the Israeli state. Unable to make sense of Arabs' grievances against the United States, Peter urges Hossam, "You have to try to understand us." Hossam responds that US foreign policy needs to use the "appropriate" language to allow for effective cross-cultural communication.

Hossam denounces the US exercise of hard power as a sign of imperialism, while Sarah and Peter present it as a form of liberal internationalism.[24] The film makes an allegorical reference to Hossam's rejection of this argument when he is shown first purchasing a

17. The baby doll nightgown laid over a US military tank in a poster for *Laylat el-Baby Doll* (2008). © Good News.

baby doll nightgown in New York to give to his wife, in the hopes of stimulating their sex life, but is later shown unable to actually hand her the gift. Thus, the baby doll gown represents Hossam's ability to realize his dream of becoming a father, but finding time to spend with his wife amid the chaos of a night fraught with the contradictions and consequences of US and Arab geopolitics proves impossible. The film's poster shows the nightgown laid over a US tank, using the piece of clothing to symbolize that "which is American and western and does not belong on the Arab body" (figure 17).[25] In another sense, the poster symbolizes how the United States represents both life and death for Arabs and Arab diasporas. The gown is a promising symbol of fun that could have led to pregnancy and childbirth, but the tank is a grim symbol of chaos that yields destruction and death.

At the beginning of the film, Hossam is shown dancing in a scene that intercuts iconic images of America, such as the Wall Street bull statue (US economic might), the Statue of Liberty (freedom), the former twin towers in New York (foreshadowing 9/11), food and other products (luxury), and medical bills (US promise of fertility for Hossam's wife). These symbols are introduced in the beginning because the rest of the film essentially critiques everything that America stands for, as hinted through these symbols. Economic might is critiqued through the Egyptian elite and how they really do not care about their own people and their cause. The whole mission of peace and its being co-opted by businesspersons speaks to that. The reference to liberty is challenged through the US role in Iraq and support of Israel. The American dream for Iraqis, for instance, is not realized; instead, people are suffering. Hossam's own dream remains unfulfilled as he never manages to impregnate his wife. Ultimately, the United States emerges in the film as a superpower that has co-opted Arab revolutionaries and rendered them docile. Throughout the film, Hossam serves as a reminder of this desperate conclusion.

Importantly, Hossam is critical not just of his fellow Americans, but also maintains a critical attitude in his encounters with other Arabs and Muslims. He challenges Shokry over the legitimacy of targeting innocent civilians and eventually convinces him to denounce it as a heinous act of terror. Responding to Shokry's initial praise of Awadain as a hero, Hossam emphasizes that "the one who is trying to blow up a ship of civilian tourists is a terrorist." He categorically rejects any rhetoric justifying violence. He denounces the plan to blow up the hotel in order to avenge Awadain's experience of injustice in the Abu Ghraib prison. "I am a tourist, not a terrorist expert," he maintains, "but the most hideous crime against humanity is that we try to find excuses for terrorism." To validate his critique, Hossam recounts his post-9/11 victimization and cites it as an example of how oppression should not justify violent resistance. Even when being used later by Awadain as a body shield against the bullets of the police force, Hossam does not hesitate to attempt to convince him to acknowledge the tragic scale of his actions and to hand himself over to authorities. He praises Awadain's heroic past of fighting for Arab causes against oppression and injustice and pleads that he refrain from ruining that history by turning to violence.

Hossam's character highlights the challenges underwriting the Arab diasporic experience in negotiating the US and Arab geopolitical terrains and their underlying narratives. Located as he is between the two worlds, so to speak, he must constantly confront the question of his allegiance. Like Layla, Hossam's loyalty is repeatedly questioned as he contests US and Arab polarizations. Shokry advises him to forsake the alienating culture of the United States and connect more with his Arab and Muslim backgrounds. Awadain accuses him of being "an American agent" who has betrayed his people. Sarah and Peter continue to address him as an Arab and do not recognize his American cultural citizenship. These varied forms of misrecognition reveal the double-layered Otherness that Hossam must negotiate and that his Arab diasporic agency seeks to disrupt. Unlike Layla, Hossam insists on continually voicing his interstitial perspective in direct conversations. This is not to denounce the circumstances defining Layla's similar interstitial experiences, but rather to illustrate the varied perspectives that can result when US-based Arab diasporas interrogate US and Arab encounters. Each character reveals different potential grounds to subvert Egyptian mainstream representation patterns in search for more complex articulations of Arab immigrant and Arab American cultural citizenship.

Conclusion

Laylat el-Baby Doll is a novel effort in Egyptian cinema to present distinct insights into US-based Arab diasporic activism in the post-9/11 context. Released in 2008, the film deviates from the polarizing imagery that has shaped Egyptian filmmaking, which frames Arab immigrant and Arab American cultural Otherness through a repertoire of sensational binaries. It proposes alternative representation strategies that are more reflective of the diasporic public spheres within which its Arab diasporic characters continue to negotiate for a sense of cultural citizenship in a globalized yet heavily nationalistic world. Rather than presenting the characters of Layla and Hossam as the passive figures to which Arab audiences have grown accustomed while watching Egyptian films, the film utilizes the silver screen as a powerful medium to communicate hybridity in the life of its characters. These characters function as interlocutors wrestling with issues of paramount concern to many in the Arab immigrant and Arab American communities, particularly within the "war on terror" context.

Laylat el-Baby Doll, I conclude, offers a distinct projection of what Nadine Naber labels "diasporas of empire" in her descriptions of US-based Arab diasporas in relation to the US simultaneous articulations of imperial violence in the Arab region (invasions, drones, bombs, etc.) and in the United States (racial profiling, xenophobia, detention, etc.).[26] Naber's call for collapsing the abroad-domestic distinctions to understand the US exercise of power is significant in both critiquing imperial violence and theorizing diasporic resistance. The Arab diasporic characters of Layla and Hossam could be considered manifestations of this spatial collapse. The film's transnational framework certainly invites critical readings of Arab diasporic activism at the intersection of US-Israeli aggressions and Egyptian narrations of resistance.[27] It presents Layla and Hossam as two Arab diasporas whose engagement with US and Arab geopolitics grounds two different migrant experiences, which lead them to develop distinct forms of diasporic agency. Thus, through its projections of Layla and Hossam, the film offers a subversive narrative that foregrounds the importance of disrupting national boundaries in imagining Arab diasporic experiences.

Laylat el-Baby Doll ends with a song that challenges the polarizing politics of nationalism and advocates instead forms of reconciliation that incorporate all the lived realities within and across the US and Arab geopolitical divides, including those of the Arab diaspora:

Why? Why can't I see?
Though my eyes are open
How can I sing
If my soul is hurt?
How and why
Do we prey on each other?
Enough space is there for us!

Layla and Hossam—similar to the Samir character in *Traitor* in chapter 3—exhibit a sense of diasporic activism that disrupts nationalistic constructions of loyalty and belonging. In this context, a different type of cultural citizenship emerges as illustrative of Arab diasporic agency. This sense of citizenship builds on Sunaina Maira's notion of "flexible citizenship," which she defines as "a manifestation of both postnational and denationalized citizenship, for it emerges in response to changes in the institution of citizenship within nation-states as well as shifts in power on national and global scales."[28] In conceptualizing this sense of citizenship, I emphasize the importance of considering the nuances surrounding the Arab diasporic public spheres as occupied by various voices representing Americanness and Arabness, notions that are constantly conceived and redefined across the United States and the Arab world.

Both *Traitor*, analyzed in chapter 3, and *Laylat el-Baby Doll* offer alternative ways of imagining Arab American cultural citizenship. The characters of Samir, Layla, and Hossam challenge the dictates of nationalist politics and resist the polarizing tendencies of US and Arab post-9/11 responses. Samir challenges racial profiling and fights terrorism in ways that do not compromise his religious adherences or sense of patriotism. Layla advocates for an Arab American investment in peaceful activism and pays the ultimate price of her life for standing against Israeli oppression. Hossam demonstrates a concern for US national security while maintaining a critique of US domestic and foreign policies. The three characters, in short, represent complex forms of Arab immigrant and Arab American subjectivity, and their inclusion in the US and Arab cinematic landscapes suggests the limited emergence of new voices and narrative possibilities of Arab Americans. This emergence is parallel to a growing trend among Arab American filmmakers themselves toward self-representation, the subject I turn to in chapter 5.

5

Renarrating the American Dream in Arab American Films

MOUSTAPHA AKKAD (1930–2005), known for producing the *Halloween* film series (1978–2002), is perhaps the most recognized Arab American to proactively engage with the Hollywood filmmaking industry in the pre-9/11 context. He is best recognized in the Arab world for directing two canonical films that celebrate Muslim and Arab histories. The first, *Mohammad, Messenger of God*—filmed simultaneously in Arabic as *al-Risālah* (1976) and in English as *The Message* (1976), with two distinct casts from the Arab world and the United States, respectively—portrays the life of the prophet of Islam and delivers an important insight into the birth of the religion. The second film, *Lion of the Desert* (1980), narrates the real-life story of Omar Mukhtar (played by Anthony Quinn) and his role in leading resistance against the Italian colonial presence in Libya. Akkad's filmic contributions reflected an Arab American consciousness in mediating such histories through a US cultural industry replete with anti-Arab reductive imagery.[1] As a diasporic filmmaker, Akkad stressed the need for works like his to act as a bridge between the Arab and Muslim worlds and the West. Speaking of *The Message*, he once said:

> Besides its production values as a film, it has its story, its intrigue, its drama. Beside[s] all this, I think there was something personal, being a Muslim myself who lived in the West, I felt that it was my obligation, my duty, to tell the truth about Islam. . . . I thought I should tell the story that will bring this bridge, this gap to the West.[2]

Akkad's struggle to secure financing for his films in Hollywood prompted him to tour the Arab world in search of support. He eventually gained governmental funding from Libya, Kuwait, and Morocco, but not without controversy.[3]

The absence of enthusiasm in Hollywood to support Arab American filmmakers has been an institutionalized problem in an industry that lacks the appetite to entertain nonmainstream perspectives, particularly ones that feature critical voices and ethnic community narratives. And producers and filmmakers in Egyptian cinema, as this book illustrates, are not interested in moving beyond the cinema's nationalist impulses and limitations. This could possibly explain the weak presence of Arab American filmmakers in both Hollywood and Egyptian cinemas, forcing filmmakers, like Akkad, to search for alternative means of support. Since 9/11 the growth of Arab and Arab American independent film festivals, particularly in the United States, has provided Arab American filmmakers with a valuable alternative to mainstream filmmaking, with some limited success in distribution.[4] And the prospect of providing support for Arab Americans seems promising with the competitive rise of such content-streaming services as Netflix, Amazon, and Hulu; Egyptian American Ramy Youssef's TV series *Ramy* (2019–present) is a good example.

This chapter examines the post-9/11 rise of a new generation of Arab American filmmakers who are invested in self-narratives of Arab American cultural citizenship. Unlike Akkad's interest in bridging East-West binaries through historical epics, the filmmakers examined in this chapter contribute to a burgeoning Arab American filmic trend rooted in an emerging urgency to self-narrate contemporary issues in the Arab American community, particularly in relation to their post-9/11 struggles and aspirations. There are, of course, many post-9/11 Arab American films, but only three films are central to this chapter's analysis: Hesham Issawi's *AmericanEast* (2007), Cherien Dabis's *Amreeka* (2009), and Sam Kadi's *The Citizen* (2012). What guides my choice of these specific films is their exhibition of two main characteristics in the growing Arab American filmic trend; both characteristics add important dimensions to this book's search for various meanings of Arab American cultural citizenship in film.

The first characteristic of post-9/11 Arab American filmmaking is the offering of a counternarrative to existing Arab American images in Hollywood and Egyptian films. Films produced by this new generation exhibit certain "accented" elements, to borrow Hamid Naficy's description of exilic and diasporic filmmaking, with their "distinct images and spectatorial environment."[5] This emergent body of work has yet to receive much critical analysis. My reading builds on Michael Najjar's remarks about the trend:

> Arab American filmmakers, like their counterparts in theater and performance, have committed themselves to the eradication of negative stereotyping, to writing fully dimensional characters who eschew the traditional representations of Arabs on screen, and to telling deeply personal stories that provide insight into the lives of Arabs in America.[6]

This chapter, therefore, highlights how self-representation empowers Arab American directors to move beyond the respective tropes of polarization of the Arab American imagery in both Hollywood and Egyptian cinemas. It also examines how Arab Americans negotiate a complex sense of identity, mediated through such particularities as nationality, religion, gender, and generation. And crucially, the chapter tells a story of Arab Americans within the contexts of 9/11 and terrorism.

The second characteristic of this new body of Arab American filmmaking is a consistent engagement with the "American dream"—a construct meant to uphold a US nationalist project—as the primary anchor for Arab American cultural citizenship. Unlike Hollywood's films, which imagine Arab Americans as threatening aliens or homegrown terrorist suspects, and the films of Egyptian cinema, which portray them as disillusioned with the American dream or the embodiment of an alternative "Egyptian Dream," emergent Arab American filmmaking presents Arab immigrant characters seeking to fulfill their own aspirations in the United States, but not without providing insightful critiques of the American dream notion as a celebratory site of inclusion in American society. In the three films analyzed in this chapter, the lead Arab immigrant characters strive variously to fulfill material desires (e.g., houses, jobs, cars) and seek belonging to the United States, but they are forced to navigate both a racialized system and a post-9/11 reality that equally challenge their inclusion in American cultural citizenship.

Thus, this chapter traces post-9/11 efforts to capture some of the Arab American filmic narratives of cultural citizenship vis-à-vis the American dream by analyzing three films: Egyptian American directed *AmericanEast*, Palestinian American directed *Amreeka*, and Syrian American directed *The Citizen*. But to contextualize my analysis and showcase the importance of these filmic efforts, let us first look at the typecasting challenge of Arab American actors in Hollywood, a systematic problem in US filmmaking that capitalizes on a sense of Arab Americans' post-9/11 visibility that renders them professionally invisible.

The Dilemma of Casting in Hollywood

Unlike Egyptian cinema, Hollywood has demonstrated an interest in featuring Arab and Arab American actors in roles dedicated to mediating Arab American subjectivity. In an industry lacking a genuine commitment to diversity, however, this mediation has been problematic.[7] Historically speaking, casting lead Arab characters has not necessarily demanded authenticity. As early as *The Sheik* (1921) and as late as *Prince of Persia* (2010) and the TV drama *Tyrant* (2014–16), non-Arab actors like Rudolph Valentino, Jake Gyllenhaal, and Adam Rayner have dominated Hollywood's casting for Arab lead roles.[8] "It's been a tradition," states Muslim American actor Aasif Mandvi. "I can't play white people, but white people can play me."[9] Several terms, including "role stratification," "role segregation," and "whitewashing," have captured this tradition in an industry where casting is structured into layers that leverage white actors to play all types of roles, including cultural Others, but confine nonwhites within stereotypical ethnic roles.[10]

Such casting practices lead to a sense of "symbolic annihilation" of Arab Americanness in Hollywood,[11] mainly shaped by US-based power dynamics of whiteness. The abundance of works advancing one-dimensional portrayals of Arabs and Arab Americans has been an attractive option to Middle Eastern–looking actors. Mizrahim actors, for instance, played "dubious Middle Eastern roles of either fanatic terrorists or of noble savages," as Ella Shohat observes, in films like *Rambo III* (1988), *Steal the Sky* (1988), *Not without My Daughter* (1991), and *True Lies* (1998).[12] The reliance of Hollywood filmmakers on actors willing to play superficial caricatures of Arabness has contributed to an ongoing process of racialization. This process has forced many Arab and Arab American actors to perform one-dimensional roles, which perpetuate images that continue to disenfranchise them and effectively deny them full articulations of their cultural citizenship.[13] At its most extreme, this marginality means complete denial of visibility. In the 1996 film *Executive Decision*, for example, Arab actors were billed simply as "terrorists," and not even properly acknowledged in the credits.[14] Other forms of erasure are more subtle; for example, continually asking actors to impersonate stereotypical characters of other ethnic and cultural backgrounds, as if distinctions among cultures and traditions were negligible.

Recognizing the fissure between Arab American actors and their ethnic and religious communities—and the resulting conversation about what responsibility the former has toward the latter—further complicates one's understanding of the casting dilemma. John Michael explores the contours of this fissure among Arab Americans:

> It is remarkably difficult to specify in general terms what the relationship between individual and group identity is. On the one hand, attempts to reduce the former to the latter, to see individuals as primarily members of groups, tend to lapse into racist or essentialist errors and violence like Orientalism and the practices it continues to legitimate. On the other hand, attempts to call the salient existence of group identities or allegiances into question . . . fail to describe a crucial part of our lives together. Many, perhaps all of us, experience

> ourselves as individuals and our place in the world through our complex, conflicted, and compelling sense of our identification with or belonging to various and heterogeneous groups.[15]

Thus, the calculation that goes into accepting or rejecting stereotypical roles is marked by a tension that actors experience between their obligations to their individual aspirations and to their community.

This tension leads to variance in conceiving the very idea of success in Hollywood. Is success realized once actors of Middle Eastern or South Asian origins stop always being seen as ethnic actors playing racialized roles and start just being actors; the desire, in a sense, for the white privilege of being nonracialized. For instance, the Pakistani British actor Riz Ahmed, known for his lead roles in the acclaimed films *The Road to Guantanamo* (2006) and *The Reluctant Fundamentalist* (2012) and his Emmy-winning role in the TV mini-series *The Night Before* (2015), has described success in Hollywood as having a career not defined by his ethnicity, where his character's story is not "intrinsically related to his race," he is not projected as "a terror suspect," and his name "might even be Dave."[16] And there are several examples illustrating this definition of success in Hollywood. Actors of Arab descent like Zoe Saldana, Vince Vaughn, F. Murray Abraham, Paula Abdul, Jerry Seinfeld, Shannon Elizabeth, Salma Hayek, Catherine Keener, and Wentworth Miller have received recognition without playing recycled Arab roles, for they have not explicitly identified, marketed, or probably perceived themselves as Arab Americans to begin with. A few other Arab American actors, such as Omar Sharif, Jay Abdo, Tony Shalhoub, Michael Nouri, Omar Metwally, and Rami Malek have also been able to outperform the negative roles specified for their ethnicity but not without playing several stereotypical roles in their careers.

While this definition of success is important at the individual level, it is problematic because it does not resolve Hollywood's default narrative of whiteness as the gateway to American cultural citizenship, effectively denying Arab and Muslim American narratives of belonging. Consider for example Mr. Robot (2015–present), a popular television series whose creator and producer, Sam Esmail, and its lead actor, Rami Malek, are both Egyptian Americans. Malek's character, Elliot, is set in a perpetual mode of a white individual's inner-conflict struggle as he fights both mental illness and corporate greed by hacking the financial system and producing chaos. (One wonders whether Elliot could still gain the same character privilege in narration, distribution, and reception if he were presented as an Arab or Muslim American in the series.)

For the 2015–16 Emmy Awards, the show was nominated for "Outstanding Writing for a Drama" and "Outstanding Drama" but lost to *Game of Thrones*; Malek, however, won an Emmy for "Best Actor in a Drama Series." Malek is the second Arab American to win an Emmy award in a lead role; the first was Tony Shalhoub, who won awards in comedy for three consecutive years (2003–6). Being the first Arab American to win the award in this category and the first minority to win it since 1998, Malek's win was welcome news during a year when the Academy Awards were accused of becoming an exclusive white club.[17] "I play a young man who is, I think like many of us profoundly alienated," remarked Malek in his acceptance speech. In the backstage press conference, Malek provided an account of his parents' struggle as immigrants to secure a better lifestyle for him. Reflecting on the sense of alienation he referred to earlier, he continued, "We live in a world right now where so many of us feel voiceless, like we are not being heard by our government, we are not being heard by our society."[18]

Esmail's and Malek's rise within the mainstream entertainment industry underlines individual successes in gaining recognition beyond their ethnic backgrounds. In 2019 Malek also won an Oscar in the "Best Actor" category for his lead role of Freddie Mercury, Queen's lead singer, in *Bohemian Rhapsody* (2018). Such successes, however valuable, do not intervene directly in Hollywood's film narratives and images of the Arab American community. To do so in Hollywood, the options remain limited: play simplistic stereotypical ethnic roles or aspire to play complex nonethnic roles. In this context, the Arab American actors' and directors' search for recognition of their talent, not their background, clashes with an existential white-based hegemonic approach to filmmaking that itself is at odds with increasing demands from audiences for nonwhite narratives and skills. Consider, for example, how even when Disney's *Aladdin* (2019) featured a diverse cast of diasporic actors like Egyptian Canadian Mena Massoud, Ugandan British of Indian descent Naomi Scott, Tunisian-Dutch Marwan Kenzari, and Iranian American Nasim Pedrad—while problematically darkening other white actors—the film could not shy away from recycling an offensive white-based imagery that continues to instruct generations of Americans to connect with the good characters speaking in American accents and fear, or even hate, those speaking in heavy Arabic accents.[19]

Most Arab and Arab American actors have struggled against a casting practice that feeds on their vulnerability in the entertainment realm. Their roles are usually subsidiary and deeply entrenched in a racial hierarchy—despite evidence suggesting consumer demand for more diversity in lead roles.[20] Furthermore, even if networks are committed to diversity initiatives, Middle Eastern actors are considered white according to the US census. Thus, as Arab American writer and director Cherien Dabis points out, the casting of Middle Easterners is not prioritized "in the writers' room or in front of the camera."[21]

For some Arab American actors, success in Hollywood does not lie in transcending their ethnic identity but in claiming it and producing changes around its portrayals. This approach emerges out of frustration with the industry's ill treatment of Arab and Muslim American imagery. Sayed Badreya is one of the most recognizable—and invisible—Arab American actors, given his twenty-year career of playing primarily terrorist roles, most notably in popular films like *True Lies* (1994), *Executive Decision* (1996), *The Insider* (1999), *Three Kings* (1999), *Iron Man* (2008), and *You Don't Mess with the Zohan* (2008). A native of Egypt with a degree in film from New York University, he once articulated his frustration with Hollywood's casting practices, most appropriately conveyed through his own children when they asked him when he would finally play the "nice guy."[22] "For fourteen years," he noted wryly, "I have one line: 'In the name of Allah I will kill you.' That's it! Every movie I go in, and somehow I end up with that line."[23]

Badreya and other Arab and Arab American actors share a belief in the possibility of producing change from within. "You don't fight the system in Hollywood," he once argued. "You become part of the system so you can change it from the inside."[24] "If I don't do it," says Iraqi American actress Yasmine Hanani, "someone who knows less about my language and culture will."[25] In addition to the industry's institutional challenges, the possibility of producing this change in Hollywood is undercut by the scarcity of "bankable Arab American actors" in producing films for mainstream audiences.[26] There is already a limited casting privilege in the case of prominent Syrian actor Ghassan Massoud, Egyptian stars like Khaled Nabawy, Kal Naga, and Amr Waked, as well as Palestinian actors like Hiam Abbass, Ali Suliman, Kais Nashif, and Ashraf Barhom, in part because of these actors' careers in other cinemas. Nabawy's role choices, for instance, are informed by his successful acting career in Egypt. When asked about the rationale behind his decision to appear in such films as *Kingdom of Heaven* (2005), *Fair Game* (2010), and *The Citizen* (2012), he responded:

> I do what I believe. If I love a role, I will take it. If I don't love it, I will not take it. And I will not encourage anyone not to be himself. Just be yourself. Don't try to please everyone. Please yourself.[27]

But options for actors like Saïd Taghmaoui, Sammy Sheik, Omar Metwally, Haaz Sleiman, and Jay Abdo are limited in Hollywood, and the process for claiming one's Arab diasporic voice is slow. And the ability of lesser-known actors who are still seeking recognition to produce change in Hollywood is minimal, since they often compromise their roles to pay their bills, with hopes of gateways to career success. Some actors, like Egyptian American Ahmed Ahmed, have made a conscious decision to stop playing the "terrorist" role. In Ahmed's case, the decision eventually pushed him to explore stand-up comedy as a rewarding and subversive venue.[28]

In this challenging context, independent filmmaking has been the primary site for Arab American filmmakers and actors to embrace their own dreams and in doing so foreground their own insights and critiques of the American dream as a US national promise deeply entrenched in white privilege, institutional racism, and discrimination against people of color. The following sections analyze three post-9/11 Arab American films and trace critiques of the American dream as well as articulations of an Arab American sense of cultural citizenship in each. Unlike *Mr. Robot* and *Bohemian Rhapsody*, the films surveyed below feature Arab Americanness not only in terms of acting but also through narratives that empower the actors to perform their ethnicity in disruptive ways. The films propose various, but not conclusive, narratives that could provide the mainstream industries in Hollywood and Egypt with insight into Arab Americans' concerns and priorities. They also speak to the rising need in producing narratives of Arab Americans at the interplay of the individual and the community.

Visibly Invisible and Invisibly Visible

Knowledge production during the "war on terror" era, argues Hamid Dabashi, requires a sense of alterity deeply embedded in resistance, an alterity that does not conform to the traditional dialectics of "self" and "Other."[29] Since 9/11, Arab American filmmakers, I argue, have used their films as a means of activism in search of a sense of agency and cultural citizenship that emphasizes their belonging to the United States but not without critiquing the premise of the American dream and the deeply embedded alienating forces of institutionalized racism that renders it unattainable to people of color, particularly Arab and Muslim American communities. This resistance is a vital response to Hollywood's homogenous and hegemonic portrayals of these communities.

The sense of urgency to collaborate in subverting the filmmaking establishment in Hollywood led two Arab immigrants to collaborate in hopes for change. The heated backlash against the Arab and Muslim communities in post-9/11 America made it possible for long-time actor Sayed Badreya to join hands with Hesham Issawi, a graduate of Columbia College's film school (Chicago) and director of documentary shorts, in a short-lived yet important collaboration. Issawi directed their first short film, *T for Terrorist* (2003), in which Badreya played the role of an Arab immigrant actor being pushed by a Hollywood director to play a threatening and hateful Arab, a plot modeled on Badreya's grievances about his being typecast. Later on, the collaboration developed into the feature film *AmericanEast* (2007), one of the first Arab American filmic attempts to subvert Hollywood's portrayals of Arab American subjectivity in the post-9/11 context.[30] Tony Shalhoub joined the collaboration as an executive producer and an actor. The film, which combines "family melodrama with political commentary and elements of a thriller,"[31] was produced by Distant Horizon and Zahra Pictures and was first premiered in the New York–based Hamptons International Film Festival in 2006. Although this indie did not gain movie-theater screening privilege, it was distributed by Metro-Goldwyn-Mayer in DVD format.

That Badreya and Issawi are the originators of the film's plot speaks of their concerted effort to encode in *AmericanEast* their demand for nuanced roles played by Arab and Arab American actors. "The opportunity to make this film and have people in America see it makes me optimistic," remarked Badreya.[32] "We wanted to make a movie about us," affirmed Issawi. "Arabs in America . . . understand the price of freedom," he contended, "but they know they're being watched."[33] Shalhoub further articulated the vision behind *AmericanEast* while stipulating the need for Arab American filmmakers to reclaim their voice:

> We wanted [to] inspire other young filmmakers in the Arab American community to begin to see it's possible that there might be an appetite in the market for these kinds of stories. So many times, we see Arab Americans and Muslims portrayed [with] negative stereotypes in the news, in television, and mainstream movies. This is an attempt to offset those images and to demonstrate it's possible to get these other stories told.[34]

AmericanEast's intervention lies in its timely critique of Hollywood's casting practices, which it advances in two ways. First, it allows Sayed Badreya to play the lead role of Mustafa and, in so doing, affords him a level of agency as an actor he has otherwise been denied in mainstream filmmaking.[35] Second, it features a substory of

Omar (Kais Nashif) as a part-time employee and a part-time Hollywood actor confined within terrorist-related stereotypical roles. The two characters in the film share a struggle to realize their dreams in the backdrop of a turbulent, post-9/11 environment rife with institutional discrimination, cinematic disenfranchisement, and anti-Arab as well as Islamophobic public backlash. The film provides the audience with insights into the social context of the two characters to develop a multidimensional understanding of their identities and the subtlety of their hardships.

Badreya plays the role of an Arab immigrant widower named Mustafa Marzoke struggling to balance the various dictates of his Arabic identity and the daily demands of life in Los Angeles. He finds himself pressed against familial, cultural, and political subtexts as he races to pay off his debts and become a successful businessperson. He is forced to navigate a post-9/11 setting with a terror alert level set to "red," while FBI agents are increasingly invested in interrogating ties between his Islamic background and terrorism. He also finds himself entangled by obligations to raise his Americanized family—two children and a sister—according to Egyptian traditions. Equally challenging are Mustafa's hardships in managing his Habibi café and in running his one-taxi company. Throughout the film, the camera captures the multitude of personal struggles and experiences of individuals inhabiting Mustafa's home and businesses in a layered narrative that recognizes their multidimensional lives and further complicates the audience's connection with and disconnection from Mustafa.

Mustafa's family members are caught between their American culture and Egyptian heritage as they become occupied with their individual concerns. His nearly ten-year-old son, Mohammed (Richard Chagoury), struggles to come to terms with his own identity as a Muslim American. He asks his father a series of questions as he hears news reporting Muslims implicated in terrorism: "Why am I a Muslim? Why did you have to name me Mohammed? Can we get a Christmas tree?" These questions capture the anxiety of a Muslim American child forced to seek conformity in post-9/11 trying times. Mohammed presents a serious challenge to Mustafa as the former ponders converting to Christianity. Mohammed is seen attracted to a balloon decorated with "Jesus Loves You." He even quits praying next to his father. He tells his father that he does not want to go to the mosque and cites the reason through a question: "Did Muslims kill all those in the towers?" Adding to Mustafa's pressure of preserving his familial identity is his daughter, Leila (Tay Blessey), the older of the two children, who escapes the pressure of working in the café through the company of her American girlfriend and by smoking marijuana. Both Mohammed and Layla are under mounting pressure of being viewed with suspicion, especially after the FBI arrests and interrogates their father on two separate occasions.

Mustafa's sister, Salwah (Sarah Shahi), struggles on her own against her family's tradition of marrying her Egyptian first cousin. The arranged marriage would have ensured that Mustafa upheld his family marriage tradition and reclaimed his father's land from the suitor's grip. Salwah rejects Mustafa's desperate concerns about her being thirty years old and a Muslim living in the United States. She contests the idea of an arranged marriage on grounds of cultural differences. Although she shares the same Egyptian heritage as her suitor, she refuses to compromise her independence, which is captured in the film through her driving her own car, working as a nurse, and running her own one-chair beauty salon in the back room of Mustafa's café. She rejects her suitor's plans for her to quit her work and life in the United States and return to Egypt to become a housewife. She rejects being thought of as a commodity or as a "business," as her suitor once refers to their engagement.

The family's multiple stories add more complexity to Mustafa's character, which further develops through his relationships with FBI agents, café customers, and potential business partners. He experiences continued harassment from US law enforcement agencies. At the airport, he is arrested while frantically searching for his son and yelling "Mohammed" out loud. His behavior raises suspicion, and he is held for interrogation. FBI Agent Stevens (Ray Wise) investigates Mustafa's charity donations to Egypt, and having arrived at no serious concern about him, he advises, "Be mindful of how you act or speak in

18. Mustafa arrested in his café in *AmericanEast* (2007). © Distant Horizon.

public." Agent Stevens directs his assistant to trace Mustafa's monetary transfers, bank statements, emails, library accounts, subscriptions, and postal records. At some point Mustafa allows bearded men with white thobes to pray in the back room of his café, which further raises the FBI's suspicions. In a disturbing scene, FBI agents storm Mustafa's café and arrest him. A close-up of the arrest shows humiliating treatment of Moustafa at gunpoint as the agents strip him of his rights as an American citizen; he is now no more than a terrorist suspect (figure 18). The mystery surrounding his connection to terrorism is cleared when Agent Stevens questions him at an undisclosed location. When pressured for a reason about his transactions through the third-party *hawala* (money transfer) system, Mustafa confesses that he has been paying his father's debt to reclaim his lost land. He is released, but his assets are frozen until the investigation is complete, which adds more pressure on him.

Mustafa never loses sight of his desire to succeed and fulfill the United States' promise of social mobility. "I still believe in this country," he shares with his family upon release. But little is he aware of his disadvantaged position: as a visibly invisible American citizen and an invisibly visible Arab immigrant. The film, therefore, presents the American dream as a floating, if not fleeting, mode of imagination that Arab Americans cling to in a white-privileged society that denies minorities the full benefits of American cultural citizenship and consistently marginalizes them as aliens. Mustafa's desire to fix his family café to sell it so that he can start a successful restaurant is the film's basic storyline. As the plot complicates, however, the film locates Mustafa at the disjuncture between the nationalist promises of the American dream and the realities of being an Arab immigrant in the post-9/11 United States.

And the portrayal of Mustafa's business is symbolic of this disjuncture. The café is falling apart—the air conditioner doesn't work, the water pipes are leaking, and the restaurant is dimly lit and filled with hookah smoke. It evokes an ethnic feel through decorations of Arab flags, hookahs, awkwardly phrased English signs, Arab celebrity photos, and religious icons. Although Mustafa is desperate to create an image of a business, there are few customers. Located in a small neighborhood in Los Angeles called "Little Arabia," the café is more of a social club than a real restaurant. The few Middle Eastern customers who do patronize the café add an important layer of ethnic flavor as they gather and discuss social and political issues, despite the grammatically flawed sign in English that reads "no political or religious allowed in this establishment."

Murad (Anthony Azizi) is a hot-headed customer, representing the voice of angry Arabs who are critical of Israel, the US government, and Arab dictators. He finds conspiracy in everything and refuses to be accommodating or compromising. Fikry (Erick Avari) is an old Christian Arab who enjoys reading newspapers, watching TV, and providing commentary on social and political news. YaYa (Mike Batayeh) is a handyman who does part-time jobs writing signs and fixing leaks. Slick Ali (Haaz Sleiman) is a constantly angry customer who does not like how the food is prepared or how the café is run. Abdulla (Sammy Sheik) is a waiter who objects to his boss's loose management style; he does not want Mustafa to give free food or to allow people to pray in the café. In the café, Mustafa is kept busy socializing with his few customers and fixing leaks, inching slowly toward his dream restaurant.

But Mustafa's dream restaurant is only made possible through a partnership with his Jewish American friend, Sam (Tony Shalhoub). Minorities cannot fulfill their aspirations by merely working hard, the film proposes. Interethnic and interreligious alliances among minorities could offer an important resolution to overcome the US system of racialized hierarchy. But to do so, minority communities have to bypass differences to realize success and inclusion. Both Mustafa and Sam face the challenge of maneuvering through their communities and transcending politicalized misperceptions of Muslims and Jews. Their partnership invites much criticism from Mustafa's Middle Eastern American customers and Sam's family.[36] The film exposes, in the words of one reviewer, "the prejudice that exists on all sides, including the Arab American community."[37] Perhaps Sam's message to his family strikes the film's tone of the importance of minority alliance:

> I know Mustafa and I know that he is the same kind of man. We are tied together by the same forefather. More importantly, I believe we are tied together now, here. We're Americans. We can make a difference. We can change things. Maybe [we] show the catastrophe is not the foregone conclusion. The everyday act of breaking bread together is more powerful than all the hate.

The film further dramatizes this tone through a cartoon montage that briefly sketches the history of violence and peace in Jerusalem. The narrator, Mustafa's daughter, concludes that hatred exists because of the absence of "cool dudes" like Saladin, under whose rule Muslims, Jews, and Christians lived in peace. The United States, the film implies, has the potential to function as a space where the idea of coexistence, which Saladin represents, could emerge. Far from perfect, however, an alliance between minorities, as the one between Mustafa and Sam, could be a good start. The name of their business "American East," rendered by the handyman YaYa as "AmERICAnEAST," connotes the possibility of resisting the US racialized system via a blend that rejects "America" versus "East" binaries.

Perhaps the most critical aspect of the film's narrative about the American dream is its jarring portrayal of the character of Omar (Kais Nashif) and his fatal ending. Omar works as a part-time driver in Mustafa's one-taxi business as he seeks to fulfill his dream of pursuing an acting career in Hollywood. Omar struggles to move beyond being typecast as a terrorist. One day, he is excited to learn that he is going to play a role in a television show called *American Safety.* Minutes before shooting, Omar learns that the doctor role has been canceled and he will instead play the usual terrorist role with "more accent" and "scary" appearance as the director instructs him. His American dream, like Mustafa's, is challenged by racially institutionalized forces beyond his control. Omar first hesitates to perform, unconvinced about the logic behind imagining terrorists invading a hospital. Terrorists want to "strike fear in the heart of America," the white director responds. He is not convinced, but the director reminds him that it is just "a show." His dream is on the verge of collapse as he reluctantly enacts his lines: "Everyone on their knees. You're being taken hostage. We are the soldiers of Allah!"

Omar is in love with a white girlfriend, Kate (Amanda Detmer). Their love renews his hope of being accepted as an actor capable of performing roles beyond the ones that racialize his ethnic and religious backgrounds. After all, he is working hard to realize his dreams. One day, Omar receives a call to audition for a non–Muslim-related major role. He is thrilled to speculate on the financial stability—and independence from Mustafa's taxi—that will enable him to marry his girlfriend. On his way, he stops by a café, where a white teenager suspects him of being a terrorist because of his looks. Irritated, Omar responds with anger. "Yes, I am a terrorist and if you don't get out of my face," he yells, "I will blow the place up." He decides to sit down and drink his coffee but is soon surrounded by the police. A few hours later, he is released but after losing the opportunity to audition for his dream role.

Desperate to earn his living, especially after Mustafa fires him from the taxi-driving job, Omar decides to go back and play his typecast character. In a state of boiling anger and frustration, he

19. Omar experiences regret in *AmericanEast* (2007). © Distant Horizon.

demands revisions to his role. The producer refuses to acknowledge Omar's request, and in a very dismissive tone, he asks Omar to leave. Having lost his two jobs and his hopes of having a successful acting career, Omar responds angrily. The producer calls security to get the "maniac" away from him. Omar promptly knocks out a security guard and snatches the gun from another. The situation turns into one in which "an Egyptian-born, Muslim actor," as the media characterizes him, holds the film crew against their will.

A shot of Omar holding a gun regretfully underscores how he has fallen a victim to a racial hierarchy that perpetually casts him as alien. The shot reveals a contrast in lighting moods that casts a shadow over Omar and sheds bright light on his captives, as if to suggest that Omar is both visibly invisible and invisibly visible (figure 19). He addresses the producer, whom he has tied up: "Why didn't you just listen?" "It's just a TV show," the director states. "It doesn't mean anything." "It means everything," Omar responds. FBI agent Stevens storms in and promises to listen. Omar sees this as his peaceful way out to reconnect with his pregnant fiancée, Kate. As soon as he drops the gun, however, a sniper shoots him dead. The news is devastating to Kate and to Omar's café community. Media personnel rush to the café, asking Mustafa questions that attempt to link Omar to any Middle-Eastern terrorist organization. The community is in a state of anger and emotional breakdown. Murad charges the media correspondent with filming "our suffering for your entertainment." Mustafa smashes glasses and has a breakdown in his own café.

Omar's stereotypical role in *American Safety*—being typecast as the threatening Middle Easterner who should be quarantined by US law enforcement—is ironically juxtaposed in *AmericanEast* with Omar's depiction in the media as the threatening Middle Easterner. The media now portrays him in the same venue as the character he plays. The film uses this juxtaposition to show how Omar, the character and the typecast character, is codified in a system that does not pay attention to nuance and relies heavily on superficial understandings of Arabness and Islam as interchangeable codes for fear and terrorism. Omar, in a sense, serves as an embodiment of the demands on many Arab and Muslim American actors to perform a version of post-9/11 visibility that keeps them, paradoxically, invisible. Actor Riz Ahmed captures this paradox when he points out the parallels between auditioning in the casting room and being interrogated at US airports:

> The pitfalls of the audition room and the airport interrogation room are the same. They are places where the threat of rejection is real. They are also places where you are reduced to your marketability or threat-level, where the length of your facial hair can be a deal-breaker, where you are seen, and hence see yourself, in reductive labels.[38]

AmericanEast's display of Mustafa's and Omar's lives produces a multilayered reading of the film's Arab American characters' concerns and priorities, rarely glimpsed in the polarizing narratives of Hollywood and Egyptian cinemas. The film offers a critique of the fetishization of the American dream as a timeless promise by pointing to how characters such as Mustafa and Omar are forced to personally endure the ramifications of the country's racialized hierarchy, and how expressing willingness to belong does not seem enough for inclusion. The film's ending still affords Mustafa the chance to realize his ambition to open a restaurant, but this is only made possible through his alliance with another minority, Sam. Meanwhile, Omar stands as testimony to a minority's disillusionment in the material promises of the American dream, and his realization that he has fallen victim in American society to an institutionalized white gaze that sees him either as a stereotype of a terrorist or an actual terrorist. Perhaps one could read Mustafa's realization of his dream and Omar's failure as a statement of how it might be easier for Arab Americans to run a restaurant than to break into the film industry!

AmericanEast registers an Arab American attempt to communicate the complexity of the Arab American story to a wider audience. In a CNN interview, Shalhoub urged the Arab American community of actors, writers, and directors to be proactive in initiating conversation about these issues in their own work. The film, he stressed, offered a "slice-of-life story" that captured different emotional experiences and added more meaning to portrayals of terrorism.[39] Equally important, *AmericanEast* critically features characters who are caught between their deep-seated desires to belong to their American homeland and their post-9/11 challenging realities of living, dreaming, and contributing as immigrants of Arabic and Islamic backgrounds in a multicultural, but racially hierarchal, society.

Unfulfilled Dreams

Cherien Dabis, a graduate of Columbia University's film school, is an Arab American director whose film *Amreeka* premiered at Sundance in 2009 and was awarded the FIPRESCI Critics' Prize at Cannes the same year.[40] *Amreeka* generated distribution interest from National Geographic and was screened on campuses across the United States. In many ways, it builds upon and advances the promise of Arab American filmmaking in scriptwriting, directing, and acting that was first demonstrated in Issawi's *AmericanEast*. *Amreeka* is inspired by a traumatic experience that Dabis witnessed in the immediate aftermath of the first Gulf War in 1990. Born in Omaha, Nebraska, and raised in Celina, Ohio, Dabis's Americanness was challenged in high school when her family experienced the effects of prejudice firsthand. Dabis recounts how her father's success as a physician was abruptly disrupted when "almost overnight he became the enemy."[41] Rumors spread like wildfire, prompting her father's patients to discontinue their relationship because they did not want help from "an Arab doctor." Another rumor spread that her seventeen-year-old sister threatened to kill the US president, which prompted Secret Service agents to investigate her school. Dabis describes the mounting pressure against her family at the time:

> A friend in high school came up to me and said, "My brother could go to war and die because of you." The local newspaper was publishing letters to the editor about "the Arabs in town." It just blew up to the point where there was no escaping it. . . . We really got death threats. Quite a lot of them. They were anonymous, handwritten notes left in our mailbox, saying things like, "We'll get Saddam and we'll get you too." Or, "Love it or leave it." My dad actually kept them all.[42]

This traumatic experience served as a wake-up call for Dabis. "I felt a huge amount of responsibility," she stressed, "because, in many ways, my drive to become a filmmaker originated with the desire to tell my family's story and represent authentic Arab Americans."[43]

Amreeka examines the lives of a multigenerational Arab American family in the post-9/11 context with some echoes from Dabis's past. One of the most notable aspects of the film is its host of Arab and Arab American actors, seasoned and novice. The acting is commanding—strong and convincing. Muna Farah (Nisreen Faour) is a Palestinian single mother whose love for her teenage son, Fadi Farah (Melkar Muallem), drives her to leave her home in search of peace in the United States. She joins her sister Raghda Halaby (Hiam Abbass) and her family—husband Nabeel Halaby (Yussef Abu Warda) and Raghda's three children, Salma (Alia Shawkat), Lamis (Selena Haddad), and Rana (Jenna Kawar)—in their house in the Chicago suburbs.

Throughout the film, the audience learns about each of the characters and develops a sense of the complexity surrounding images of Arab diaspora in the United States. The Arab and Arab American actors and characters in the film speak of a critical dimension in the post-9/11 burgeoning filmmaking experience that foregrounds writing and casting as a double-layered measure of cinematic intervention.

The significance of this film lies in its disruptive portrayals that depart from US and Arab mainstream representation codes and casting practices. As both scriptwriter and director, Dabis addresses issues of relevance to Arab diasporic multilayeredness in the United States. A product of a diasporic Palestinian cinema—a cinema that Nurith Gertz and George Khleifi characterize as "heterogeneous" and interactive with "a mosaic of classes, generations, genders, regions, and nations"—*Amreeka* highlights three layers that underscore the issue of heterogeneity in the Arab American community: immigrant generational difference, importance of national background, and distinction in religious identity.[44]

One dimension of Arab American heterogeneity is conveyed through the film's portrayal of generational differences within the same immigrant household. Nabeel and Raghda are consumed by their various priorities. Nabeel is overwhelmed by the impact of racial profiling on his career and sense of belonging. He is also haunted by the unraveling politics of the US invasion of Iraq, and he obsessively follows the news. He emerges critical of US foreign policy in the Arab world and expresses his resentment of the government's use of his tax dollars to finance its military adventures in the region. Raghda experiences a bitter sense of nostalgia for her Palestinian homeland. She reproaches Muna for deciding to give up on her roots and insists that no justification could ever account for her departure. Having failed to go back herself, Raghda strictly observes her Palestinian traditions and forces her children to abide by them. When her adolescent daughter refuses to acknowledge Raghda's Arab parenting style and reminds her that they live in America, Raghda angrily warns her, "This is Palestine," in reference to their house. As a result of their own hardships,

Nabeel and Raghda struggle to communicate with each other, adding more strain to their relationship.

As a newly arrived immigrant herself, the lead character, Muna, is preoccupied with her desire to secure financial independence. Having lost her life savings, which she had placed in a food can that the US customs officers removed upon her arrival at the airport, she is anxious to contribute to the living expenses of her host family. Despite being educated and having experience working in banking, her search for a job reaches a dead end. When she eventually lands a job at the fast food chain White Castle, she is embarrassed and informs her family that she was hired at a bank close to her real place of work. Later, she is targeted by some of Fadi's high school classmates who have already posed trouble for him. She also develops a relationship with Fadi's school principal. As the plot unfolds, Muna emerges resilient and succeeds in restoring peace for her family.

While Nabeel, Raghda, and Muna invest their time and energy wrestling with their own struggles, the young children also wrestle with issues of immediate concern to their ages and personalities. Fadi must patiently follow the directions of his cousins, who worry he will look "fresh off the boat" at the high school. Fadi sustains abuse and harassment that culminates in his arrest. At the police station, he is subjected to extraordinary measures in response to security concerns about his Arab background. Meanwhile, his cousin Salma (Alia Shawkat), who attends Fadi's classes and constantly defends him, is preoccupied with her own teenage rebellion, which takes the form of smoking marijuana, having an African American boyfriend, and challenging her mother's strict observations of Palestinian tradition. The audience also learns a bit about Salma's much younger sisters, Lamis and Rana, through their fight over who gets the bigger side of the room they share. The film's multiple storylines advance simultaneously, immersing the audience in the multigenerational layers that define this Arab American household.

The second issue examined in the film is that of Arab state nationalism as a critical identity marker within the Arab American community. The camera follows the story of the migrating single parent, Muna, and her son Fadi, as they leave their home in the Palestinian territories and join their relatives in Chicago. We see their life prior to their departure into diaspora: Muna works in a bank and Fadi goes to school. They are consumed by the socioeconomic struggles under the Palestinian-Israeli political realities. Israeli checkpoints and intensive inspection procedures interrupt their daily commute to Bethlehem. Muna is hesitant to travel and leave her mother behind; she also fears being disconnected from her home. Fadi, however, is determined to convince her otherwise. Leaving their homeland, he stresses, is bittersweet but necessary. Living as a prisoner in one's own country, he argues, is not worth the sacrifice. Fadi's urging and increasing intimidation by Israeli soldiers eventually convince Muna to migrate.

Muna's experience demonstrates the importance of Arab state nationality in defining the specificity of the Arab American image.[45] Dabis's own Palestinian roots are evident in her portrayal of Muna and Fadi. Her first childhood encounter with Palestine impressed upon her the imprisonment associated with being Palestinian. "We were harassed and given so much trouble at the Israeli border," she remembers. "We were held for twelve hours, [and I was] strip-searched at the age of eight."[46] Dabis's choice, then, to depict Muna's and Fadi's struggle as Palestinians prior to capturing their experience in the United States is a welcome intervention in the mainstream decontextualized representations of Arab migration in both Hollywood and Egyptian cinemas. It invites viewers to learn about the transnational space that shapes the lives of Arab immigrants, an interactive space that renders them disconnected from, but still indelibly shaped by, the conditions of their countries of origin. To register this sense of diasporic consciousness, Dabis injects a twisted line of humor when Muna responds to a question posed by a US border officer about her occupation. Misunderstanding the question, she responds in the affirmative, "Yes, it is occupied" in reference to the Occupied Territories. Muna's confusion reveals her anxiety about the formally unrecognized status of her homeland and illustrates the need to attend to Arab immigrants' national background.

20. Fadi is humiliated at an Israeli checkpoint in *Amreeka* (2009). © National Geographic Entertainment.

Dabis also offers a pointed critique of the double-layered discrimination that an immigrant family like Muna and her son are bound to experience both in their country of origin and in the United States.[47] Depicting Fadi, for instance, as a victim of an Israeli soldier's abusive power—he is forced by an Israeli soldier to step out of the vehicle and lift his shirt—provides the necessary background to understand the intense impact of the anti-Arab harassment that Fadi will soon experience in his new home. The image of innocent Fadi, surrounded by three armed soldiers, one of whom is pointing his rifle at Fadi, is heart-wrenching (figure 20). Fadi's experience resonates with Edward Said's reflections on the unique hardships that Palestinian Americans experience:

> The life of an Arab Palestinian in the West, particularly in America, is disheartening. There exists here an almost unanimous consensus that politically he does not exist, and when it is allowed that he does, it is either as a nuisance or as an Oriental. The web of racism,

> cultural stereotypes, political imperialism, dehumanizing ideology holding in the Arab or the Muslim is very strong indeed, and it is this web which every Palestinian has come to feel as his uniquely punishing destiny.[48]

These dual experiences of discrimination in Fadi's life, whether in his Palestinian homeland or his newly adopted home in the United States, cannot be understood without describing the national identity of the Palestinian American community, a characteristic missing from the simplified portrayals of Arab Americans in both Hollywood and Egyptian cinemas.

Amreeka's third contribution to diversifying the Arab American image is the light the film sheds on the Christian background of Muna's family. Like any other community, Arab Americans subscribe to a variety of religious identities, including secular and atheistic tendencies. This constitutes a necessary intervention against Hollywood's longstanding conflation of Arab and Muslim identities into one homogenous category. Such conflation projects Muslim and Arab identities as interchangeable when, in reality, Arabs make up less than 20 percent of the world's 1.6 billion Muslims, and most Muslims live in Indonesia, India, Pakistan, Bangladesh, Malaysia, China, Iran, and Turkey—none of which are Arab countries. Contributors to the Gallup-based survey *Who Speaks for Islam?* and the study of Muslim cultural politics *Being Young and Muslim* navigate the multitude of global Muslim voices and demonstrate how Islam transcends the boundaries of color, language, and ethnicity.[49] Many scholars have offered a comprehensive history of American Muslims as "a community of communities," to echo Muqtedar Khan's description, informed by Americans of non-Arab backgrounds like South Asian Americans, East Asian Americans, and African Americans, as well as converts from other backgrounds, including Native Americans, Latino/a Americans, and Americans of European descent.[50]

This is not to dismiss the intersections of Muslim and Arab subjectivities.[51] In fact, *Amreeka* foregrounds these intersections through the hardship that Muna and her sister's family undergo as part of the post-9/11 backlash. Her brother-in-law, Nabeel, the family's patriarch, suddenly finds himself experiencing a crisis in his career as a physician. His patients, not recognizing his Christian background and considering him as a Muslim threat, decide to boycott him in a frenzy of polarized "you are with us or against us" calculations. His wife—Muna's sister, Raghda—refuses to hang the American flag in their yard, in protest of the US invasion of Iraq (2003). This further hinders Nabeel's ability to communicate his patriotism to his grief-stricken neighbors, wrapped in a commodification process that once transformed 9/11 into a brand and the American flag into a signifier of allegiance.[52] Nabeel's masculinity is also challenged when he can't provide his family with the sense of security they need. He refuses to buy a gun and opts for a baseball bat as a myth-debunking gesture to the relationship between Arabs and violence. The family experiences financial troubles, struggling to pay off their mortgage and retain their credit cards. Worse still, the family continues to receive anonymous death threats in the mail, and the children are subjected to harassment at school. Specifying the family's Christian background, therefore, adds an important dimension to the complexity of Arab diasporic subjectivity and emphasizes how religious difference has mattered less in the post-9/11 backlash against Middle Easterners.

If generation, nationality, and religion are the primary axes shaping the lives of *Amreeka*'s Arab immigrant characters, the characters' post-9/11 experiences underscore the filmmaker's critique of the American dream limitations. Even though the film ends on a happy note with the whole family dining in a restaurant, it does not shy away from critiquing the disconnect between the promise of inclusion embedded in the premise of the American dream and the bitter consequences of anti-Arab racism that deny the characters the full articulations of their cultural citizenship. Muna, Nabeel, and Raghda may have been lured by the American dream's promise of social mobility and inclusion, codified in the film through their diasporic aspirations to improve their lives and attain home away from the suffocating conditions in the Palestinian territories, but their lives are shaped by US racialized and alienating forces that constantly question their own sense of belonging.

Muna fails to secure a job that matches her credentials and banking work experience. Her immigrant struggle against anti-Arab racism in the United States forces her to forsake her dream and adapt by accepting work at a White Castle. Nabeel fails to sustain his clinic as he is caught between forces that scar his Arabness and Americanness. He feels helpless that his tax dollars fuel US wars in Iraq and feels equally helpless to defend his family from threats and to keep his patients from fleeing. And Raghda loses faith in the American promise of justice and freedom as she re-creates for her family a Palestinian experience of resistance against her American neighbors' signs of anti-Arab hatred. She defines inclusion in American society as more than hanging the American flag in her backyard. The film further foreshadows the kind of disruptive forces in the children's lives that will shape their struggles—be that inclusion in the case of Fadi or reconciling the Palestinian and American identities in the case of Salma.

The film could be critiqued for whitewashing the characters' struggle by relying on a happy ending in which the family dine together and enjoy music, food, and hookah. This very ending, however, suggests how the Arab American filmmaker imagines the family's belonging to the United States itself as a critical component of her characters' Palestinian loss-of-home storyline, one that values finding home away from the harsh reality of living under Israeli control as an important measure of success. The film's message seems to be that the whole family chooses to live in and belong to the United States despite all the racism, discrimination, and struggle.

Americanness as a Constitutional Right

The release of *The Citizen* in 2012 marked a development in the evolution of Arab American filmmaking, furthering the promise of a rising generation of directors and actors committed to communicating their post-9/11 visibility in disruptive ways. Syrian American Sam Kadi, the film's director, gave up a career in engineering to pursue filmmaking. The way he reacted to 9/11, he recollected, was by "switching from being an engineer to being a filmmaker, to tell a story, to tell people what we thought and what I thought myself about 9/11, and how I reacted to it."[53] Kadi graduated from the Motion Picture Institute of Michigan in 2007. For three years he worked on the script for *The Citizen* with his writing partners, Jazmen Brown and Samir Younis, the latter of whom helped provide more insight into the post-9/11 Arab American experience in New York. The film was produced by 3K Pictures and Why Me Film, was featured at many film festivals, and received several awards.[54] It is distributed in the United States by Monterey Media and in the Arab world by Gulf Film.

In the words of Rebecca Romani, *The Citizen* is a "tale of being the wrong person in the wrong place at the wrong time."[55] It follows the life of Ibrahim Jarrah (Khaled Nabawy), a Lebanese immigrant who wins the green-card lottery and arrives in the United States on September 10, 2001, one day prior to the tragic attacks. Before his arrival, Ibrahim is forced to move from one Arab country to another in search of peace and prosperity. As a teenager, he flees the Lebanese civil war to Aleppo but comes up against the deteriorating economic situation in the Syrian city. When he receives a job offer in Kuwait, he takes it, in the hope of finally leading a decent life. Four months later, Iraqi forces invade Kuwait. Throughout all his hardships, Ibrahim dreams of immigrating to the United States, where he imagines himself succeeding at work, establishing a family, and securing a sense of home and belonging. But no sooner does he arrive—on his second day—than he wakes up to the collapse of the twin towers, a tragic incident that challenges his resilience and accelerates his awareness of the racialized undertones of his newly adopted homeland.

That day Ibrahim rushes out onto the street, feeling helpless but wanting to help. He enters a grocery store run by a South Asian American named Mo (Rizwan Manji), and the two talk as they stare, fixated, at the television screen. Mo is concerned that his brother, who owns a kiosk at the bottom of one of the towers, might be hurt. Ibrahim consoles him by invoking his own faith in Americans and assuring Mo that someone will surely help his brother. "You have to wake up, buddy," Mo responds. "The people flying those planes look like us. No one is going to help my brother." Long familiar with harassment and discrimination in the United States, Mo anticipates the anger and fear that will be directed at people like him and Ibrahim. Indeed, his statement is interrupted by a white boy breaking the store's glass with a rock, yelling "Terrorists! Sand Niggers! Go back to your country." The scene exaggerates the speed of the backlash,[56] but its dramatic message is clear. The attacks on 9/11 ushered in a period of anxiety and fear of Arabs, Muslims, and any others who might be mistaken as "Middle Eastern." But far from being entirely new, the backlash simply exacerbated conditions that already pushed people like Mo and Ibrahim to the margins of society.

Ibrahim's encounter with Mo at this moment is significant because it represents an early test of his faith in America. He has been in the United States only for one day, and he seems disconnected from reality, at least in Mo's eyes. "What makes you an expert in how this country works?" Mo asks him. He goes on to explain:

> I've been a citizen for many years. And not a single day has passed that someone hasn't given me a dirty look because of the way that I look. What happened today is just gonna make things worse. If I were you, I'll keep a low profile.

Not yet disillusioned, Ibrahim rejects the warning and reads it as Mo's failure to act like "a real citizen." "You're a part of this country," Ibrahim retorts. "You should help, not hide." Hiding, he reasons, suggests wrongdoing, and he is guilty of none. Mo issues his final warning, telling Ibrahim that this logic is close to "fantasy." His words serve to foreshadow the forms of racial profiling that he and Ibrahim will face. In later scenes, Mo appears clean shaven; his beard would have invited unwelcomed troubles.

Ibrahim's character, nonetheless, is resilient and resistant to claiming any sort of victimization. This resolve is put to the test as he endures various hardships at the hands of authorities. On the following day—his third day in the country—immigration officers break into his motel room and arrest him while he is praying. What happens, though, looks less like an arrest than a kidnapping, as Ibrahim is snatched from his prayer mat, his head is covered with a mask, and he is thrown into a dark van. A concerned friend tries to learn his whereabouts but gets nowhere. The film vividly depicts the collapse of institutional order and constitutional norms that followed in the wake of the attacks.[57] Subjected to interrogation, Ibrahim asks for a lawyer, only to be told, "terrorists don't get lawyers." He is held in solitary confinement for six months without any charges and is dressed in an orange suit like those used at Guantanamo Bay. Because Ibrahim has the same last name as one of the hijackers and arrived only one day prior to 9/11, the authorities are convinced that it is more than a coincidence.

Remarkably, even when he is finally released, Ibrahim's resolve to realize his aspirations in the United States is strengthened, not shaken. He takes English classes, where he learns phrases like "land of the free and home of the brave" and words like "legal," "legality," "equal," "equality," "civil," and "civility." He dates a Lebanese immigrant who eventually chooses to return to her homeland to take care of her mother and who does not understand Ibrahim's determination to become a citizen of a country that puts him through so much pain and anguish. He struggles to find a job and is advised by a Muslim interviewer to change his name. He eventually finds work at Mo's gas station, where he continues to challenge Mo's views on various issues. He helps an African American homeless man find a job and even brings him home, but Ibrahim does not feel dismayed when the guest steals his valuables and runs away. When Ibrahim is beaten after trying to defend a young Jewish man, the *New York Post* hails him as an "immigrant hero." When asked why he wants to help others, he recalls his father's advice: "To reach your dreams, plant your good deeds." Ibrahim eventually marries a white woman named Diane (Agnes Bruckner), who helps him navigate life in the United States. By the end of the film, Ibrahim appears to have made it: he has a thriving business, he drives a nice car, and he has a home with Diane and their child.

Despite its happy ending, the film still critiques racialized imbalances in American society and observes that excluding Arab and Muslim Americans from American cultural citizenship creates a constitutional problem, one that the nationalist rhetoric of the American dream evades. The film develops this argument when Ibrahim's right

21. Ibrahim fighting for his right to citizenship in court in *The Citizen* (2012). © 3K Pictures.

to American citizenship—and his worthiness for the designation—is called into question in court. After passing the naturalization test, Ibrahim receives a letter from the immigration office instructing him that he has been recommended for deportation to his country of origin. The letter reads, "You are hereby summoned to appear in court to respond to the charges filed against you and either accept or contest your deportation." His initial reaction is one of disappointment. For the first time, Ibrahim questions the United States' broken promise of inclusion to him as an immigrant. He seems to give up and even burns some of his immigration paperwork but decides to fight his deportation in court. "I respect the laws of this country in a way only an immigrant can," he declares as he prepares for the fight of his life. In court, he shows up well-groomed and with serious looks that reflect his commitment to claiming his legal citizenship (figure 21). After pressure from allies and activists, the court hearings are allowed to go from private to public in a symbolic gesture of the public's concern about the fate of the Arab immigrant patriot.

The prosecutor challenges Ibrahim's right to US citizenship on the grounds that he represents a threat to the United States, despite the fact that he was released and cleared of all terrorism-related charges after being detained with no access to legal representation. The prosecutor asks Ibrahim about his participation in an antigovernment rally on the morning of his arrival to the country—a memory that Ibrahim cherishes for its symbolic reminder of his freedom of speech in the United States. "Considering your nationality and the fact that you were shouting anti-American rhetoric on the streets of New York the day before September 11," the prosecutor continues, "why should God-fearing Americans believe that someone like you wishes no harm to their country?" Ibrahim responds with a set of rhetorical questions that essentially articulate an Arab immigrant rallying cry for legal and cultural citizenship:

> Would you please clarify? When you say "anti-American," do you mean that criticizing the president means that someone doesn't care about this country? And when you say "someone like me," do you mean someone from a part of the world that you fear because simply you do not wish to understand? And when you say "God-fearing Americans," do you mean that I worship an inferior God to yours? And when you say "the day before 9/11," do you mean that I'm somehow connected with this event?

By responding in this way, Ibrahim claims his American constitutional values. The film foregrounds an active sense of agency that denounces US hypernationalism as itself anti-American. When Ibrahim follows his reflections with the firm statement, "I cannot answer such an un-American question because I am here in the United States of America where the Bill of Rights must be respected," he reminds the audience of the existing contradictions between the rhetoric of lofty values enveloping the idea of Americanness and the racialized mapping of the country's population.

The Citizen offers a narrative that embraces the Americanness of Arab immigrants and their entitlement to respect and inclusion in their adopted home. This entitlement, the film proposes, should not be awarded out of sympathy but as a right. The film thus picks up and continues the important conversation initiated by *AmericanEast* and sustained by *Amreeka*. It is also a personal statement that reflects the overlapping activist investments of the lead actor and the director.

In a joint interview, the two men talk about what the film means for them.[58] For actor Nabawy, the film presents an opportunity to show the American audience the complexity of the Arab experience. "We know the West more than the West knows about us," he stated. He decided to participate in the film in part because of its educational mission to challenge misrepresentations. A film like this, he believes, helps "fix the image for the American people." "We are not the nineteen ones behind 9/11," he continued. "We are 300 million, and it's the right [thing] that we fix this."[59]

Nonetheless, *The Citizen's* line of critique is often underwhelming. The film often seems to be a tribute to the American dream rather than a critique of it. The film's romanticized portrayal of Ibrahim's engagement with the United States prompted cultural commentator E. Nina Rothe to praise it as "a film tribute to a great country, to our slightly dusty 'American dream' and an homage by one of its adoptive Arab sons to the land he loves." In a way, the film presents Ibrahim as the embodiment of what it means to be American and how other Americans have drifted away from this idealism. According to one of the film producers Rothe interviewed, the film moves away from politics and religion and foregrounds freedom and justice as holy American principles that "everyone who lives in the United States enjoys."[60] Director Kadi himself speaks of this tribute:

> The entire movie was built on the American dream theme. A lot of people thought after 9/11 this dream has vanished or will never exist anymore. What I really felt [was] that the American dream never dies. And the reason I say this [is] because I feel that this country [the United States] has been built on a solid structure, on a solid foundation, a Constitution that if we always refer to this country will be in a good shape. I believe right now we are going through circumstances that might make the American dream a little harder to accomplish, but that only means is that we have to work harder to earn it.[61]

The film's critique of the American dream is therefore not based on the problematic nature of its rhetoric but on its relevance to the post-9/11 Arab and Muslim immigrant experiences. Kadi discusses how

Ibrahim's experience with America and his struggles echo his own life and the lives of many other immigrants that he knows.

The celebratory framing of the American dream, despite the film's critiques, risks perpetuating the same nationalist rhetoric that promotes the narrative of US exceptionalism without critiquing the subtlety of the challenges that make it impossible for many minorities to realize their dreams within an institutionally racialized society. The film ends up feeling like a "Hallmark Special" that looks back at the 9/11 tragedy and the painful consequences it had on several communities but moves beyond that to a happy ending that somehow suggests a disconnect between those painful consequences and the present reality of continued racial profiling, Islamophobia, and anti-Arab racism.[62] In this respect, *The Citizen* is in line with films such as *In America* (2002), *Under the Same Moon* (2007), and *A Better Life* (2011) that "depict the American system as heartbreakingly stacked against newcomers who want nothing more than a modest, non-threatening, thoroughly patriotic version of the American dream," in the words of a senior editor of *The Dissolve*. This sense of patriotism is delivered at the cost of idealizing characters to the level of superficiality. Ibrahim is "a paper saint," the review continues, "and the people around him are similarly artificial—particularly Diane, who represents America's charitable impulse and its limitations."[63] Ibrahim, according to Frank Scheck of the *Hollywood Reporter*, is portrayed "with such an unrelentingly saintliness that he mostly comes across as a symbol of anti-Arab discrimination."[64]

Nonetheless, it should not be discounted that *The Citizen* offers an Arab American narrative of cultural citizenship that is critical of exclusionary attitudes that view Arab Americans as fundamentally un-American. By laying claim to the protections of the Constitution and the promises of the American dream, the lead character in *The Citizen* articulates a form of Arab American patriotism unimaginable in mainstream cinemas of Hollywood and Egypt.

Conclusion

"[It] feels to me this is our time," said Arab American actor Shalhoub in an interview at the 2008 Arab and South Asian film festival when asked about the emerging Arab American filmmaking experience. "It's now or never really for the Arab American community," he continued, "It's time for all of us to . . . embrace the fact that . . . the time is ripe, and we'll have to become proactive . . . to billboard the idea that if we . . . don't initiate it ourselves, it's not gonna happen." Films analyzed in this chapter examine an emerging filmmaking trend that sends serious messages to other screenwriters and directors involved in portrayals of the Arab American community, demanding more complicated, multilayered images and narratives. The characters in such films are "actual human beings with the same hopes, dreams, and desires as would be found in any other film."[65] These works constitute personal responses to the mainstream dehumanization and homogenization of Arab American culture. By demonstrating the range of possible genres and narratives, a new generation of Arab American filmmakers is breathing authenticity, cultural specificity, and fully dimensional humanity into the stories told by, about, and for Arab Americans. They underscore the array of possible storylines and perspectives made possible by self-representation.

In an unprecedented challenge to the nationalist projections of the Arab American image in Hollywood and Egyptian cinemas, several Arab American filmmakers have emerged since 9/11 to play a critical role in claiming their hijacked narratives and images. *AmericanEast* presents Arab American actors in the lead roles so often denied in Hollywood and Egyptian filmmaking. *Amreeka* highlights Arab American heterogeneity in terms of national background, religious identity, and migration generation. And *The Citizen* envisions Arab Americans claiming legal and cultural citizenship as constitutional rights.

Unlike Hollywood and Egyptian filmmakers, who condition their portrayals of the relationship between Arab Americans and the American dream to the nationalist narratives of their respective societies, these Arab American filmmakers have complicated, albeit in limited ways, this relationship. While it is true that the lead Arab immigrant characters in *AmericanEast*, *Amreeka*, and *The Citizen* may have enjoyed happy endings, with their dreams fulfilled or reconciled, the films are filled with situations and images that continue to confront the very idea of dreaming in a discriminatory society that constantly questions the presence of Arab immigrants in the country. The fact that the filmmakers and many of the actors have struggled to make their voices heard in mainstream filmmaking industries that seem dismissive of their works is a testimony to many of the critiques that the films themselves communicate.

The Arab American directors examined in this chapter have projected their Arab American agency in these films and provided counternarratives that emphasize the variety of the Arab American community. These films do not necessarily present themselves as exclusively representative of all Arab Americans, but they certainly forge critical diasporic spaces informed by a post-9/11 emerging Arab American consciousness and forms of subjectivity that defy the sensational projections of Hollywood and Egyptian filmmaking. In doing so, they are enacting various forms of activism through self-representation but are somehow still limited within the contexts of 9/11 and terrorism. What does it mean to produce Arab American films that go beyond such a context? The book's epilogue reflects on this question.

Epilogue

A CENTRAL EFFORT of this book has been to examine modes of thinking, narration, and creativity in Hollywood, Egyptian, and Arab American filmmaking in support of two main arguments regarding Arab American cultural citizenship. The first argument theorizes moving beyond US Orientalist and racialized histories in defining Arab American Otherness by further considering how Arab state nationalist narratives play a critical role in alienating Arab Americans. There exists a process of Otherness of Arab Americans, I argue, as a result of polarizing conceptions of "Self" and "Other" in both US and Arab state nationalist narratives of identity and belonging. The first two chapters of the book develop this argument through charting and critiquing the ways in which Arab Americans have been projected and consumed in Hollywood and Egyptian cinemas.

On the one hand, Hollywood filmmakers have evolved from portraying Arabs in the United States solely as aliens committed to undermining US national security and foreign policy in the 1970s, to a somewhat more nuanced post-9/11 repertoire of images that includes Arab American characters as homegrown terrorists, but also as patriots fighting terrorism or as victims of racial profiling. On the other hand, the Egyptian cinema's representations of Arab Americans since the 1990s consider themes of nation, class, gender, and generation but still problematically reduce them to polarized abstractions as either glorified Egyptians or denigrated Americans. Even in their most complicated forms, the two filmic sites remain superficial, constraining heterogeneous Arab Americans in a liminal space in which the broad categories of Arabness or Americanness appear as mutually exclusive and clashing opposites. Crucially, the US and Egyptian nationalist narratives underwriting these representations play an important role in shaping the cinematic elision of Arab American cultural citizenship in both industries.

The second argument of this book is that there exist post-9/11 efforts in Hollywood and Egyptian cinemas, but more importantly in Arab American filmmaking, that represent Arab Americans with complexity, realism, and fluidity. Chapters 3 through 5 examine films that reflect critical narratives of Arab American cultural citizenship that wrestle with nationalist constructions of identity and belonging in the United States and Egypt. The book, therefore, critiques how Arab American cultural citizenship has been tethered to the US and Egyptian nation-state in Hollywood and Egyptian mainstream cinemas, but also analyzes filmic efforts to capture existing dynamics in the representation of Arab Americans that wrestle with US and Arab nationalist narratives.

Chapter 3 locates such a dynamic in the character of Samir Horn (Don Cheadle) in Jeffrey Nachmanoff's *Traitor* (2008), whose nuanced Arab, Black, Muslim, and American identities offer a complicated portrayal of Arab American subjectivity as one traversing good Muslim/bad Muslim, Arab/African, national/international, domestic/foreign, and local/empire binaries. Chapter 4 captures two other dynamics through the characters of Layla Khoury (Ghada Abdulrazeq) and Hossam al-Ashry (Mahmoud Abdel Aziz) in Adel Adeeb's *Laylat el-Baby Doll* (The Baby Doll Night, 2008), whose fatal and neoliberal modes of diasporic experiences of activism in US, Arab, and Israeli geopolitics reflect a filmic awareness of some of the transnational configurations of Arab American cultural citizenship. And chapter 5 maps several dynamics in the narration of Arab American cultural citizenship that both critique the nationalist underpinnings of the American dream and reflect Arab American meanings and interpretations of the notion—be that through interethnic and interreligious alliances among minorities in Hesham Issawi's *AmericanEast* (2007), claiming America as home in Cherien Dabis's *Amreeka* (2009), or demand for American constitutional rights in Sam Kadi's *The Citizen* (2012).

This book ends with a note of hope for furthering filmic possibilities of narrating Arab American cultural citizenship in disruptive ways, particularly through Arab American films. A key site of narration with a great potential for filmic subversion is problematizing the notion of multiculturalism in the United States, which is often wrapped in a depoliticized and celebratory narrative of ethnic diversity that expects each immigrant and ethnic minority group to "preserve its own heritage (as long as it speaks English)"—to echo Vijay Prashad's critique—without treating such heritage as "a living set of social relations but as a timeless trait."[1] Hollywood's post-9/11 positive portrayals of Arab Americans surveyed in chapter 3, for instance, are merely sympathetic, and they draw on a flawed sense of multiculturalism that renders such portrayals no more than tokens for inclusion in films that primarily entertain white perspectives.

Hollywood's portrayals of Arab Americans, even in their most positive forms, are limited insofar as they remain linked to issues of foreign policy and national security. The industry presents Arab Americans through a fixed set of stereotypical conceptions of Arabness and Islam and continues to restrict portrayals of Arab Americans to the context of terrorism. Arab American filmmaker Cherien Dabis, for instance, once shared how her efforts to develop an authentic show about a Muslim family in Dearborn, Michigan, the Arab American capital of the United States, were soon challenged in the marketplace by demands to include more conventional storylines. It was suggested, for example, that the family should face false accusations of terrorism; they would not be depicted as terrorists, but the story would add intrigue nonetheless. Dabis eventually lost interest in the show because of her stand that "we can't keep showing Muslims as terrorists, even if it's just a false accusation."[2] Thus, it is important to witness the emergence of an Arab American filmmaking that showcases the possibility of representation beyond the politics of terrorism or racial profiling.

Consider the Arab American filmmaker Rola Nashef's independent film *Detroit Unleaded* (2013). The film departs not only from Hollywood's rigid narratives but also from the other Arab American films analyzed in chapter 5 (*AmericanEast*, *Amreeka*, and *The Citizen*)

22. Sami and Naj in love behind the bulletproof cage in *Detroit Unleaded* (2013). © Gas Afterhours.

that invest in critical but saturated cinematic imagery of 9/11, geopolitics, and terrorism. In *Detroit Unleaded*, Nashef breaks away from these issues as she grapples with Arab American individuals' efforts to negotiate the dynamics of their gendered roles in their community as they search to fulfill their own aspirations for freedom in the United States.[3] And the film's choice of Detroit, a city that embodies a made-in-the-USA economic struggle shaped through the rise and fall of the so-called "Motor City," stands as a testimony to the crushed realities and resulting struggles to realize individuals' own dreams, each in his or her own way.

A romantic comedy, *Detroit Unleaded* features a love story between Sami (EJ Assi) and Najlah (Nada Shouhayib). Due to his father's sudden death, Sami is forced to forsake his dreams of going to college in California. He finds himself running his family gas station to support his mother. To protect himself from the violent armed robberies that also claimed his father's life, Sami installs a cage-like, bulletproof glass shield. Naj (shortened form of Najlah), who works in a nearby family cell-phone business, falls in love with Sami and pays frequent visits to his bulletproof cage, where they spend platonic romantic time and laugh away the pressures of their lived realities as individuals tied to their family obligations (figure 22). Naj's relationship with Sami is filled with references to one of many gendered patterns in the

Arab American community, which presupposes family interventions and dictations. It sheds lights on "the dissonance between American hookup culture and home-country traditions."[4] Naj's over-protective brother, Fadi, (Steven Soro) draws strict boundaries around her social life. In one scene, Naj flees a nightclub in fear of being spotted by her brother, even though he himself indulges frequently in casual relationships.

To keep her relationship with Sami secret, Naj weaves a web of lies to make sense of her absence from work and home. In one emotionally charged scene, her brother Fadi humiliates her when he discovers her at the gas station. In a sense, Naj's independence is "compromised by family ties that are both comforting and constricting."[5] Ultimately, though, she emerges triumphant in claiming her own Arab American feminine agency. She challenges her brother's controlling reproach and his threats toward Sami by deciding to leave with Sami in search of a life defined by their own sensibilities. It is not entirely clear whether they will continue their relationship, but the film concludes instead by emphasizing their act of leaving Detroit together in search of their own dreams.

Another gendered dynamic unfolds through the character of Sami's mother, Mariam (Mary Assel), who has been dependent on men her whole life. With her husband now dead, Mariam lives a life of solitude and grieving. She is unable to socialize with her welcoming neighbors. She constantly demands help from her son to run errands for her, and she is hesitant to obtain a driver's license as the first step toward securing a sense of independence for herself. She struggles to retain her role as a mother and seems less inclined to reconcile her femininity and individuality. It is only when Sami informs her of his decision to leave the state that she comes to terms with her feminine identity, suddenly emerging as a "newborn" woman full of confidence and command over her own destiny. After years of passivity, captured visually through shots of a laid-back lifestyle in her dimly lit house, Mariam finally reclaims her own feminine agency. Her triumph is revealed through close-up shots of her driving around, thereby transgressing the limits of her self-imposed, Arab-structured traditional gendered role as a mother. The newly emancipated Mariam no longer hesitates to introduce herself to her neighbors, and she finds meaning in initiating communication with others in her community.

Nashef's critique of gendered formations also develops through the character of Sami, whose gendered role obligates him to maintain the family business at the expense of his own plans. The bulletproof glass, in this case, is literal and metaphorical, symbolic of the "ever-present yet unspoken fear that violence could claim his life at any minute."[6] His "cage" experience at the gas station, which hinders his ability to pursue both romance and a career of his own, also forces him to perform his gendered role of earning income and supporting his mother. In writing this role, Nashef drew on her personal observation of the Arab American community in Detroit: "In every neighborhood, I would encounter Arab men behind the glass, their voices muffled and their images distorted."[7] The cage in Sami's case represents the double-layered imperatives of economic necessity and gendered expectations. It is not until he decides to redefine his own destiny that he manages to break away from his monotonous lifestyle. To realize his ambitions, he first needs to confront his mother. This speaks to the interconnectedness of work responsibility and family obligation that underwrites the lives of many Arab Americans. Once he reconciles these gendered expectations with his dreams, Sami successfully gains his sense of individuality and independence.

The cage image in *Detroit Unleaded* stands for the sense of entrapment surrounding Arab American women like Naj and Mariam and men like Sami. Nashef imagines the film as a call to transcend the barriers between individuals and their community. "It is a metaphor for how we constantly are put in boxes or create boxes for ourselves," she explains. "It's about breaking out of that box."[8] The act of breaking away from one's cage is specific to each character, whether it is the past for the mother, the dating taboo for Naj, or leaving the gas station for Sami. Breaking away from their cages, therefore, represents a statement in favor of empowerment that transcends the community's impact on their gendered roles and demonstrates their ability to master their own reality. Nashef's calls for disruption do not promote divorcing oneself from one's tradition; rather, she points to the need to develop ways of adapting tradition to one's own life. "We're not trying to rebel against Arab tradition and we don't want to reject our families," she states. "It is more like expanding the tradition, making it more fluid."[9] The possibility of this disruption is contingent on the characters' willingness to reconcile the dictations of the collective and the individual in their lives. Naj, Mariam, and Sami present three various articulations of this reconciliation and three different examples of Arab American subjectivity.

Nashef's recruitment of twelve Arab American actors likewise reflects her interest in presenting relatable portrayals for the community. Her portrayal of Arab Americans as everyday people reflects her embrace of a more inclusive sense of multiculturalism, one that shapes her effort to translate an aspect of Arab American culture for a mainstream audience.[10] Equally important, Nashef also keeps in mind the Arab American youth as a primary audience for the film. Watching Arab American actors in lead roles is inspiring, as is witnessing their culture being projected as "fun," "hip," "cool," "hot," and "sexy." It is also important for the audience to experience the specificity of their Arab American culture with all its norms, rules, and taboos.[11] Nashef's work, therefore, demonstrates the possibility of complicating understanding of American multiculturalism through empowerment of Arab American actors and projections of Americanness as well as Arab Americanness away from national security or foreign policy themes.

Another key site of narration with a great potential for filmic subversion in narrating Arab American cultural citizenship is decentering nationalist representations of belonging—be they American or Arabic—by emphasizing instead how Arab Americans' difference is multisited and emerges from the various contexts they inhabit, both physically and culturally. This understanding underlines my interest in dynamic Arab American perspectives that move beyond the American rhetoric of patriotism and the Arabic appeals to nostalgia. It speaks to my definition of Arab American cultural citizenship as an ever-changing amalgamation of thoughts, attitudes, and positions that results from Arab Americans' cross-cultural and multidimensional positionality.

To illustrate this point, let's consider *May in the Summer* (2013), written and directed by Cherien Dabis, who also directed the 2009 film *Amreeka* (chapter 5). The film captures the turbulence of a moment in the life of May Brennan (who is also played by Dabis in her acting debut), an Arab American author who travels back to her natal home in Jordan for a summer to prepare for her marriage to a New York–based academic named Ziad (Alexander Siddig). Once she is in Jordan, the audience learns about the fissures in May's life that lead her to give up on her love for Ziad and cancel the wedding. May's Christian mother Nadine (Hiam Abbass), who has developed deep resentment against intercultural marriages following her divorce from May's cheating American father Edward (Bill Pullman), is adamant in rejecting May's planned marriage to Ziad because he is Muslim. May's interaction with her father rekindles the ever-burning flames of her parents' failed marriage. During their reunion, May sees in her Jordanian American sisters Dalia (Alia Shawkat) and Yasmine (Nadine Malouf) the vigor of youth rebellion and search for independence. Her experiences during the trips to the Dead Sea and the desert in Jordan add more meaning to her life—whether through watching a flying fighter jet that reminds her of Israeli aggressions across the sea or her realization of the unexplored venues of romance and passion in her life. "Her once carefully structured world appears to unravel as she grapples with her own truths," to quote the film's synopsis, leading her "to question the direction her life is taking."[12] The choice of the image for the background of one of the film's posters (figure 23) lends a symbolic meaning to what might otherwise be a quick shot of May's breathing outside air while being transported through a car in Jordan. The poster offers a glimpse of May's confusion as she searches for her "self" while she moves through US-Jordan experiences and challenges.

Despite its appealing promises, *May in the Summer* lacks complexity; its simplistic treatment of pertinent issues (i.e., tradition, family history, and identity) doesn't allow for in-depth analysis.[13] However,

23. The poster of *May in the Summer* (2013) is symbolic of May's search for her "self" through her US-Arab experiences and challenges. © Displaced Pictures.

the film makes it possible to envision Arab American filmmaking narrations of the community's cultural citizenship at the crossroads of US and Arab cultures in Arab American films. There is no mention of 9/11, terrorism, or Arab immigrants' struggles to realize their American or Egyptian dreams, as in the case of many of the films surveyed in this book; the film makes the case instead for the significance of Arab American self-representation in a transnational context. And as Arab and Arab American film festivals continue to emerge and grow in Michigan, California, Minnesota, Boston, Houston, Chicago, New York, and other cities and states, there is hope now more than ever in witnessing the emergence of more Arab American filmmakers whose work reflects the complexity of their community's cultural citizenship vis-à-vis the United States and the Arab world that they navigate. Indeed, there is great potential for Arab American films to present sophisticated, realistic, and fluid Arab American imagery, unlike those in Hollywood and Egyptian cinemas that overstate the nation as the locus of identity and citizenship.

And the trajectory for mainstreaming Arab American self-representations is promising. The Hollywood Bureau of the Muslim Public Affairs Council (MPAC) has organized summits to help Arab and Muslim American youth develop a better understanding of the mainstream industry. The office itself has provided consultations to major studios regarding imagery and cultural sensitivity. Muslims on Screen and Television (MOST) is also another tool that provides Hollywood filmmakers with resources about Islam and Muslims.[14] These efforts have resulted in some positive changes in television works like *Grey's Anatomy*, *Army Wives*, *Madam Secretary*, and *Tyrant*.[15] Even though the changes in these works are cosmetic, as they do not seriously challenge the platform, they still demonstrate how Hollywood filmmakers can sometimes accommodate critiques and concerns. Self-representation certainly remains the best possible route for serious image change in Hollywood and even Arabic-language cinemas. It is also encouraging to see Arab American directors like Sami Kadi and Rola Nashef taking advantage of tax incentives provided in Detroit and producing their own features drawing from localized sources.

It would be remiss not to acknowledge here the other cultural means through which Arab Americans have been telling their own stories in nuanced and complex ways. Since 9/11, Arab American presence in comedy, with performers including Ahmed Ahmed, Dean Obeidallah, Maysoon Zayid, Aron Kader, Mo Amer, and others, has been noted and well-received.[16] In music, Syrian American Omar Offendum, Sudanese American Amir el Khalifa (Oddisee), and Libyan American Khaled M., among many others, have developed an engaging genre of diasporic hip-hop that reflects the artists' consciousness about their East-West experiences. The Iraqi American heavy metal band Acrassicauda features a similar transnational engagement. The poetics of Suheir Hammad's performances stands as a popular example of the power of Arab American words and performances, most visibly captured in theater. Whether in the comedic plays of the Michigan-based AJYAL Theatrical Group, the aesthetic performances of the Minnesota-based New Arab American Theater Works, or the critical works of the Chicago-based Silk Road Rising, Arab American voices are expressing various critiques that enhance understanding of identity and politics. Playwrights Jamil Khoury, Kathryn Haddad, Yussef El Guindi, and Leila Buck, among others, are at the forefront of mediating a complicated sense of Arab American cultural autonomy that is not subservient to a specific national framework but operates within its own paradigm.[17] Even more distinct is the presence of Arab Americans in literature, which is backed by a long and rich history of visibility that dates to the Arab American Pen League (roughly 1915–32).[18] The workshops and symposia provided by literary organizations such as the Radius of Arab American Writers and Mizna ensure the sustenance of established and emerging writers and performers. Support for Arab American growth is further solidified through the scholars invested in the community, served by the Arab American Studies Association (founded in 2012) and supported by Syracuse University Press, the Arab American National Museum, the University of Michigan's Arab American Studies programs in Ann Arbor and Dearborn, the Arab American Cultural Center at the University of Illinois in Chicago, and the Moise A. Khayrallah Center for Lebanese Diaspora Studies, among others.

In this context of productivity and agency, it seems natural for Arab Americans to claim their voices and narratives in film in ways that defy US and Egyptian hegemonic representations—whether those representations were and are driven by institutionalized racism, restrictive multiculturalism, or reductive Arab state nationalism. This requires registering Arab American lead characters as active rather than passive players in defining their own subjectivity. It also entails proactive efforts on the part of writers, actors, directors, producers, and others involved in the filmmaking process to project the paradoxical and multiscalar dimensions of Arab American identity.

The urgency for Arab American presence in filmmaking, and the reason behind selecting this medium for analysis in this book, lies in the industry's multilayered importance in contemporary popular culture. Films are accessible to audiences regardless of their language competency, educational status, or cultural background. They serve as educational tools in a world increasingly centered around, if not mobilized by, mediated images and messages. They also have the power to function as tools for visibility, podiums for authenticity, and mirrors of reality. And when adding the enriching effects of genres, it becomes obvious that the medium of film is a vehicle of thoughts and emotions that is often packaged as "mere" entertainment, but that carries the power to voice social commentary, mobilize public sentiments, and patrol the boundaries of national and cultural realms of belonging. Thus, the production of Arab American aesthetics in film becomes a critical component of gaining visibility and retaining agency.

Although this book does not address the mechanics of production, the dynamics of circulation, or the intricacies of reception, I invite both researchers interested in exploring the role of Arab Americans in film and filmmakers invested in the issue of cultural citizenship to consider this work as a starting point for future theory and practice. How might future films dramatize Arab Americans' constructions of identity without overriding existing nationalistic voices? How are Arab Americans producing their own aesthetic values and filmmaking techniques? In what ways have filmmakers negotiated with existing funding sources, and what is gained or lost in the process? How possible is it for Arab American filmmakers to create their own audience at the core of American and Arab viewership? To intervene in filmmaking with a critical consciousness of cultural citizenship requires scholars and filmmakers to engage with these questions.

Additionally, the comparative framework of this book, which advocates the necessity of unsettling the "national" as a category of analysis while interrogating Arab American subjectivity, needs further development in the field of Arab American Studies. The book emphasizes the need to examine the simultaneous projection of Arab

American images in Hollywood, Egyptian, and Arab American films, but adding other sites for comparison could yield different insights into how they cross-pollinate and challenge one another. More scholarship is needed that equally engages the Arab world as a critical site of inquiry for Arab American identity formation. A study of Muslims' struggle against Islamophobia in the United States, for instance, could benefit from exploring the conditions generating both radicalization and anti-Islamism in the Arab world. Unpacking the issue of activism, to mention another example, would likewise benefit from multisite comparisons, spanning the national, postcolonial, and diasporic.

Importantly, comparative analyses should not simply be about merely adding more sites but should also examine how sites influence one another. At the same time, comparisons across fields might need to be cautious about assuming an analysis from one industry will necessarily transfer to another, for each genre has its own dynamics, and each nationalist industry, as this book highlights, operates within its own imperatives. Future scholarship surrounding the interplay of Arab Americans and filmmaking could further develop comparative readings of such specific topics as nation, family, class, gender, sexuality, race, and disability. Meanwhile, there is a need to explore the filmic experiences of Arab American communities, broadly defined beyond the United States to include Arab migrating experiences in the Americas. Inquiries such as these could potentially fully elaborate, if not even redefine, the parameters of Arab American cultural citizenship.

Finally, future scholarship around Arab American filmmaking should consider methodological frameworks not employed in this book. The broad, historical surveys of Hollywood and Egyptian films capture the discursive dynamics of the book's cinematic sites, while the content analyses in chapters 3 through 5 provide close readings of specific films in order to unpack the complexity of narrative and image-making. More critical evaluations of individual films are needed to make sense of various forms of cultural citizenship. Conducting interviews with Arab American producers, directors, actors, writers, festival organizers, and film scholars should also yield valuable insights into the very process of representation. And ethnographic methods of audience study groups or surveys of consumption trends could tackle issues not sufficiently addressed in this book.

In closing, I want to articulate one of this book's driving forces—namely, generating more interest among scholars and filmmakers to engage with the book's under-studied field. My comparative and transnational case study of Arab American representation recognizes the power of film to offer various, often conflicting views of Arab Americans' cultural citizenship. Central to this investigation has been my emphasis on the need for simultaneous interrogations of relevant collective memories and emerging cross-cultural disruptive filmic efforts to recapture the cultural citizenship of the Arab American community in disruptive ways. I very much hope that this effort opens the door for further scholarly interventions and more nuanced films as imagined in this epilogue and beyond.

Notes

Bibliography

Filmography

Index

Notes

Introduction

1. The Benghazi attacks were the most notorious, claiming the lives of American ambassador J. Christopher Stevens and Foreign Service officer Sean Smith, and sparking the Benghazi controversy in Washington, DC.

2. See Naff, *Becoming American*; Michael Suleiman, *Arabs in America*; Abraham and Shryock, *Arab Detroit*; Boosahda, *Arab-American Faces and Voices*; Jamal and Naber, *Race and Arab Americans*; Bayoumi, *How Does It Feel?*; and Cainkar, *Homeland Insecurity* (2009).

3. See Alsultany and Shohat, *Between the Middle East*; Naber, *Arab America*; Berman, *American Arabesque*; Fadda-Conrey, *Contemporary Arab-American Literature*; Hassan, *Immigrant Narratives*; and Bawardi, *Making of Arab Americans.*

4. Naber, "Imperial Whiteness," 1113–14.

5. Fadda-Conrey, *Contemporary Arab-American Literature.*

6. To learn more about Odeh's case, see the dedicated website http://justice4rasmea.org. To read about Trump's tweet, see Allyn, "Congresswomen Denounce Trump Tweets."

7. See, for instance, the case of Khaled Hassan, who was subjected to the coercion practices of Egyptian authorities: Sudarsan Raghavan, "Jailed in Egypt, American Limo Driver Attempts Suicide," *Washington Post*, August 9, 2019, https://www.washingtonpost.com/world/jailed-in-egypt-american-limo-driver-attempts-suicide/2019/08/09/90e32b40-bac5-11e9-aeb2-a101a1fb27a7_story.html.

8. See May, *Screening Out the Past*; Friedman, *Unspeakable Images*; Rony, *Third Eye*; Denzin, *Reading Race*; and Fuller, *Hollywood Goes Oriental.*

9. Naficy, *An Accented Cinema.*

10. This reading draws from Stuart Hall's theory of ideology; see Hall, "Culture, Media," "Ideology and Communication Theory," and *Representation*; also, Makus, "Stuart Hall's Theory."

11. See "McCain Responds to 'Arab' Epithet at Rally: 'Obama a Decent Family Man,'" *The Uptake* (blog), *Huffington Post*, November 10, 2008, http://www.huffingtonpost.com/the-uptake/mccain-responds-to-arab-a_b_133820.html.

12. The Barbary Coast referred to the land of the Berbers residing across North Africa. This includes today's Morocco, Algeria, Tunisia, Libya, and Mauritania.

13. Schueller, *US Orientalisms*, 47.

14. Marr, *Cultural Roots*, 40.

15. Allison, *Crescent Obscured*, 59. For more about this early history, see Sha'ban, *Islam and Arabs.*

16. Obenzinger, *American Palestine*. See also Davis, *Landscape of Belief*, and Vogel, *To See a Promised Land.*

17. Trafton, *Egypt Land.*

18. Steet, *Veils and Daggers.*

19. Michalek, "Arab in American Cinema," 3.

20. Hajji, *Arabs in American Cinema*, 9.

21. See *The Arab* (1915), *The Garden of Allah* (1916), *Intolerance* (1916), *Cleopatra* (1917), *Salome* (1918), *An Arabian Knight* (1920), *A Son of the Sahara* (1924), *The Son of the Sheik* (1926), and *A Son of the Desert* (1928).

22. McAlister, *Epic Encounters*, 1–39.

23. Michalek, "Arab in American Cinema," 3.

24. Shaheen, *Reel Bad Arabs*, 2.

25. See Abraham, "Anti-Arab Racism"; Salaita, *Anti-Arab Racism in USA*; Naber, "Introduction: Arab Americans"; Pennock, *Rise of Arab American Left*; Yaqub, *Imperfect Strangers*; and Feldman, *Shadow over Palestine.*

26. Said, "Declaring War on Islam."

27. Said, *Covering Islam*; Kamalipour, *US Media in Middle East*; and Hudson and Wolfe, *American Media and Arabs.*

28. Alsultany, *Arabs and Muslims in the Media*; Jarmakani, *Imagining Arab Womanhood* and *An Imperialist Love Story*; Sabbagh, *Sex, Lies & Stereotypes*; Stockton, "Ethnic Archetypes"; Gottschalk and Greenberg, *Islamophobia*; and Richards and Omidvar, *Muslims and American Popular Culture.*

29. Elnaccash, "Egyptian Cinema: A Historical Outline," 52.

30. Thabet, *Industrie du film Egyptien*; as quoted in Allagui and Najjar, "Framing Political Islam."

31. Saad, *Mūjaz tārīkh al-sīnimā al-Miṣrīyah.*

32. Shafik, *Arab Cinema*, 12.

33. "Rising Stars."

34. Examples include the International Film Festival of Marrakech (2001), the Beirut International Film Festival (2003), the Jordan Short Film Festival (founded in 2004), the Abu Dhabi Film Festival (2007), Muscat International Film Festival (2007), the Gulf Film Festival (2008), the Karama Human Rights Film Festival (2009), the Doha Tribeca Film Festival (2009–12), and the Kuwait International Film Retreat (2013).

35. To read more about the primary issues circulating in Egyptian popular culture, see Armbrust, *Mass Culture and Modernism.*

36. An insightful reading into this complexity is available in Khalaf and Khalaf, *Arab Society and Culture.*

37. To learn more about Egypt's historical context, see Cook, *Struggle for Egypt*; Sowers and Toensing, *Journey to Tahrir.* To examine the role of traditional and alternative media in echoing the protests globally, refer to Nanabhay and Farmanfarmaian, "From Spectacle to Spectacular."

38. Dawn, *From Ottomanism to Arabism.*

39. The founding members were Egypt, Iraq, Jordan, Lebanon, Syria, and Saudi Arabia. The League sought to mediate a broad sense of *al-'uruba* premised on common Arab beliefs, thoughts, attitudes, and values. Later, Arabian Peninsula countries (Bahrain, Kuwait, Oman, Qatar, United Arab Emirates, and Yemen), North African countries (Algeria, Libya, Mauritania, Morocco, Tunisia, and Sudan), and Horn of Africa countries (Djibouti and Somalia) joined. When the recognition-seeking state of Palestine and the archipelago island of Comoros joined, the number of Arab League members reached twenty-two: https://www.nationsonline.org/oneworld/arab_league.htm.

40. Coury locates Egyptian Arab nationalism in a history that predefined the Free Officer Movement (1952) and the subsequent rise of Nasser; see Coury, "Who 'Invented' Egyptian Arab Nationalism?"

41. Khouri, *Arab National Project*, xi.

42. The "Arab Dream" is deeply rooted in the Arab collective memory of a glorious past. The nineteenth-century literary movement of *al-nahḍa* (cultural awakening) first mobilized this dream of a consolidated Arab identity, which then evolved into demands for sovereignty from the Ottoman Empire rule during World War I. The dream faltered, however, as British and French mandates resulted in more conquered and divided Arab nation-states. See Sharabi, *Arab Intellectuals and the West*; Choueiri, *Arab Nationalism*; Alangari, *Struggle for Power*; and Khalidi et al., *Origins of Arab Nationalism.* To learn about Arab history, refer to Hitti, *History of the Arabs* and Hourani, *History of the Arab Peoples.*

43. For an Arab reading of the Crusades, refer to Maalouf, *Crusades through Arab Eyes.*

44. Shmeit, *Youssef Chahine*, 193, as quoted in Khouri, *Arab National Project*, 43.

45. For a thorough treatment of post-1967 Arab intellectual history, see Abu-Rabi', *Contemporary Arab Thought*; for a discussion of disillusionment with the pan-Arab dream, see Rubin, "Pan-Arab Nationalism" (1991) and Ajami, *Dream Palace.*

46. In 1972 the attempt to create a Federation of Arab Republics uniting Libya, Egypt, and Syria failed. Similarly, proposals for other unions like the 1958 Arab Federation (Iraq and Jordan), the 1958 United Arab States (United Arab Republic and

Kingdom of Yemen), and the 1972 Arab Islamic Republic (Libya and Tunisia) met with failure. For more about the history of Arab nationalism and unity attempts, see Dawisha, *Arab Nationalism in the Twentieth Century.*

47. The word "Arab" was only official for a limited period in the Yemen Arab Republic (1962–90), Libyan Arab Republic (postrevolution–1977), Socialist People's Libyan Arab Jamahiriya (1977–86), and the Great Socialist People's Libyan Arab Jamahiriya (1986–2012).

48. The concepts still reverberated through Hizb al-Ba'th al-'Arabi al-Ishtiraki (the Arab Ba'th Socialist Party), which peaked upon achieving power in Syria and Iraq, but then receded when the party failed to deliver Arab unity as promised. Like Nasser, the party also lost support when it embraced state nationalist military authoritarianism. Other factors behind the decline of the Ba'th party include the US invasion of Iraq (2003) and the Syrian Civil War (2011).

49. Hammond, *Popular Culture*, 2.

50. Seib, *Aljazeera Effect.*

51. Kraidy and Khalil, *Arab Television Industries.*

52. By "imagined," I am borrowing Anderson's sense of the term; see *Imagined Communities.*

53. See, for example, Armbrust, *Mass Mediations*; Hafez, *Arab Media*; Sabry, *Cultural Encounters*; Valassopoulos, *Arab Cultural Studies*; and Hamamsy and Soliman, *Popular Culture in the Middle East.*

54. Poetry in Abu-Lughod's *Veiled Sentiment*, film in Arasoughly's *Screens of Life*, media in Lynch's *Voices of the New Arab Republic*, television in Sakr's *Arab Television Today*, music in Lohman's *Umm Kulthum*, and posters in Khatib's *Image Politics in the Middle East.*

55. See Yasir Suleiman's *Arabic, Self and Identity* for a more in-depth reading of the power of Arabic as an identity marker.

56. Mastered by the prolific Palestinian-Egyptian director Ahmed el-'Erian, the operetta follows the musical style of Michael Jackson's "We Are the World." The "Arab Dream" theme was later sustained in the 2008 follow-up operetta *el-Ḍamir el-'Arabi* (The Arab Conscience).

57. The operetta received much attention from Arab television channels, particularly in the aftermath of the second Palestinian *intifaḍa* (uprising) in the period 2000–2005.

58. Culhane, *East/West, an Ambiguous State of Being.*

59. Hassan el-Banna (1906–49) established el-Ikhwān el-Muslimūn in 1928 to propose a mainstream role for religion to play in state and society. El-Jamā'ah el-Islamiyyah draws from the salafi school of Wahhabism. See el-Fadl, *And God Knows the Soldiers*, chapter 1.

60. For more about the Islamist appeal of the *ummah*, see Mahmood, *Concept of an Islamic State*.

61. Gilsenan, *Recognizing Islam*, 216.

62. Wickham, *Mobilizing Islam*, 98, 107.

63. A viable source of influence in Qutb's writings is the South Asian Islamic thinker Syed Abul A'ala Maududi (1903–79), who called for an Islamic revivalist revolution against Western forms of liberalism in Muslim land: Maududi, *Tajdid-o-Ihya-i-din*. Also see Calvert, *Sayyid Qutb*.

64. President Sadat allowed Islamists some freedom in order to weaken the remnant forces of the Socialist left, a policy that backfired and claimed his own life; see Jamal Mohammed Ahmed, *Intellectual Origins*, chapter 2.

65. According to Tsourapas, Sadat's government relied more on regional emigrants for remittances. The remittances were central to the Egyptian economy and reached more than 14 percent of the GDP of the Egyptian Central Bank. "Remittances from workers in Saudi Arabia," observes Tsourapas, "accounted for 42.7% of net private transfers to Egypt in 2012, followed by Kuwait (21.3%) and the United Arab Emirates (12.2.%)"; see Tsourapas, "Why Do States Develop Multi-tier Emigrant Policies?," 2203–4.

66. The war is often referred to as Yom Kippur War, Ramadan War, or October War.

67. Van Nieuwkerk, *A Trade Like Any Other*, 64.

68. Appeal to morality also corresponded with increasing pressures from the cinema's audiences in conservative oil-rich countries.

69. Abu-Lughod, "Finding a Place for Islam," 494. For a reading of how art is intertwined with politics in Egyptian cinema, see Baker's "Combative Cultural Politics."

70. Mehrez, *Egypt's Culture Wars*, introduction; and Aboulnaga, *Al-Mouthaqaf al-Intiqali*, chapter 1.

71. The ultraconservative Salafi party, Hizb el-Nur, ironically joined the call.

72. Khatib, *Filming the Modern Middle East*, chapter 4.

73. Allagui and Najjar, "Framing Political Islam."

74. Armbrust, "Islamists in Egyptian Cinema," 925.

75. Bhabha, *Location of Culture*, 245–46.

76. Volpp, *Culture of Citizenship*, 574.

77. Rosaldo, "Cultural Citizenship in San Jose," 57.

78. Rosaldo, "Cultural Citizenship and Educational Democracy," 402.

79. Naber, "Ambiguous Insiders," 37–58.

80. Ong, "Cultural Citizenship as Subject-Making," 738.

81. See Flores and Benmayor, *Latino Cultural Citizenship*; Tuan, *Forever Foreigners or Honorary Whites?*; and Chen and Churchill, *Film, History and Cultural Citizenship*.

82. See Siu, "Diasporic Cultural Citizenship"; Bauböck, *Transnational Citizenship*; and Ong, *Flexible Citizenship.*

83. See Maira, *Missing*; Prashad, *Karma of Brown Folk*; Naber, *Arab America*; and Fadda-Conrey, *Contemporary Arab-American Literature.*

84. See, for example, Witteborn, "Situated Expression."

85. See Alsultany and Shohat, *Between the Middle East*, 2013.

86. See Hegel, Miller, and Findlay, *Phenomenology of Spirit*; Gramsci, *Prison Notebooks*; and Foucault, *Archaeology of Knowledge.*

87. To read about American exceptionalism, see Noble, *Death of a Nation*; Kane, *Between Virtue and Power*; and Hodgson, *Myth of American Exceptionalism.* To examine US-style Orientalism, see Said, *Orientalism*; Schueller, *US Orientalisms*; Little, *American Orientalism*; Lockman, *Contending Visions*; Gerges, *America and Political Islam*; and Klein, *Cold War Orientalism.*

88. The term Occidentalism has been proposed to make sense of Arab-based conceptions of the West. See El-Enany, *Arab Representations of the Occident* and Mohamed, *Arab Occidentalism.*

89. The call to transnationalize the field of American studies was made by then-president of the American Studies Association, Janice Radway, in a keynote speech in which she questioned the politics of naming the field. The speech was delivered during the annual convention in 1998 bearing the theme "American Studies and the Question of Empire: Histories, Cultures, and Practices." In the same year, *American Quarterly* published a set of essays on "empire," "internationalization," "globalist discourse," and "black transnationalism." See Radway, "What's in a Name?" and Gross, "Transnational Turn." For examples of the "transnational turn" in relation to the Middle East, see Edwards and Gaonkar, *Globalizing American Studies* and Lubin and Kraidy, *American Studies Encounters the Middle East.*

1. Hollywood's Portrayals of Arab Americans

1. Toby Miller defines the cultural citizen as "the virtuous political participant who is taught how to scrutinize and improve her or his conduct through the work of cultural policy"; see Miller, *Well-Tempered Self*, xxi.

2. Althusser, "Ideology," 85–126.

3. Rosaldo, "Cultural Citizenship and Educational Democracy," 402.

4. See Richard, *Contemporary Hollywood's Negative Hispanic Image*; Guerrero, *Framing Blackness*; Alsultany, *Arabs and Muslims in the Media*; Marchetti, *Romance and the "Yellow Peril"*; Shaheen, *Reel Bad Arabs*; Lester Friedman, *Jewish Image in American Film*; Rollins and O'Connor, *Hollywood's Indian*; Lee, *Orientals*; and Casty, *Communism in Hollywood.*

5. Lary May, *Big Tomorrow*, 1.

6. See Shaheen, *Reel Bad Arabs* and *Guilty*; Bernstein and Studlar, *Visions of the East*; Semmerling, *"Evil" Arabs*; and Alsultany, *Arabs and Muslims in the Media.*

7. Said, *Orientalism.*

8. McAlister, *Epic Encounters*, 1–39.

9. Bayoumi, *How Does It Feel to Be a Problem?*, 5.

10. Bayoumi, 5.

11. Sturken, *Tangled Memories*, 2–3.

12. The silent cinema entertained Orientalist images of Arab Americans in the short film *Arabian Dagger* (1908), which shows less interest in the peddler than in his dagger.

13. Gualtieri, *Between Arab and White*, 142–43.

14. Gualtieri, 142–43.

15. Naff, *Becoming American*, 2.

16. Gualtieri, *Between Arab and White*, 2.

17. See Bayoumi, "Racing Religion."

18. Ford, "Why I Wrote a Syrian Play?," as quoted in Gualtieri, 141.

19. Hajji, *Arabs in American Cinema*, 11–12.

20. McAlister, *Epic Encounters.*

21. Michalek, "Arab in American Cinema," 3.

22. *The Sheik* inspired other films like *Arabian Love* (1922), *The Tents of Allah* (1923), *The Arab* (1924), and *Fazil* (1928); invited satire from *The Shriek of Araby* (1923), *She's a Sheik* (1927), and the *Felix the Cat* cartoons (1926–28); and created momentum for films like *The Tales of a Thousand and One Nights* (1922) and *The Thief of Bagdad* (1924).

23. Ngai, *Impossible Subjects*, 28–29.

24. See Cainkar, *Homeland Insecurity*, 79.

25. Examples of films produced in the 1940s include *Arabian Nights* (1942), *Ali Baba and the Forty Thieves* (1944), *A Thousand and One Nights* (1945), and *Bagdad* (1949).

26. Refer to this book's filmography for more notable films produced in the 1950s and the 1960s.

27. Pennock, *Rise of the Arab American Left*, 5.

28. Yaqub, *Imperfect Strangers*, 7, 13.

29. See also *The Golden Voyage of Sinbad* (1974), *Sinbad and the Eye of the Tiger* (1977), *The Spy Who Loved Me* (1977), and *March or Die* (1977).

30. See also *The Black Stallion Returns* (1983), *The Sheltering Sky* (1990), *Ruby Cairo* (1992), *A Kid in Aladdin's Palace* (1997), and *The 13th Warrior* (1999).

31. "Sirhan Sirhan."

32. Yaqub, *Imperfect Strangers*, 5.

33. Yaqub, 92.

34. McAlister, "Cultural History," 440.

35. Boggs and Pollard, "Hollywood and the Spectacle of Terrorism," 337.

36. Yaqub, *Imperfect Strangers*, 93–96.

37. The Cabinet Committee to Combat Terrorism included the directors of the CIA and the FBI along with the secretaries of state, defense, justice, and transportation, and senior officials.

38. Yaqub, *Imperfect Strangers*, 98.

39. Adam Liptak and Michael D. Shear, "Trump's Travel Ban Is Upheld by Supreme Court," *New York Times*, June 26, 2018, https://www.nytimes.com/2018/06/26/us/politics/supreme-court-trump-travel-ban.html.

40. Said, "Arab Portrayed," 2, 6.

41. Stewart, "How Cannon Films."

42. Shohat, *Israeli Cinema*.

43. See *The Hitman* (1991), *Delta Force 3* (1991), *American Ninja 4* (1991), *American Samurai* (1992), *The Human Shield* (1991), and *Chain of Command* (1993). Also, other films gratuitously injected stereotypical images of and slurs about Arabs and Muslims in plots that had nothing to do with either group: e.g., *Firewalker* (1986), *Allan Quatermain and the Lost City of Gold* (1986), *Surrender* (1987), *Bloodsport* (1988), and *American Ninja 3* (1989).

44. See *Double Edge* (1992), *Deadly Heroes* (1993), *Operation Delta Force 5* (1999), *Delta Force One* (2000), *The Order* (2001), and *Air Marshall* (2003).

45. Shaheen, *Reel Bad Arabs*, 27.

46. Other comedies include *Best Defense* (1984), *In the Army Now* (1994), and *Ernest in the Army* (1998).

47. That this film features an African American actress should not come as a surprise as many Hollywood filmmakers, including Spike Lee, have empowered marginalized groups like African Americans at the cost of denigrating Arabs and Muslims.

48. Susan Akram, Steven Salaita, and Nadine Naber locate this fear within a US history of anti-Arab racism.

49. OAPEC members included Saudi Arabia, Algeria, Bahrain, Egypt, United Arab Emirates, Iraq, Kuwait, Libya, Qatar, and Syria.

50. Mearsheimer and Walt, *Israel Lobby*.

51. Yergin, *Prize*, 784.

52. Pfeiffer and Lisa, *Films of Sean Connery*, 160.

53. Shaheen, *Reel Bad Arabs*.

54. "Arab Students Sit in Here for a Hard Line on Israel," *New York Times*, March 11, 1968, https://www.nytimes.com/1968/03/11/archives/arab-students-sit-in-here-for-a-hard-line-on-israel.html.

55. The film received four Academy Awards and was praised for the originality of its screenplay.

56. Fitzpatrick, "Network," 36.

57. 9/11 generated a very important moment for the television industry to play a viable role in spurring such a sense of patriotism; see Spiegel, "Entertainment Wars."

58. Barthes, *Mythologies.*

59. Yaqub, *Imperfect Strangers*, 279.

60. Yaqub, 279.

61. Hight, "'It Isn't Always Shakespeare,'" 235–36.

62. The operation was initially reported as "Arab scam."

63. Yaqub, *Imperfect Strangers*, 277.

64. Naber, "Introduction," 35.

65. Nancy Anderson, "Believe That Fonda Believes," *Evening Outlook*, December 11, 1981.

66. Michalek, "Arab in American Cinema," 9.

67. Other comedies include *First Family* (1980), *Cannonball Run* (1981), *Things Are Tough All Over* (1982), *Cannonball Run 2* (1984), and *St. Elmo's Fire* (1985).

68. For a reading of Hollywood's history of associating Arabs with animals, see Mahdi, "Marked Off."

69. See Pennock, *Rise of Arab American Left*; Feldman, *Shadow Over Palestine.*

70. The National Association of Arab Americans was founded in 1972, the American-Arab Anti-Discrimination Committee in 1980, and the Arab American Institute in 1985.

71. In 1972 Arab American attorney Abdeen Jabara sued the FBI for monitoring his post-1967 pro-Palestinian activism. With support from the American Civil Liberties Union, the FBI disclosed surveillance by the National Security Agency.

72. Abraham, "Anti-Arab Racism," 180.

2. Images of Arab Americans in Egyptian Cinema

1. For works that deal with Egyptian cinema's subversion of Hollywood, see El-Bendary, "*Ugly American*" and El-Alaoui, *Arab, Arab-American, American.*

2. Bhabha, *Location of Culture*, 245–46.

3. Khatib, *Filming the Modern Middle East*, 1.

4. Shafik, *Popular Egyptian Cinema*, 87.

5. I draw from Fredric Jameson's conception of national allegory in "Third-World Literature in the Era of Multinational Capitalism" (65–88) to make sense of the nationalist coded imagery in the surveyed films. Doing so is by no means an endorsement of Jameson's generalized observation that "all . . . third-world texts" should "necessarily" be read as national allegories. For a critique of this observation, see Ahmad, "Jameson's Rhetoric of Otherness," 3–25.

6. Although scholars tend to embed the "American dream" concept in the earliest stages of US nation-state formation, Cyril Ghosh argues that it emerged in the twentieth century as a secularized linking of "work, virtue, and happiness" that early Puritans advanced in their efforts to establish a form of exceptionalism and identity for their colonies. See Ghosh, *Politics of the American Dream*, 7. For more about the concept, see Cullen, *American Dream*; Jillson, *Pursuing the American Dream*; Krickus, *Pursuing the American Dream;* and Samuel, *American Dream.*

7. *Amricany min Ṭanṭa* (An American from Tanta, 1954) was perhaps the earliest known Egyptian film to critique the American dream and imagine an alternative Egyptian dream.

8. See Max Friedman, *Rethinking Anti-Americanism.*

9. O'Conner, *Anti-Americanism*, chapter 1.

10. Hammond, *What the Arabs Think*, 41.

11. Qutb, "'The America I Have Seen,'" 9–10.

12. Abaza, "Shopping Malls," 97–122.

13. El-Sargany, "From Alexandria to New York," 55.

14. The film is an adaptation of Yūsuf al-Qa'īd's self-published novel *Yaḥduth fi Miṣr Alān* (Happening in Egypt Now, 1976). Salah Abouseif, the father of realism in Egyptian cinema, sought to adapt the novel at the time of its initial release, but the Egyptian censorship authority denied his request for filmmaking permission on the premise that the film would disrupt Egypt's newly formed strategic relations with the United States. Abouseif changed the title to *Yaḥduth fi Rīf Miṣr* (Happening in Egypt's Countryside), but the censorship authority rejected this too, saying the story offended Egypt's strategic relations with other countries. The novel was republished many times later and, despite pressures to delete the word "Now" from the title, al-Qa'īd retained it as a way to register his continuing critique of the US role in the Arab world. See Yūsuf al-Qa'īd, "Salah Abouseif bayn ma yaḥhduth fi Miṣr alan wa al-ḥarb fi bar Miṣr" (Salah Abouseif between Happening in Egypt Now and the War in Egypt [novels]), *Oman Daily*, February 9, 2017, https://www.omandaily.om/?p=437370.

15. Messiri, *Ibn al-Balad.*

16. The compound is based on President Sadat's dream of building a church, a synagogue, and a mosque in one site so that Christians, Jews, and Muslims could find a space for peaceful interaction.

17. Chahine and Massad, "Arts and Politics," 88.

18. Khatib, *Filming the Modern Middle East*, 86.

19. *Hallo Amrīka* dominated the box office during its release; see "Fi Īradāt al-Eid: Adel Imam Yatafawak 'la al-Jamī'," *Al-Jazeera*, January 12, 2000. http://www.al-jazirah.com/2000/20000112/at1.htm.

20. Shafik, *Popular Egyptian Cinema*, 79–82.

21. This is one of four films recounting the six-decade filmmaking career of the critically acclaimed director Youssef Chahine.

22. Gamal El-Ghitani describes New York as a city of foreigners in his novel *Madinat al-Ghoraba*.

23. The same screenwriter, Midhat el-Adl, wrote *Si'di fi el-Game'a el-Amrīkyya* and *Amrīka Shika Bika*. *Si'di fi el-Game'a el-Amrīkyya* has been credited for sparking Egyptians' interest in movies and producers' appetite for filmmaking given its unprecedented box-office revenue of more than E£25 million. See Mahmoud Hussein, "Limatha yu'ad film Si'di fi el-Game'a el-Amrīkyya noqtat taḥwoul bil-sinema?" (Why was Sa'eedi fil Gamaa el-Amrekeia a Turning Point in Cinema?), *Limaza*, December 28, 2018, https://www.limaza.com/صعيدي-في-الجامعة-الأمريكية/.

24. Notably, in real life, the public relations office of the institution denied Hamed's request to film on campus because of image concerns. See Isslam Nash'at, "Idārat al-Jama'a Mana't Taswīiruh wa al-Raqāba I'taraḍat 'ala al-Scenario: Si'di fi el-Game'a el-Amrīkyya, film yastathmir ta'aluk Henidi" (The University's Administration Rejected Filming and Censorship Authorities Objected to the Scenario: Si'di fi el-Game'a el-Amrīkyya, a Film That Invests in Henedi's Shining), *Al-Bayān*, May 17, 1998, http://www.albayan.ae/five-senses/1998-05-17-1.1009625.

25. Khalidi, *Sowing Crisis*, 164.

26. It is not clear, however, whether the films have had any success in this effort; since 2012, as many as 3,465,000 Egyptian migrants in the years 2013–14 have sought to escape the country's sociopolitical and economic unrest. See Social Affairs Sector of the Arab League, "Al-Taqrīr al-Iqlīmi lil-Hijra al-dwaliyya al-Arabbiyaa"; and Sabri, "Al-Shabāb al-Arabi wa Riḥlat al-baḥth 'an al-Jawaz al-Badīl" (documentary).

3. Challenging Hollywood's Terrorism Syndrome

1. Maira, *Missing*, 84.

2. Maalouf, *In the Name of Identity*, 30–38.

3. Rutherford, "Interview with Homi Bhabha," 207–21.

4. Volpp, "The Citizen and the Terrorist." Also see Beydoun, *American Islamophobia*.

5. This closely resembles Du Bois's "double consciousness," a conceptualization of the African American collective struggle to maintain a consciousness of authenticity in a white sociocultural system; see Du Bois, *Souls of Black Folk*.

6. Mitchell, "911," 571.

7. Butler, *Precarious Life*, xi.

8. Berlant, *Queen of America*, 27.

9. G. W. Bush, "A Nation Challenged: President Bush's Address on Terrorism before a Joint Meeting of Congress," *New York Times*, September 21, 2001.

10. Lewis, "Roots of Muslim Rage"; Huntington, "Clash of Civilizations?"

11. Personal narratives provided in Bayoumi, *How Does It Feel?*

12. Tirman, "Security the Progressive Way."

13. Cainkar, *Homeland Insecurity.*

14. PATRIOT is an acronym for Uniting and Strengthening America by Providing Appropriate Tools Required to Intercept and Obstruct Terrorism.

15. For more about the Arab and Muslim American post-9/11 civil rights crisis, see Detroit Arab American Study Team, *Citizenship and Crisis*; Hagopian, *Civil Rights in Peril*; and Elaasar, *Silent Victims.*

16. Richard Winton and Teresa Watanabe, "LAPD's Muslim Mapping Plan Killed," *Los Angeles Times*, November 15, 2007.

17. Amanda Reavy, "Islamic Group Finds Town's Emergency Drill Offensive," *State Journal-Register*, May 8, 2008, https://www.sj-r.com/x1820415277/Islamic-group-finds-town-s-emergency-drill-offensive.

18. Wilkins, *Home/Land/Security*, 1.

19. See Alsultany, "Selling American Diversity."

20. The White House, Office of the Press Secretary, "Remarks by the President at Islamic Society of Baltimore," February 3, 2016, https://www.whitehouse.gov/the-press-office/2016/02/03/remarks-president-islamic-society-baltimore.

21. For a reading of the racial violence on the day following September 11, 2001, see Muneer Ahmed, "Homeland Insecurities."

22. Ibish, *1998–2000 Report on Hate Crimes*; Ibish, *Report on Hate Crimes.*

23. See Civil Rights Reports by the Council of American-Islamic Relations, https://www.cair.com/resources/cair-civil-rights-reports/.

24. In *Good Muslim, Bad Muslim*, Mahmood Mamdani describes such involvement in Afghanistan as constituting the earliest transnational organizing model for subsequent terrorist organizations like al-Qaeda and ISIS.

25. Salaita, "Ethnic Identity," 154.

26. Perhaps the earliest film to utilize this strategy was *Wild Geese II* (1985), directed by Peter Hunt. In this British action-thriller film—based on Daniel Carney's novel *The Square Circle* (1982)—a Lebanese American protagonist John Haddad (Scott Glenn) wages war against Palestinian terrorists who claimed the lives of his own family.

27. Alsultany, *Arabs and Muslims*, 14.

28. Alsultany, 29.

29. Some of the post-9/11 films that humanize Arab Americans, albeit briefly, and do not present them through the lens of terrorism include *Kitchen* (2001), *Enough* (2002), *The Final Cut* (2004), and *A Day without a Mexican* (2004).

30. For a broader examination of Hollywood's engagement with terrorism, see Dodds, "Screening Terror."

31. Johsi, "Racialization of Hinduism," 212.

32. In the five days following 9/11, 125 bias incidents were directed against Sikh Americans. In 2012 a white supremacist, Wade Page, stormed the Sikh temple in Oak Creek, Wisconsin, and opened fire, killing six and injuring four individuals. See Falcone, "Seeking Recognition"; Steven Yaccino, Michael Schwirtz, and Marc Santora, "Gunman Kills 6 at a Sikh Temple Near Milwaukee," *New York Times*, August 5, 2012, http://www.nytimes.com/2012/08/06/us/shooting-reported-at-temple-in-wisconsin.html.

33. Arjana, *Muslims in Western Imagination*, 172–77.

34. Arjana, 177. For more about post-9/11 works, see Riegler, "'Mirroring Terror.'"

35. "Traitor—Jeffrey Nachmanoff Interview."

36. Bayoumi, "The Race Is On."

37. Bayoumi, "The Race Is On."

38. Goldberg, "Islam 'Hijacked' by Terror."

39. Mousalli, *Images of Islam*; Massad, *Islam in Liberalism*.

40. Fischer, "Exclusive Interview."

41. IMDb, http://www.imdb.com/title/tt0988047/business.

42. Michael Phillips, "This 'Traitor' Is Intriguing," *Chicago Tribune*, August 27, 2008, http://articles.latimes.com/2008/aug/27/entertainment/et-traitor27.

43. "Traitor—Jeffrey Nachmanoff Interview."

44. Peter Bradshaw, "Film Review: *Traitor*," *Guardian*, March 26, 2009, http://www.theguardian.com/film/2009/mar/26/traitor-film-review.

45. tedsltg, "Political Anti-American Agenda."

46. joneswil, "Christians Are Terrorists Just Like Muslims."

47. khaldoun_rayyan, "Review from an Arab Muslim."

48. Federal Bureau of Investigation, "Terrorism 2002–2005."

49. This is exhibited in the lack of media coverage of terrorist attacks against Muslim Americans; see the Chapel Hill case and the Islamberg case. In these cases, Muslim Americans fell victims to cold-blooded attacks that did not receive the media coverage that would often be allocated to incidents in which the perpetrators are Muslims.

50. Stratton, "At the Movies: *Traitor*."

51. Guy Pearce, quoted in Powers, "A Look at Traitor."

52. Puar and Rai, "Monster, Terrorist, Fag," 117–48.

53. Huntington, "Clash of Civilizations?"

54. Parsley, *Silent No More*.

55. Corn, "McCain's Pastor Problem."

56. To learn about the US racial structure, read Omi and Winant, *Racial Formation*.

57. Puar and Rai, "Monster, Terrorist, Fag."

58. Petin, *"I'm Not an American,"* 75.

59. Asad, *On Suicide Bombing.*

60. Curtis, "Islamism."

61. Petin, *"I'm Not an American,"* 72.

62. Bhabha, *Location of Culture*, 50–51.

63. Douglas, "Don Cheadle Turns Traitor."

64. A. O. Scott, "In a World of Extremists, Shades of Gray Add Ambiguity," *New York Times*, August 26, 2008, http://www.nytimes.com/2008/08/27/movies/27trai .html.

65. Qur'an, 5:32.

4. Disrupting Egyptian Depictions of Arab Americans

1. The company supported *The Yacoubian Building* (2006) along with six other popular films through 2009.

2. Mahmoud Goma'a, "Akthar al-Aflām bi-Tareekh al-Sinima al-Masriyya Taklufa Yafshal" (The Most Expensive Film in Egyptian Cinema's History Loses), *Al-Jazeera*, June 27, 2008, https://www.aljazeera.net/news/cultureandart/2008/6/27 /أكثر-الأفلام-بتاريخ-السينما-المصرية.

3. Maha Hussein, "El-Shinawi: Sinario 'Laylat el-Baby Doll' Ḍa'īf wa Khali min al-mut'ah" (El-Shinawi: Laylat el-Baby Doll's Scenario Is Weak and Not Entertaining), *al-Sharq al-Awsat*, June 6, 2008, http://archive.aawsat.com/details.asp?section =25&article=473749&issueno=10783.

4. Naber, "Imperial Whiteness," 1108.

5. Appadurai, *Modernity at Large*, 4.

6. Appadurai, 21–22.

7. Maira, *Missing*, 10.

8. Bhabha, *Location of Culture*, 2.

9. Raz-Krakotzkin, "Zionist Return to the West," 175.

10. Levy, "Historicizing the Concept," 454.

11. Shohat, *Taboo Memories*, 201–32.

12. For more about the Arab-Jew image in Egyptian cinema, read al-Harmarnah, "Discovering the Other." A reading of the Arab-Israeli conflict in Palestinian and Israeli filmmaking is available in Stein and Swedenburg, *Palestine, Israel.*

13. Shohat, *Taboo Memories*, 335.

14. Shohat, "Reflections by an Arab Jew."

15. See Saliba, "On Rachel Corrie." Corrie was in Gaza as a member of the International Solidarity Movement, which defends Palestinian rights.

16. Goodman, "My Name Is Rachel Corrie."

17. Israel has received $130 billion from the United States in financial aid since 1949 in addition to a recent pledge of $3 billion on top of military and political aid.

For a brief summary of Israeli influence on the US Congress, see Giraldi, "Should AIPAC Register?"

18. The song is by the Egyptian popular singer Sha'bān Abd el-Raḥim, who is known for his simple lyrics and performance style. For more about the impact of Abd el-Raḥim's popular music, see Gordon, "Singing the Pulse," 73–88.

19. This reductive reading obscures the fact that the Israeli lobby is not a singular entity but rather a cluster of individuals and organizations. Advocacy organizations, special interest groups, think tanks, neoconservatives, Christian Zionists, and Jewish Zionists form a coalition, which—though not unified under a central leadership—tends to exert influence across the US political spectrum and cultural sphere. The Zionist Organization of America, the Conference of Presidents of Major American Jewish Organizations, the American Israel Public Affairs Committee, the Washington Institute for Near East Policy, the Anti-Defamation League, the Jewish Institute for National Security Affairs, and the Middle East Forum are but some of the organizations included in this coalition. See Mearsheimer and Walt, *Israeli Lobby*, 112.

20. The CIA's manuals were legalized through the infamous "Bybee Lee's memo" of the US Department of Justice that redefined torture in violation of the Geneva Convention and the United Nations' Act of Torture.

21. For works that examine the deployment of sexuality in the imperial and anticolonial discourses see McClintock, *Imperial Leather*; Puar, *Terrorist Assemblages*; and Massad, *Desiring Arabs*.

22. The premise of the theory is that economic prosperity is the desired ultimate end toward which a nation-state progresses, primarily through its elite, and that multinational corporations are essential to this progression; hence, conflicts or tensions would jeopardize the elite's stability; Thomas Friedman, *Lexus*.

23. These are not Vilnai's exact words. His statement is as follows: "As the rocket fire grows, and the range increases—and they haven't yet said the last word on this—they are bringing upon themselves [Palestinians] a greater Shoah [Hebrew word for Holocaust] because we will use all our strength in every way we deem appropriate, whether in air strikes or on the ground"; see Donald Macintyre, "Israel's Warning: Rocket Fire from Gaza Will Result in a Palestinian 'Holocaust,'" *Independent*, March 1, 2008, http://www.independent.co.uk/news/world/middle-east/israels-warning-rocket-fire-from-gaza-will-result-in-a-palestinian-holocaust-790004.html.

24. For a reading of debates around US foreign policy between imperial internationalism and liberal internationalism, refer to Ikenberry et al., *Crisis of American Foreign Policy*.

25. Mohamed, *Who Defines Me*, 176.

26. Naber, "Imperial Whiteness," 1108.

27. In *The Anarchy of Empire*, Amy Kaplan dates American imperialism back to the nineteenth century. For a reading of US imperialist presence in the Middle East,

read Bacevich, *American Empire*; Khalidi, *Resurrecting Empire*; and Gerges, *Obama and the Middle East.*

28. Maira, *Missing*, 101.

5. Renarrating the American Dream in Arab American Films

1. Unfortunately, Akkad passed away in 2005 without completing a third film, his much-anticipated epic *Saladin*, which narrates the Crusades' religious wars from a Muslim perspective. Akkad was killed in al-Qaeda-planned triple bombings in Jordan that also took the life of his daughter. See Firas Al-Atraqchi, "Halloween Producer's Epic Plan," *Al-Jazeera*, September 2, 2007, http://www.aljazeera.com/news/americas/2007/08/2008525173723311875.html.

2. Abu-Zannad, "Moustapha Akkad: Biography."

3. A controversy that surrounded *The Message* did not emanate from Hollywood but from Muslim governments. The script, though initially approved by Al-Azhar in Egypt and the Supreme Islamic Shiite Council in Lebanon, was met with complete rejection from the Muslim World League in Saudi Arabia. After pressure from Saudi Arabia, Kuwait and Morocco withdrew their support for the film, which eventually gained full support from the Libyan leader Muammar al-Qaddafi. The film, which has become a celebrated classic work about Islam, was initially banned in the Muslim world and met screening challenges in US movie theaters due to threats by a Hanafi black-nationalist Muslim group that kidnapped twenty-two hostages and threatened to burn theaters that screened the film. See the documentary *From Aleppo to Hollywood* (2007).

4. Examples of such festivals include the Arab American Film Festival (Arab American National Museum), the Arab Film Festival (California and Minnesota), the Palestine Film Festivals (Boston, Houston, and Chicago), the New York Arab and South Asian Festival, and the Middle Eastern Film Festival (New York City), among others.

5. Naficy, *An Accented Cinema*, 4–9.

6. Najjar, *Arab American Drama*, 192–93.

7. See Bunche Center for African American Studies, Hollywood Diversity Reports for 2014, 2015, and 2016.

8. Fienberg, "Why It Matters." Also see Nance, *How the Arabian Nights.*

9. Melena Ryzik, "Can Television Be Fair to Muslims?" *New York Times*, November 30, 2016, https://www.nytimes.com/2016/11/30/arts/television/can-television-be-fair-to-muslims.html.

10. See Wong, *On Visual Media Racism.*

11. I am using Gerbner and Gross's term, "Living with Television," 182.

12. Shohat, *Israeli Cinema*, 257.

13. For an account about modes of racialization in Hollywood, see Alsultany, *Arabs and Muslims in the Media.*

14. Shaheen, *Reel Bad Arabs*, 188.

15. Michael, "Beyond US and Them," 709.

16. Riz Ahmed, "Typecast as a Terrorist," *Guardian*, September 15, 2016, https://www.theguardian.com/world/2016/sep/15/riz-ahmed-typecast-as-a-terrorist.

17. Eadeh, "Rami Malek."

18. See "Rami Malek Emmys 2016 Full Backstage Speech," streamed live on September 18, 2016, YouTube video, 7:15, https://www.youtube.com/watch?v=SzzB9d1SPFA.

19. Kimberly Yam, "Disney Admits to Darkening White Actors' Skin for 'Aladdin,' Sparking Outrage," *HuffPost*, January 10, 2018, https://www.huffpost.com/entry/disney-aladdin-skin-darkening_n_5a54e36fe4b003133eccb275; Alsultany, "How the New 'Aladdin.'"

20. See Bunche Center for African American Studies, Hollywood Diversity Reports for 2014, 2015, and 2016.

21. As quoted in Ryzik, "Can Television Be Fair to Muslims?"; Dabis is a contributing producer to some episodes in two popular television series, *Empire* (2015–present) and *Quantico* (2015–18).

22. Cardillo and Potter, *Casting Calls.*

23. Sanchez, *Out in the Open.*

24. Cardillo and Potter, *Casting Calls.*

25. Ashraf Khalil, "But Can You Play a Terrorist?" *Los Angeles Times*, October 4, 2007, http://articles.latimes.com/2007/oct/04/entertainment/et-arabactors4.

26. Najjar, *Arab American Drama*, 192–93.

27. "The Citizen: A 9/11 Story by Sam Kadi and Khaled Nabawy," streamed live on October 31, 2012, YouTube video, 6:10, https://www.youtube.com/watch?v=UzRB9A7Qh_E.

28. Ahmed Ahmed, "Riz Khan's One on One," *Al-Jazeera English*, June 28, 2011, http://www.aljazeera.com/programmes/oneonone/2011/06/201162183836517768.html.

29. Dabashi, *Post-Orientalism.*

30. Andre Degas's *Kitchen* (2001) was probably the earliest post-9/11 Arab American television film.

31. Clavin, "A Movie on Muslims In America."

32. Clavin, "A Movie on Muslims In America."

33. Jeffrey Fleishman, "Director Shines a Light on Arabs' Plight in America," *Los Angeles Times*, December 23, 2007, http://articles.latimes.com/2007/dec/23/entertainment/ca-american23.

34. Tony Shalhoub, "Interview at New York Arab American and South Asian Festival," streamed live on October 11, 2012, YouTube video, 8:18, https://www.youtube.com/watch?v=7YuKXWuK3cI.

35. Following this recognition, Badreya played a lead role in the subsequent Swiss independent film *Cargo* (2009).

36. In a parallel between fiction and reality, some of the same heated responses were voiced by those who attended the film's screening at the Egyptian Film Festival in 2007. Reflecting on the news conference following the screening, director Issawi recalled, "It was hell. I was getting attacked by everybody. 'How dare you try to make normalization with Israel.' And this was coming from journalists and critics." See Hanania, "Film Review."

37. Hanania, "Film Review."

38. Riz Ahmed, "Typecast as a Terrorist."

39. Sanchez, *Out in the Open.*

40. "FIPRESCI" stands for the Fédération Internationale de la Presse Cinématographique International Federation of Film Critics.

41. June Stein, "Cherien Dabis."

42. June Stein, "Cherien Dabis."

43. June Stein, "Cherien Dabis."

44. Gertz and Khleifi, *Palestinian Cinema*, 8.

45. Archer, "Coming to *Amreeka*."

46. June Stein, "Cherien Dabis."

47. For a detailed account of this double-layeredness, refer to Armstrong's reading of Said's *Out of Place: A Memoire* in "Being 'Out of Place,'" 97–121.

48. Said, *Orientalism*, 27.

49. Esposito and Mogahed, *Who Speaks for Islam?*; Herrera and Bayat, *Being Young and Muslim.*

50. Khan, *American Muslims*. Examples of works exploring the Muslim American community include Haddad and Esposito, *Muslims on the Americanization Path?*; Haddad, *Muslims in the West*; Barrett, *American Islam*; Bukhari et al., *Muslims' Place*; Leonard, *Muslims in the United States*; Wormser, *American Islam*; and Hasan, *American Muslims.*

51. See Haddad, *Not Quite American?*; Geaves et al., *Islam and the West Post 9/11*; Abdo, *Mecca and Main Street*; Wolfe, *Taking Back Islam*; Ernst, *Islamophobia in America*; Howell, *Old Islam in Detroit*, and Bakalian and Bozorgmehr, *Backlash 9/11.*

52. Walmart sold 116,000 flags on September 11, 2001. Total flag sales in 2001 reached $51.7 million. The flag emerged as an identity marker and was displayed everywhere—on stickers, websites, magnets, mouse pads, lapel pins, clothing articles, TV images, and car decals; see Heller, "Introduction: Consuming 9/11," 16–19.

53. "Ethnic Stereotypes in Casting by Khaled Nabawy."

54. The film was screened at the Hollywood Film Festival, the Boston Film Festival, the International Family Film Festival, Michigan's Uptown Film Festival, California's Arab Film Festival, the Cinequest Film Festival (California), the Gotham Screen International Film Festival (New York), the Tri-Media Film Festival (Colorado), and the Abu Dhabi Film Festival.

55. Romani, "Review."

56. There were no reported incidents of harassment against Arabs or Muslims that took place at the same time as the towers' collapse. Only when the attackers were revealed to be al-Qaeda did public violence occur.

57. See chapter 3 for more discussion of this process.

58. "Ethnic Stereotypes in Casting."

59. "Ethnic Stereotypes in Casting."

60. E. Nina Rothe, "The Citizen: Four Men, a Movie and the American Dream," *Huffington Post*, October 19, 2012, http://www.huffingtonpost.com/e-nina-rothe/the-citizen-four-men_b_1984701.html.

61. "The Citizen: A 9/11 Story by Sam Kadi and Khaled Nabawy."

62. Romani, "Review."

63. Robinson, "The Citizen."

64. Scheck, "The Citizen."

65. Najjar, *Arab American Drama*, 188.

Epilogue

1. Prashad, *Karma of Brown Folk*, 111–12.

2. Ryzik, "Can Television Be Fair to Muslims?"

3. For works about Arab American gender, see Abdulhadi, Alsultany, and Naber, *Arab and Arab American Feminisms*.

4. Neil Genzlinger, "Love among the Gas Pumps," *New York Times*, November 21, 2013, http://www.nytimes.com/2013/11/22/movies/detroit-unleaded-a-low-octane-comedy.html.

5. Simon, "Film Review."

6. Lapin, "Detroit Unleaded."

7. Laurier, "Detroit Unleaded."

8. Danny Peary, "Rola Nashef on Her Untraditional 'Detroit Unleaded,'" *Sag Harbor Express*, November 20, 2013, http://sagharborexpress.com/rola-nashef-on-her-untraditional-detroit-unleaded.

9. Peary, "Rola Nashef."

10. Amerlang, "Rola Nashef."

11. Peary, "Rola Nashef."

12. See the synopsis in Cherien Dabis's website, http://cheriendabis.me/may-in-the-summer.

13. Stephanie Merry, "'May in the Summer' Movie Review: Marriage, Symbolism and a Missed Opportunity," *Washington Post*, August 28, 2014, https://www.washingtonpost.com/goingoutguide/movies/may-in-the-summer-movie-review-marriage-symbolism-and-a-missed-opportunity/2014/08/27/fe15c4c0-2a10-11e4-8593-da634b334390_story.html.

14. MPAC, https://www.mpac.org/; MOST, http://www.mostresource.org/.

15. Harbin, "Hollywood Reworks Muslim Stereotypes."

16. In 2003 Dean Obeidallah and Maysoon Zayid founded the New York Arab-American Comedy Festival. Arab American comedian Amer Zahr premiered the now yearly 1001 Laughs Dearborn Comedy Festival in Dearborn in 2013. The Muslim Funny Fest has been hosting its annual ritual of gathering Muslim comedians since 2015. And comedic productions such as the *Arab-American Comedy Tour* (2006), *Axis of Evil Comedy Tour* (2008), *Just Like Us* (2010), and *Allah Made Me Funny* (2008), along with the documentary *The Muslims Are Coming* (2013), speak to an audience eager to see and hear Arab and Muslim Americans' own critical and comedic perspectives.

17. See Najjar, *Arab American Drama*.

18. Three surveys (Steven Salaita's *Modern Arab American Fiction*, Waïl Hassan's *Immigrant Narratives*, and Carol Fadda-Conrey's *Contemporary Arab-American Literature*), and four anthologies (Gregory Orfalea's and Sharif Elmusa's *Grape Leaves*, Joanna Kadi's *Food for Our Grandmothers*, Munir Akash's *Post-Gibran*, and Susan Atefat-Peckham's *Talking through the Door*) capture this tradition. Chief among post-9/11 writers are Mohja Kahf, Joseph Geha, Rabih Alameddine, Diana Abu-Jaber, Frances Khirallah Noble, Randa Jarrar, Evelyn Shakir, Susan Muaddi Darraj, Laila Halaby, and Laila Lalami.

Bibliography

Abaza, Mona. "Shopping Malls, Consumer Culture and the Reshaping of Public Space in Egypt." *Theory, Culture & Society* 18, no. 5 (2001): 97–122.

Abd el-Raḥim, Sha'bān. "Ana Bakrah Israel." In *ma Te'darsh* (cassette) by Sha'bān Abd el-Raḥim and Mustafa Sha'bān. Cairo: al-Wādi, 2000.

———. "Ya 'Aam 'Arabi Isḥa." In *illi Khaif Yerūḥ—Ya 'Aam 'Arabi* (cassette) by Sha'bān Abd el-Raḥim. Cairo: Dream 4, 2004.

Abdo, Geneive. *Mecca and Main Street: Muslim Life after 9/11*. New York: Oxford Univ. Press, 2006.

Abdulhadi, Rabab, Evelyn Alsultany, and Nadine Naber, eds. *Arab and Arab American Feminisms: Gender, Violence, and Belonging*. Syracuse: Syracuse Univ. Press, 2011.

Aboulnaga, Shereen. *Al-Mouthaqaf al-Intiqali: Min al-Istibdād ila al-Tamarud*. Cairo: Rawafid, 2014.

Abraham, Nabeel. "Anti-Arab Racism and Violence in the United States." In *The Development of Arab-American Identity*, edited by Ernest McCarus, 155–209. Ann Arbor: Univ. of Michigan Press, 1994.

Abraham, Nabeel, and Andrew Shryock, eds. *Arab Detroit: From Margin to Mainstream*. Detroit: Wayne State Univ. Press, 2000.

Abu-Lughod, Lila. "Finding a Place for Islam: Egyptian Television Serials and the National Interest." *Public Culture* 5, no. 3 (Spring 1993): 493–513.

———. *Veiled Sentiment: Honor and Poetry in a Bedouin Society*. Berkeley: Univ. of California Press, 1986.

Abu-Rabi', Ibrahim M. *Contemporary Arab Thought: Studies in Post-1967 Arab Intellectual History*. London: Pluto Press, 2004.

Abu-Zannad, Ahmad. "Moustapha Akkad: Biography." Internet Movie Database (IMDb), based on 1976 interview. http://www.imdb.com/name/nm0002160/.

Ahmad, Aijaz. "Jameson's Rhetoric of Otherness and the 'National Allegory.'" *Social Text* 17 (Autumn 1987): 3–25.

Ahmed, Jamal Mohammed. *The Intellectual Origins of Egyptian Nationalism.* London: Oxford Univ. Press, 1960.

Ahmed, Muneer. "Homeland Insecurities: Racial Violence the Day after September 11." *Social Text* 20, no. 3 (Fall 2002): 101–15.

Ajami, Fouad. *The Dream Palace of the Arabs: A Generation's Odyssey.* New York: Vintage Books, 1998.

Akash, Munir, ed. *Post Gibran: Anthology of New Arab American Writing.* Syracuse: Syracuse Univ. Press, 2000.

Akram, Susan M. "The Aftermath of September 11, 2001: The Targeting of Arabs and Muslims in America." *Arab Studies Quarterly* 24, nos. 2–3 (Spring/Summer 2002): 61–118.

Alangari, Haifa. *The Struggle for Power in Arabia: Ibn Saud, Hussein and Great Britain, 1914–1924.* Reading, UK: Ithaca Press, 1998.

Alaoui, Lalla Khadija Fritsch el-. *Arab, Arab-American, American: Hegemonic and Contrapuntal Representations.* PhD diss., Technischen Universität Dresden, 2005.

Allagui, Ilhem, and Abeer Najjar. "Framing Political Islam in Popular Egyptian Cinema." *Middle East Journal of Culture and Communication* 4, no. 2 (2011): 203–24.

Allison, Robert. *The Crescent Obscured: The United States and the Muslim World, 1776–1815.* New York: Oxford Univ. Press, 1995.

Allyn, Bobby. "Congresswomen Denounce Trump Tweets Telling Them To 'Go Back' To Their Home Countries." NPR, July 14, 2019. https://www.npr.org/2019/07/14/741630889/congresswomen-denounce-trump-tweets-telling-them-to-go-back-to-their-home-countr.

Alsultany, Evelyn. *Arabs and Muslims in the Media: Race and Representation after 9/11.* New York: NYU Press, 2012.

———. "How the New 'Aladdin' Stacks Up Against a Century of Hollywood Stereotyping." The Conversation, May 26, 2019. https://theconversation.com/how-the-new-aladdin-stacks-up-against-a-century-of-hollywood-stereotyping-115608.

———. "Selling American Diversity and Muslim American Identity through Nonprofit Advertising Post-9/11." *American Quarterly* 59, no. 3 (September 2007): 593–622.

Alsultany, Evelyn, and Ella Shohat, eds. *Between the Middle East and the Americas: The Cultural Politics of Diaspora*. Ann Arbor: Univ. of Michigan Press, 2013.

Althusser, Louis. "Ideology and the Ideological State Apparatuses (Notes towards an Investigation)." In *Lenin and Philosophy and Other Essays*, 85–126. New York: Monthly Review Press, 2001.

Amerlang, Cosima. "Rola Nashef, Detroit Unleaded," *Screen Daily*, September 11, 2012. http://m.screendaily.com/5046450.article.

Anderson, Benedict. *Imagined Communities: Reflections on the Origin and Spread of Nationalism*. London: Verso, 2006.

Appadurai, Arjun. *Modernity at Large: Cultural Dimensions of Globalization*. Minneapolis: Univ. of Minnesota Press, 1996.

Arasoughly, Alia, ed. *Screens of Life: Critical Film Writing from the Arab World*. Quebec: World Heritage, 1996.

Archer, Michael. "Coming to *Amreeka*: Michael Archer interviews Cherien Dabis." *Guernica*, September 15, 2009. https://www.guernicamag.com/interviews/cherien_dabis.

Arjana, Sophia Rose. *Muslims in the Western Imagination*. Oxford: Oxford Univ. Press, 2015.

Armbrust, Walter. "Islamists in Egyptian Cinema." *American Anthropologist* 104, no. 3 (September 2002): 922–31.

———. *Mass Culture and Modernism in Egypt*. Cambridge: Cambridge Univ. Press, 1996.

———, ed. *Mass Mediations: New Approaches to Popular Culture in the Middle East and Beyond*. Berkeley: Univ. of California Press, 2000.

———. "Political Film in Egypt." In *Film in the Middle East and North Africa: Creative Dissidence*, edited by Josef Gugler, 228–51. Austin: Univ. of Texas Press, 2011.

Armstrong, Paul B. "Being 'Out of Place': Edward W. Said and the Contradictions of Cultural Differences." *Modern Language Quarterly* 64, no. 1 (March 2003) 97–121.

Asad, Talal. *On Suicide Bombing*. New York: Columbia Univ. Press, 2007.

Aswany, Alaa al-. *Chicago: A Novel*. New York: Harper Perennial, 2009.

Atefat-Peckham, Susan, ed. *Talking through the Door: An Anthology of Contemporary Middle Eastern American Writing*. Syracuse: Syracuse Univ. Press, 2014.

Ayubi, Naziy. "The Egyptian 'Brain Drain': A Multidimensional Problem." *International Journal of Middle East Studies* 15, no. 4 (November 1983): 431–50.

Bacevich, Andrew J. *American Empire: The Realities and Consequences of US Diplomacy*. Cambridge, MA: Harvard Univ. Press, 2002.

Bakalian, Anny, and Mehdi Bozorgmehr. *Backlash 9/11: Middle Eastern and Muslim Americans Respond*. Berkeley: Univ. of California Press, 2009.

Baker, Raymond. "Combative Cultural Politics: Film Art and Political Spaces in Egypt." *Alif: Journal of Comparative Poetics* 15 (1995): 6–38.

Barrett, Paul M. *American Islam: The Struggle for the Soul of a Religion*. New York: Farrar, Straus and Giroux, 2007.

Barthes, Roland. *Mythologies*. New York: Hill and Wang, 1972.

Bauböck, Rainer. *Transnational Citizenship: Membership and Rights in International Migration*. Cheltenham, UK: Edward Elgar, 1994.

Bawardi, Hani J. *The Making of Arab Americans: From Syrian Nationalism to US Citizenship*. Austin: Univ. of Texas Press, 2014.

Bayoumi, Moustafa. *How Does It Feel to Be a Problem? Being Young and Arab in America*. New York: Penguin, 2008.

———. "The Race Is On: Muslims and Arabs in the American Imagination." *Middle East Research and Information Project*, March 3, 2010. https://merip.org/2010/03/the-race-is-on/.

———. "Racing Religion." *CR: The New Centennial Review* 6, no. 2 (Fall 2006): 267–93.

Beinin, Joel. "Neoliberal Structural Adjustment, Political Demobilization and New Authoritarianism in Egypt." In *The Arab State and Neo-Liberal Globalization: The Restructuring of State Power in the Middle East*, edited by Laura Guazzone and Daniela Pioppi, 19–46. Reading, UK: Ithaca Press, 2009.

Bendary, Mohamed el-. *The "Ugly American" in the Arab Mind: Why Do Arabs Resent America?* Washington, DC: Potomac Books, 2011.

Berlant, Lauren. *The Queen of America Goes to Washington City: Essays on Sex and Citizenship*. Durham, NC: Duke Univ. Press, 1997.

Berman, Jacob. *American Arabesque: Arabs, Islam, and the 19th-Century Imaginary*. New York: NYU Press, 2012.

Bernstein, Matthew, and Gaylyn Studlar, eds. *Visions of the East: Orientalism in Film*. New Brunswick, NJ: Rutgers Univ. Press, 1997.

Beydoun, Khaled A. *American Islamophobia: Understanding the Roots and Rise of Fear.* Oakland: Univ. of California Press, 2018.

Bhabha, Homi. *The Location of Culture.* London: Routledge Classics, 2004.

Blatty, William Peter. *The Exorcist: A Novel.* New York: Harper & Row, 1971.

Boggs, Carl, and Tom Pollard. "Hollywood and the Spectacle of Terrorism." *New Political Science* 28, no. 3 (2006): 335–51.

Boosahda, Elizabeth. *Arab-American Faces and Voices: The Origins of an Immigrant Community.* Austin: Univ. of Texas Press, 2003.

Bukhari, Zahid H., Sulayman S. Nyang, Mumtaz Ahmad, and John L. Esposito, eds. *Muslim's Place in the American Public Square: Hope, Fears, and Aspirations.* Walnut Creek, CA: Altamira, 2004.

Bunche Center for African American Studies. *2014 Hollywood Diversity Report: Making Sense of the Disconnect.* https://bunchecenter.pre.ss.ucla.edu/wp-content/uploads/sites/97/2014/02/2014-Hollywood-Diversity-Report-2-12-14.pdf.

Bunche Center for African American Studies. *2015 Hollywood Diversity Report: Flipping the Script.* https://bunchecenter.pre.ss.ucla.edu/wp-content/uploads/sites/97/2015/02/2015-Hollywood-Diversity-Report-2-25-15.pdf.

Bunche Center for African American Studies. *2016 Hollywood Diversity Report: Busine$$ as Usual?* https://bunchecenter.pre.ss.ucla.edu/wp-content/uploads/sites/97/2016/02/2016-Hollywood-Diversity-Report-2-25-16.pdf.

Butler, Judith. *Precarious Life: The Powers of Mourning and Violence.* London: Verso, 2004.

Cainkar, Louise A. *Homeland Insecurity: The Arab American and Muslim American Experience after 9/11.* New York: Russell Sage, 2009.

Calvert, John. *Sayyid Qutb and the Origins of Radical Islamism.* New York: Columbia Univ. Press, 2010.

Cardillo, Lauren F., and Deborah Potter. *Casting Calls.* Princeton, NJ: Films for the Humanities & Sciences, 2004.

Casty, Alan. *Communism in Hollywood: The Moral Paradoxes of Testimony, Silence, and Betrayal.* Lanham, MD: Scarecrow Press, 2009.

Chahine, Youssef, and Joseph Massad. "Arts and Politics in the Cinema of Youssef Chahine." *Journal of Palestine Studies* 28, no. 2 (Winter 1999): 77–93.

Chen, Tina Mai, and David S. Churchill, eds. *Film, History and Cultural Citizenship: Sites of Production*. New York: Routledge, 2007.

Choueiri, Youssef M. *Arab Nationalism: A History; Nation and State in the Arab World*. Oxford: Blackwell, 2000.

"Citizen, The: A 9/11 Story by Sam Kadi and Khaled Nabawy." Streamed live on October 31, 2012. YouTube video, 6:10. https://www.youtube.com/watch?v=UzRB9A7Qh_E.

Clavin, Tom. "A Movie on Muslims in America." Hamptons.com, posted February 14, 2008. http://www.hamptons.com/The-Arts/On-The-Screen/2952/A-Movie-On-Muslims-In-America.html.

Cobb, Amanda J. "This Is What It Means to Say Smoke Signals: Native American Cultural Sovereignty." In *Hollywood's Indian: The Portrayal of the Native American in Film*, edited by Peter C. Rollins and John E. O'Connor, 206–28. Lexington: Univ. Press of Kentucky, 1998.

———. "Understanding Tribal Sovereignty: Definitions, Conceptualizations, and Interpretations." *American Studies* 46, nos. 3–4 (Fall/Winter 2005): 115–32.

Cook, Steven A. *The Struggle for Egypt: From Nasser to Tahrir Square*. Oxford: Oxford Univ. Press, 2012.

Corn, David. "McCain's Pastor Problem: The Video." *Mother Jones*, May 8, 2008. http://www.motherjones.com/politics/2008/05/mccains-pastor-problem-video.

Coury, Ralph M. "Who 'Invented' Egyptian Arab Nationalism? Part I." *International Journal of Middle East Studies* 14, no. 3 (August 1982): 249–81.

Culhane, Hind Rassam. *East/West, an Ambiguous State of Being: The Construction and Representation of Egyptian Cultural Identity in Egyptian Film*. New York: Peter Lang, 1995.

Cullen, Jim. *The American Dream: A Short History of an Idea That Shaped a Nation*. Oxford: Oxford Univ. Press, 2003.

Curtis, Edward E. "Islamism and Its African American Muslim Critics: Black Muslims in the Era of the Arab Cold War." *American Quarterly* 59, no. 3 (September 2007): 683–709.

Dabashi, Hamid. *Post-Orientalism: Knowledge and Power in Time of Terror*. Somerset, NJ: Transaction, 2008.

Davis, John. *The Landscape of Belief: Encountering the Holy Land in Nineteenth-Century American Art and Culture*. Princeton, NJ: Princeton Univ. Press, 1996.

Dawisha, Adeed. *Arab Nationalism in the Twentieth Century: From Triumph to Despair.* Princeton, NJ: Princeton Univ. Press, 2003.

Dawn, C. Ernest. *From Ottomanism to Arabism: Essays on the Origins of Arab Nationalism.* Urbana: Univ. of Illinois Press, 1973.

Denzin, Norman. *Reading Race: Hollywood and the Cinema of Racial Violence.* London: Sage, 2002.

Detroit Arab American Study Team. *Citizenship and Crisis: Arab Detroit after 9/11.* New York: Russell Sage Foundation, 2009.

Dodds, Klaus. "Screening Terror: Hollywood, the United States and the Construction of Danger." *Critical Studies of Terrorism* 1, no. 2 (2008): 227–43.

Douglas, Edward. "Don Cheadle Turns Traitor." ComingSoon.net, August 27, 2008. http://www.comingsoon.net/movies/features/48160-don-cheadle-turns-traitor.

Du Bois, W. E. B. *The Souls of Black Folk.* New York: Vintage Books, 1990.

Eadeh, Nisreen. "Rami Malek: First Arab American to Win an Emmy for Best Actor in a Drama Series." Arab America, posted on September 21, 2016. http://www.arabamerica.com/rami-malek-first-arab-american-win-emmy.

Edwards, Brian T., and Dilip Parameshwar Gaonkar, eds. *Globalizing American Studies.* Chicago: Univ. of Chicago Press, 2010.

Elaasar, Aladdin. *Silent Victims: The Plight of Arab & Muslim Americans in Post-9/11 America.* Bloomington, IN: AuthorHouse, 2004.

Ellison, James. *The American Captive, or Siege of Tripoli.* Boston: Joshua Belcher, 1812.

Elnaccash, Ataa. "Egyptian Cinema: A Historical Outline." *African Arts* 2, no. 1 (Autumn 1968): 52–55.

Enany, Rasheed el-. *Arab Representations of the Occident: East-West Encounters in Arabic Fiction.* London: Routledge, 2011.

'Erian, Ahmed el-. *El-Ḍameer el-'Arabi* (operetta). Ahmed el-'Erian, Music Boss, 2008.

———. *El-Ḥilm el-'Arabi* (operetta). Ahmed el-'Erian, 1998.

Ernst, Carl W., ed. *Islamophobia in America: The Anatomy of Intolerance.* New York: Palgrave Macmillan, 2013.

Esposito, John L., and Dalia Mogahed. *Who Speaks for Islam? What a Billion Muslims Really Think.* New York: Gallup Press, 2007.

"Ethnic Stereotypes in Casting by Khaled Nabawy." Streamed live on November 10, 2012. YouTube video, 3:25. https://www.youtube.com/watch?v=1DBJP5e-uEs.

Everett, David. "Slaves in Barbary." In *The Columbian Orator*, 102–18. Boston: Manning and Loring, 1797.

Fadda-Conrey, Carol. *Contemporary Arab-American Literature: Transnational Reconfiguration of Citizenship and Belonging*. New York: NYU Press, 2014.

Fadl, Khled M. Abou el. *And God Knows the Soldiers: The Authoritative and Authoritarian in Islamic Discourses*. Lanham, MD: Univ. Press of America, 2001.

Falcone, Jessica. "Seeking Recognition: Patriotism, Power and Politics in Sikh American Discourse in the Immediate Aftermath of 9/11." *Diaspora: A Journal of Transnational Studies* 15, no. 1 (Spring 2006): 89–119.

Federal Bureau of Investigation. "Terrorism 2002–2005." US Department of Justice, Federal Bureau of Investigation, n.d. http://www.fbi.gov/stats-services/publications/terrorism-2002-2005.

Feldman, Keith P. *A Shadow over Palestine: The Imperial Life of Race in America*. Minneapolis: Univ. of Minnesota Press, 2015.

Fienberg, Daniel. "Why It Matters that FX's 'Tyrant' Didn't Cast a Middle Eastern Actor in Its Lead Role." *Uproxx*, June 24, 2014. https://uproxx.com/hitfix/why-it-matters-that-fxs-tyrant-didnt-cast-a-middle-eastern-actor-in-its-lead-role/.

Fischer, Paul. "Exclusive Interview: Jeffrey Nachmanoff for 'Traitor.'" Dark Horizons, August 18, 2008. http://www.darkhorizons.com/features/552/jeffrey-nachmanoff-for-traitor.

Fitzpatrick, Kathleen. "Network: The Other Cold War." *Film & History: An Interdisciplinary Journal of Film and Television Studies* 31, no. 2 (2001): 33–39.

Flores, William V., and Rina Benmayor, eds. *Latino Cultural Citizenship: Claiming Identity, Space, and Rights*. Boston: Beacon Press, 1997.

Ford, Harry C. "Why I Wrote a Syrian Play?" *Syrian World* 2 (July 1927): 33–34.

Foucault, Michel. *The Archaeology of Knowledge and the Discourse of Language*. Translated by A. M. Sheridan Smith. New York: Pantheon Books, 1972.

———. "Governmentality." In *The Foucault Effect*, edited by Graham Burchell, Colin Gordon, and Peter Miller, 87–104. Chicago: Univ. of Chicago Press, 1991.

Friedman, Lester D. *The Jewish Image in American Film*. Secaucus, NJ: Citadel Press, 1987.

———, ed. *Unspeakable Images: Ethnicity and the American Cinema.* Urbana: Univ. of Illinois Press, 1991.

Friedman, Max Paul. *Rethinking Anti-Americanism: The History of an Exceptional Concept in American Foreign Relations.* Cambridge: Cambridge Univ. Press, 2012.

Friedman, Thomas L. *The Lexus and the Olive Tree: Understanding Globalization.* New York: Farrar, Straus, and Giroux, 1999.

Fuller, Karla Rae. *Hollywood Goes Oriental: CaucAsian Performance in American Film.* Detroit: Wayne State Univ. Press, 2010.

Geaves, Ron, Theodore Gabriel, Yvonne Haddad, and Jane Idleman Smith, eds. *Islam and the West Post 9/11.* Aldershot, UK: Ashgate, 2004.

Gerbner, George, and Larry Gross. "Living with Television: The Violence Profile." *Journal of Communication* 26, no. 2 (Spring 1976): 172–99.

Gerges, Fawaz A. *America and Political Islam: Clash of Cultures or Clash of Interests.* Cambridge: Cambridge Univ. Press, 1999.

———. *Obama and the Middle East: The End of America's Moment?* New York: Palgrave MacMillan, 2012.

Gertz, Nurith, and George Khleifi. *Palestinian Cinema: Landscape, Trauma, and Memory.* Bloomington: Indiana Univ. Press, 2008.

Ghitani, Gamal el-. *Madinat al-Ghorabaa-Matalat New Yorkiyya* (City of Foreigners: New York Observations). Giza: Dar Nahda Misr, 2010.

Ghosh, Cyril. *The Politics of the American Dream: Democratic Inclusion in Contemporary American Political Culture.* New York: Palgrave Macmillan, 2013.

Gilsenan, Michael. *Recognizing Islam: Religion and Society in the Modern Arab World.* New York: Pantheon Books, 1982.

Giraldi, Philip. "Should AIPAC Register as a Foreign Agent?" *American Conservative,* July 28, 2017. http://www.theamericanconservative.com/articles/aipac-should-register-as-a-foreign-agent.

Goldberg, Kate. "Islam 'Hijacked' by Terror." BBC News Online, October 11, 2001. http://news.bbc.co.uk/2/hi/americas/1591024.stm.

Goodman, Amy. "'My Name Is Rachel Corrie': A Debate Over Why the Play Is Not Opening in New York." *Democracy Now!,* March 22, 2006. https://www.democracynow.org/2006/3/22/my_name_is_rachel_corrie_a.

———. "Supreme Court: Torture and Rendition Victim Maher Arar Cannot Sue in US Courts." *Democracy Now!,* June 15, 2010. http://www.democracynow.org/2010/6/15/supreme_court_torture_and_rendition_victim.

Gordon, Joel. "Singing the Pulse of the Egyptian-Arab Street: Shaaban Abd Al-Rahim and the Geo-Pop-Politics of Fast Food." *Popular Music* 22, no. 1 (January 2003): 73–88.

Gottschalk, Peter, and Gabriel Greenberg. *Islamophobia: Making Muslims the Enemy*. Lanham, MD: Rowman & Littlefield, 2008.

Gramsci, Antonio, Quintin Hoare, and Geoffrey Nowell-Smith. *Selections from the Prison Notebooks of Antonio Gramsci*. New York: International, 1971.

Greene, R. H. "40 Years On, a Controversial Film on Islam's Origins Is Now a Classic." NPR, August 7, 2016. http://www.npr.org/sections/parallels/2016/08/07/485234999/40-years-on-a-controversial-film-on-islams-origins-is-now-a-classic.

Gross, Robert A. "The Transnational Turn: Rediscovering American Studies in a Wider World." *Journal of American Studies* 34, no. 3 (2000): 373–93.

Gualtieri, Sarah M. A. *Between Arab and White: Race and Ethnicity in the Early Syrian American Diaspora*. Berkeley: Univ. of California Press, 2009.

Guerrero, Ed. *Framing Blackness: The African American Image in Film*. Philadelphia: Temple Univ. Press, 1993.

Haddad, Yvonne Yazbeck, ed. *Muslims in the West: From Sojourners to Citizens*. Oxford: Oxford Univ. Press, 2002.

———. *Not Quite American? The Shaping of Arab and Muslim Identity in the United States*. Charles Edmondson Historical Lectures 26. Waco, TX: Baylor Univ. Press, 2004.

Haddad, Yvonne Yazbeck, and John L. Esposito, eds. *Muslims on the Americanization Path?* Oxford: Oxford Univ. Press, 2000.

Hafez, Kai, ed. *Arab Media: Power and Weakness*. New York: Continuum, 2008.

Hagopian, Elaine C., ed. *Civil Rights in Peril: The Targeting of Arabs and Muslims*. Chicago: Haymarket Books, 2004.

Hajji, Abdelmajid. *Arabs in American Cinema (1894–1930): Flappers Meet Sheikhs in New Movie Genre*. United States: CreateSpace Independent Publishing Platform, 2013.

Hall, Stuart. "Culture, Media and the 'Ideological Effect.'" In *Mass Communication and Society*, edited by James Curren, M. Gurevitch, and J. Woolacott, 315–48. London: Edward Arnold, 1977.

———. "Ideology and Communication Theory." In *Rethinking Communication, Vol. 1: Paradigm Issues*, edited by Brenda Dervin, Lawrence

Grossberg, Barbara J. O'Keefe, and Ellen Wartella, 40–52. Newberry Park, CA: Sage, 1989.

———, ed. *Representation: Cultural Representations and Signifying Practices.* London: Sage, 1997.

Hamamsy, Walid el, and Mounira Soliman, eds. *Popular Culture in the Middle East and North Africa: A Postcolonial Outlook.* New York: Routledge, 2013.

Hammond, Andrew. *Popular Culture in the Arab World: Arts, Politics, and the Media.* Cairo: American Univ. in Cairo Press, 2007.

———. *What the Arabs Think of America.* Oxford: Greenwood World, 2007.

Hanania, Ray. "Film Review: AmericanEast." The American Muslim, posted February 3, 2009. http://theamericanmuslim.org/tam.php/features/articles/film_review_american_east.

Harbin, Julie Poucher. "Hollywood Reworks Muslim Stereotypes." Religion News Service, May 24, 2016. http://religionnews.com/2016/05/24/cultural-advisers-help-hollywood-rework-muslim-stereotypes.

Harmarnah, Ala al-. "Discovering the Other: 'Arab/Jewish' Youth Encounters in Arab Films." In *Youth and Youth Culture in the Contemporary Middle East*, edited by Jorgen Baek Simonsen, 35–55. Aarhus: Aarhus Univ. Press, 2005.

Hasan, Asma Gull. *American Muslims: The New Generation.* New York: Continuum, 2004.

Hassan, Waïl S. *Immigrant Narratives: Orientalism and Cultural Translation in Arab American and Arab British Literature.* Oxford: Oxford Univ. Press, 2011.

Hegel, Georg Wilhelm Friedrich, Arnold V. Miller, and J. N. Findlay. *Phenomenology of Spirit.* Oxford: Clarendon Press, 1977.

Heller, Dana. "Introduction: Consuming 9/11." In *The Selling of 9/11: How a National Tragedy Became a Commodity*, edited by Dana Heller, 1–26. New York: Palgrave Macmillan, 2005.

Herrera, Linda, and Asef Bayat, eds. *Being Young and Muslim: New Cultural Politics in the Global South and North.* Oxford: Oxford Univ. Press, 2010.

Hight, Craig. "'It Isn't Always Shakespeare, but It's Genuine': Cinema's Commentary on Documentary Hybrids." In *Understanding Reality Television*, edited by Su Holmes and Deborah Jermyn, 233–51. New York: Routledge, 2004.

Hitti, Philip K. *History of the Arabs: From the Earliest Times to the Present.* 10th ed. New York: St. Martin's Press, 1970.

Hodgson, Godfrey. *The Myth of American Exceptionalism*. New Haven, CT: Yale Univ. Press, 2009.

Hourani, Albert. *A History of the Arab Peoples*. London: Faber and Faber, 1991.

Howell, Sally. *Old Islam in Detroit: Rediscovering the Muslim American Past*. New York: Oxford University Press, 2014.

Hudson, Michael, and Ronald Wolfe. *The American Media and the Arabs*. CCAS Studies in Arab-American Relations. Washington, DC: Georgetown Univ. Press, 1980

Huntington, Samuel P. "The Clash of Civilizations?" *Foreign Affairs* 72, no. 3 (Summer 1993): 22–49.

Ibish, Hussein. *1998–2000 Report on Hate Crimes and Discrimination against Arab Americans*. Washington, DC: ADC Research Institute, 2001.

———. *Report on Hate Crimes and Discrimination against Arab Americans: The Post–September 11 Backlash, September 11, 2001–October 11, 2002*. Washington, DC: ADC Research Institute, 2003.

Ikenberry, John, Thomas J. Knock, Anne-Marie Slaughter, and Tony Smith. *The Crisis of American Foreign Policy: Wilsonianism in the 21st Century*. Princeton, NJ: Princeton Univ. Press, 2009.

International Organization for Migration and the League of Arab States. *Arab Migration in a Globalized World*. Geneva: International Organization for Migration, 2004.

Jamal, Amaney, and Nadine Naber. *Race and Arab Americans before and after 9/11: From Invisible Citizens to Visible Subjects*. Syracuse: Syracuse Univ. Press, 2008.

Jameson, Fredric. "Third-World Literature in the Era of Multinational Capitalism." *Social Text* 15 (Autumn 1986): 65–88.

Jarmakani, Amira. *Imagining Arab Womanhood: The Cultural Mythology of Veils, Harems, and Belly Dancers in the US*. New York: Palgrave McMillan, 2008.

———. *An Imperialist Love Story: Desert Romances and the War on Terror*. New York: NYU Press, 2015.

Jillson, Calvin. *Pursuing the American Dream: Opportunity and Exclusion Over Four Centuries*. Lawrence: Univ. Press of Kansas, 2004.

Johsi, Khyati Y. "The Racialization of Hinduism, Islam, and Sikhism in the United States." *Equity & Excellence in Education* 39, no. 3 (2006): 211–26.

joneswil. "Message: Christians Are Terrorists Just Like Muslims." Review of *Traitor*. IMDb, December 22, 2008. https://www.imdb.com/user/ur16750987.

Kadi, Joanna, ed. *Food for Our Grandmothers: Writings by Arab-American and Arab-Canadian Feminists.* Boston: South End Press, 1994.

Kamalipour, Yahya R., ed. *The US Media and the Middle East: Image and Perception.* Westport, CT: Praeger, 1995.

Kane, John. *Between Virtue and Power: The Persistent Moral Dilemma of US Foreign Policy.* New Haven, CT: Yale Univ. Press, 2008.

Kaplan, Amy. *The Anarchy of Empire in the Making of US Culture.* Cambridge, MA: Harvard Univ. Press, 2002.

Khalaf, Samir, and John Gagnon, eds. *Sexuality in the Arab World.* London: SAQI, 2006.

Khalaf, Samir, and Roseanne Saad Khalaf, eds. *Arab Society and Culture: An Essential Reader.* London: SAQI, 2009.

khaldoun_rayyan. "A Review from an Arab Muslim." IMDb, October 17, 2010. https://www.imdb.com/review/rw2325538.

Khalidi, Rashid. *Resurrecting Empire: Western Footprints and America's Perilous Path in the Middle East.* Boston: Beacon Press, 2005.

———. *Sowing Crisis: The Cold War and American Dominance in the Middle East.* Boston: Beacon Press, 2009.

Khalidi, Rashid, Lisa Anderson, Muhammad Muslih, and Reeva S. Simon, eds. *The Origins of Arab Nationalism.* New York: Columbia Univ. Press, 1991.

Khan, M. A. Muqtedar. *American Muslims: Bridging Faith and Freedom.* Beltsville, MD: Amana, 2002.

Khatib, Lina. *Filming the Modern Middle East: Politics in the Cinemas of Hollywood and the Arab World.* London: I. B. Tauris, 2006.

———. *Image Politics in the Middle East: The Role of the Visual in Political Struggle.* London: I. B. Tauris, 2013.

Khouri, Malek. *The Arab National Project in Youssef Chahine's Cinema.* Cairo: American Univ. in Cairo Press, 2010.

Klein, Christina. *Cold War Orientalism: Asia in the Middlebrow Imagination, 1945–1961.* Berkeley: Univ. of California Press, 2003.

Kraidy, Marwan M., and Joe F. Khalil. *Arab Television Industries.* London: Palgrave Macmillan, 2009.

Krickus, Richard. *Pursuing the American Dream: White Ethnics and the New Populism.* Bloomington: Indiana Univ. Press, 1976.

Lainsbury, Andrew. *Once Upon an American Dream: The Story of Euro Disneyland.* Lawrence: Univ. Press of Kansas, 2000.

Landy, Marcia. "America under Attack: Pearl Harbor, 9/11, and History in the Media." In *Film and Television after 9/11*, edited by Wheeler Winston Dixon, 79–100. Carbondale: Southern Illinois Univ. Press, 2004.

Lapin, Andrew. "Detroit Unleaded." The Dissolve, November 21, 2013. https://thedissolve.com/reviews/389-detroit-unleaded/.

Laurier, Joanne. "Detroit Unleaded: 'This Is the American Dream?'" World Socialist Web Site, November 11, 2013. https://www.wsws.org/en/articles/2013/11/11/detr-n11.html.

"Laylat el-Baby Doll: Cinematic Chaos between Sex and Politics." Middle East Online, May 29, 2008. http://www.middle-east-online.com/?id=62686.

Lee, Robert G. *Orientals: Asian Americans in Popular Culture*. Philadelphia: Temple Univ. Press, 1999.

Leonard, Karen Isaksen. *Muslims in the United States: The State of Research*. New York: Russell Sage, 2003.

Levy, Lital. "Historicizing the Concept of Arab Jews in the Mashriq." *Jewish Quarterly Review* 98, no. 4 (Fall 2008): 452–69.

Lewis, Bernard. "The Roots of Muslim Rage." *Atlantic Monthly*, September 1990.

———. *What Went Wrong? The Clash between Islam and Modernity in the Middle East*. New York: Oxford Univ. Press, 2002.

Little, Douglas. *American Orientalism: The United States and the Middle East since 1945*. Chapel Hill: Univ. of North Carolina Press, 2002.

Lockman, Zachary. *Contending Visions of the Middle East: The History and Politics of Orientalism*. Cambridge: Cambridge Univ. Press, 2004.

Lohman, Laura. *Umm Kulthum: Artistic Agency and the Shaping of an Arab Legend, 1967–2007*. Middletown, CT: Wesleyan Univ. Press, 2013.

Lubin, Alex, and Marwan Kraidy, eds. *American Studies Encounters the Middle East*. Chapel Hill: Univ. of North Carolina Press, 2016.

Lynch, Marc. *Voices of the New Arab Republic: Iraq, Al-Jazeera, and Middle East Politics Today*. New York: Columbia Univ. Press, 2006.

Maalouf, Amin. *The Crusades through Arab Eyes*. Translated by Jon Rothschild. New York: Schocken, 1984.

———. *In the Name of Identity: Violence and the Need to Belong*. Translated by Barbara Bray. New York: Arcade, 2000.

Mahdi, Waleed. "Marked Off: Hollywood's Untold Story of Arabs/Muslims and Camels." In *Muslims and American Popular Culture*, edited by Anne R. Richards and Iraj Omidvar, 196–223. Santa Barbara, CA: Praeger, 2014.

Mahmood, Sohail. *The Concept of an Islamic State*. Lahore: Progressive, 1989.

Maira, Marr Sunaina. *Missing: Youth, Citizenship, and Empire after 9/11*. Durham, NC: Duke Univ. Press, 2009.

Makus, Anne. "Stuart Hall's Theory of Ideology: A Frame of Rhetorical Criticism." *Western Journal of Speech Communication* 54, no. 4 (Fall 1990): 495–514.

Mamdani, Mahmood. *Good Muslim, Bad Muslim: America, the Cold War, and the Roots of Terror*. New York: Three Leaves Press, 2004.

Marchetti, Gina. *Romance and the "Yellow Peril": Race, Sex, and Discursive Strategies in Hollywood Fiction*. Berkeley: Univ. of California Press, 1994.

Markoe, Peter. *The Algerine Spy in Pennsylvania*. Yardley, PA: Westholme, 2008.

Marr, Timothy. *The Cultural Roots of American Islamicism*. Cambridge: Cambridge Univ. Press, 2006.

Massad, Joseph A. *Desiring Arabs*. Chicago: Univ. of Chicago Press, 2007.

———. *Islam in Liberalism*. Chicago: Univ. of Chicago Press, 2015.

Maududi, S. Abdul A'la. *Tajdid-o-Ihya-i-din: A Short History of the Revivalist Movement in Islam*. Translated by Al-Ash'ari. Lahore: Islamic Publications, 1963.

May, Elaine Tyler. "Echoes of the Cold War: The Aftermath of September 11 at Home." In *September 11 in History: A Watershed Moment?*, edited by Mary L. Dudziak, 35–54. Durham, NC: Duke Univ. Press, 2003.

May, Lary. *The Big Tomorrow: Hollywood and the Politics of the American Way*. Chicago: Univ. of Chicago Press, 2000.

———. *Screening Out the Past: The Birth of Mass Culture and the Motion Picture Industry*. New York: Oxford Univ. Press, 1980.

McAlister, Melani. "A Cultural History of the War without End." *Journal of American History* 89, no. 2 (2002): 439–55.

———. *Epic Encounters: Culture, Media, and US Interests in the Middle East since 1945*. 2nd ed. Berkeley: Univ. of California Press, 2005.

McClintock, Anne. *Imperial Leather: Race, Gender, and Sexuality in the Colonial Contest*. New York: Routledge, 1995.

Mearsheimer, John J., and Stephen M. Walt. *The Israel Lobby and US Foreign Policy*. New York: Farrar, Straus and Giroux, 2007.

Mehrez, Samia. *Egypt's Culture Wars: Politics and Practice*. London: Routledge, 2008.

Messiri, Sawsan el-. *Ibn al-Balad: A Concept of Egyptian Identity*. Leiden: E. J. Brill, 1978.

Michael, John. "Beyond US and Them: Identity and Terror from an Arab American's Perspective." *South Atlantic Quarterly* 102, no. 4 (Fall 2003): 701–28.

Michalek, Laurence. "The Arab in American Cinema: A Century of Otherness." *Cineaste* 17, no. 1 (1989): 3–9.

Miller, Toby. *The Well-Tempered Self: Citizenship, Culture, and the Postmodern Subject*. Baltimore: Johns Hopkins Univ. Press, 1993.

Mitchell, W. J. T. "911: Criticism and Crisis." *Critical Inquiry* 28, no. 2 (Winter 2002): 567–72.

Mohamed, Eid. *Arab Occidentalism: Images of America in the Middle East*. London: I. B. Tauris 2015.

———. *Who Defines Me: Orientalism Revisited and Occidentalism Redefined in Post 9/11 Era*. PhD diss., George Washington Univ., 2011.

Mousalli, Ahmad. *Images of Islam in the Western World and Images of the West in the Islamic World*. Riyadh: Arab-PR, 2002–3.

Naber, Nadine. "Ambiguous insiders: an investigation of Arab American invisibility." *Ethnic and Racial Studies* 23, no. 1 (2000): 37–61.

———. *Arab America: Gender, Cultural Politics, and Activism*. New York: NYU Press, 2012.

———. "Imperial Whiteness and the Diasporas of Empire." *American Quarterly* 66, no. 4 (December 2014): 1107–15.

———. "Introduction: Arab Americans and US Racial Formations." In *Race and Arab Americans before and after 9/11: From Invisible Citizens to Visible Subjects*, edited by Amaney Jamal and Nadine Naber, 1–45. Syracuse: Syracuse Univ. Press, 2008.

Naff, Alixa. *Becoming American: The Early Arab Immigrant Experience*. Carbondale: Southern Illinois Univ. Press, 1985.

Naficy, Hamid. *An Accented Cinema: Exilic and Diasporic Filmmaking*. Princeton, NJ: Princeton Univ. Press, 2001.

Najjar, Michael Malek. *Arab American Drama, Film and Performance: A Critical Study, 1908 to the Present*. Jefferson, NC: McFarland, 2015.

Nanabhay, Mohamed, and Roxane Farmanfarmaian. "From Spectacle to Spectacular: How Physical Space, Social Media and Mainstream Broadcast Amplified the Public Sphere in Egypt's 'Revolution.'" *Journal of North African Studies* 16, no. 4 (2011): 573–603.

Nance, Suzan. *How the Arabian Nights Inspired the American Dream, 1790–1935*. Chapel Hill: Univ. of North Carolina Press, 2009.

Ngai, Mae M. *Impossible Subjects: Illegal Aliens and the Making of Modern America*. Princeton, NJ: Princeton Univ. Press, 2005.

Nieuwkerk, Karin van. *A Trade Like Any Other: Female Singers and Dancers in Egypt*. Austin: Univ. of Texas Press, 1995.

Noble, David W. *Death of a Nation: American Culture and the End of Exceptionalism*. Minneapolis: Univ. of Minnesota Press, 2002.

Obenzinger, Hilton. *American Palestine? Melville, Twain, and the Holy Land Mania*. Princeton, NJ: Princeton Univ. Press, 1999.

O'Conner, Brendon, ed. *Anti-Americanism: History, Causes, Themes. Volume 1: Causes and Sources*. Oxford: Greenwood, 2007.

Omi, Michael, and Howard Winant. *Racial Formation in the United States: From the 1960s to the 1990s*. 2nd ed. Routledge: New York, 1994.

Ong, Aihwa. "Cultural Citizenship as Subject-Making: Immigrants Negotiate Racial and Cultural Boundaries in the United States." *Current Anthropology* 37, no. 5 (December 1996): 737–62.

———. *Flexible Citizenship: The Cultural Logic of Transnationality*. Durham, NC: Duke Univ. Press, 1999.

Orfalea, Gregory, and Sharif Elmusa, eds. *Grape Leaves: A Century of Arab-American Poetry*. New York: Interlink, 2000.

Parsley, Rod. *Silent No More: Bringing Moral Clarity to America While Freedom Still Rings*. Lake Mary, FL: Charisma House, 2005.

Pennock, Pamela E. *The Rise of the Arab American Left: Activists, Allies, and Their Fight against Imperialism and Racism, 1960s–1980s*. Chapel Hill: Univ. of North Carolina Press, 2017.

Petin, Mika'il Abdullah-Al-Baaqee. *"I'm Not an American": Sovereign Masculinity and Images of Black Muslim Men during the War on Terror*. PhD diss., George Mason Univ., 2016.

Pfeiffer, Lee, and Philip Lisa. *The Films of Sean Connery*. New York: Citadel Press, 2001.

Powers, Kevin. "A Look at Traitor: Interview with Jeffrey Nachmanoff and Guy Pearce." Firstshowing.net, August 26, 2008. http://www.firstshowing.net/2008/a-look-at-traitor-interview-with-jeffrey-nachmanoff-and-guy-pearce.

Prashad, Vijay. *The Karma of Brown Folk*. Minneapolis: Univ. of Minnesota Press, 2000.

Puar, Jasbir K. *Terrorist Assemblages: Homonationalism in Queer Times*. Durham, NC: Duke Univ. Press, 2007.

Puar, Jasbir K., and Amit S. Rai. "Monster, Terrorist, Fag: The War on Terrorism and the Production of Docile Patriots." *Social Text* 20, no. 3 (Fall 2002): 117–48.

Qutb, Sayyid. "'The America I Have Seen': In the Scale of Human Values." In *America in an Arab Mirror: Images of America in Arabic Travel Literature, 1668 to 9/11 and Beyond*, edited by Kamal Abdel-Malek and Mouna el-Kahla, 9–27. New York: Palgrave MacMillan, 2000.

Radway, Janice. "What's in a Name? Presidential Address to the American Studies Association, 20 November 1998." *American Quarterly* 51, no. 1 (1999): 1–32.

"Rami Malek Emmys 2016 Full Backstage Speech." Streamed live on September 18, 2016. YouTube video, 7:15. https://www.youtube.com/watch?v=SzzB9d1SPFA.

Rampton, James. "The Artful Dodger Interview: Art Malik." *Independent*, January 24, 1998. http://www.independent.co.uk/life-style/the-artful-dodger-interview-art-malik-1140417.html.

Raz-Krakotzkin, Amnon. "The Zionist Return to the West and the Miazrahi Jewish Perspective." In *Orientalism and the Jews*, edited by Ivan Davidson Kalmar and Derek J. Penslar, 162–81. Waltham, MA: Brandeis Univ. Press.

Richard, Alfred Charles. *Contemporary Hollywood's Negative Hispanic Image: An Interpretive Filmography, 1956–1993*. Annotated edition. Westport, CT: Greenwood Press, 1994.

Richards, Ann, and Iraj Omidvar, eds. *Muslims and American Popular Culture*. Vol. 1, *Entertainment and Visual Culture*. Vol. 2, *Print Culture and Identity*. Santa Barbara, CA: Praeger, 2014.

Riegler, Thomas. "'Mirroring Terror': The Impact of 9/11 on Hollywood Cinema." *Imaginations: Journal of Cross-Cultural Media Studies* 5, no. 2 (2014): 103–19.

"Rising Stars: The History of Egyptian Cinema." Rising Stars Project, July 2011. https://risingstarsproject.files.wordpress.com/2011/07/history_egyptian-cinema1.pdf.

Robinson, Tasha. "The Citizen," The Dissolve, September 27, 2013. https://thedissolve.com/reviews/234-the-citizen/.

Rollins, Peter, and John E. O'Connor, eds. *Hollywood's Indian: The Portrayal of the Native American in Film*. Lexington: Univ. Press of Kentucky, 1999.

Romani, Rebecca. "Review 'The Citizen': New Film Tells Unexpected Story." KPBS, September 11, 2013. http://www.kpbs.org/news/2013/sep/11/citizen-tells-unexpected-story.

Rony, Fatimah Tobing. *The Third Eye: Race, Cinema, and Ethnographic Spectacle*. Durham, NC: Duke Univ. Press, 1996.

Rosaldo, Renato. "Cultural Citizenship and Educational Democracy." *Cultural Anthropology* 9, no. 3 (1994): 402–11.

———. "Cultural Citizenship in San Jose, California." *PoLAR* 17, no. 2 (1994): 57–64.

Rowson, Susanna. *Slaves in Algiers*. Philadelphia: Wrigley and Berriman, 1794.

Rubin, Barry. "Pan-Arab Nationalism: The Ideological Dream as Compelling Force." *Journal of Contemporary History* 26, nos. 3–4 (1991): 535–51.

Rutherford, Jonathan. "Interview with Homi Bhabha: The Third Space." In *Identity: Community, Culture, Difference*, edited by Jonathan Rutherford, 207–21. London: Lawrence & Wishart, 1990.

Saad, Abdel Moneim. *Mūjaz tārīkh al-sīnimā al-Miṣrīyah*. Cairo: GIBCO Film, 1976.

Sabbagh, Suha. *Sex, Lies & Stereotypes: The Image of Arabs in American Popular Fiction*. Washington, DC: ADC Research Institute, 1990.

Sabri, Hani, dir. "Al-Shabāb al-Arabi wa Riḥlat al-baḥth 'an al-Jawaz al-Badīl" (The Arab Youth and the Search Journey for an Alternative Passport). Aired June 15, 2016, on https://www.aljazeera.net/programs/infocus/2016/6/14/الجواز-البديل.

Sabry, Tarik. *Cultural Encounters in the Arab World: On Media, the Modern and the Everyday*. London: I. B. Tauris, 2010.

Said, Edward W. "The Arab Portrayed." In *The Arab-Israeli Confrontation of June 1967: An Arab Perspective*, edited by Ibrahim Abu-Lughod, 1–9. Evanston, IL: Northwestern Univ. Press, 1970.

———. *Covering Islam: How the Media and the Experts Determine How We See the Rest of the World*. New York: Pantheon Books, 1981.

———. "Declaring War on Islam." *Progressive*, May 1996.

———. *Orientalism*. New York: Vintage, 1994.

———. *Out of Place: A Memoire*. New York: Knopf, 1999.

Sakr, Naomi. *Arab Television Today*. London: I. B. Tauris, 2007.

Salaita, Steven. *Anti-Arab Racism in the USA: Where It Comes from and What It Means for Politics Today*. London: Pluto Press, 2006.

———. "Ethnic Identity and Imperative Patriotism: Arab Americans before and after 9/11." *College Literature* 32, no. 2 (Spring 2005): 146–68.

———. *Modern Arab American Fiction: A Reader's Guide*. Syracuse: Syracuse Univ. Press, 2011.

Saliba, Therese. "On Rachel Corrie, Palestine, and Feminist Solidarity." In *Arab and Arab American Feminism: Gender, Violence, and Belonging*, edited by Rabab Abdulhadi, Evelyn Alsultany, and Nadine Naber, 184–202. Syracuse: Syracuse Univ. Press, 2011.

Ṣāliḥ, Sanīyah ʻAbd al-Wahhāb. *Hijrat al-kafāʼāt al-ʻilmīyah min Miṣr*. Cairo: al-Haiya al-Misriyyah al-Amah lil-Kitab, 1990.

Samuel, Lawrence R. *The American Dream: A Cultural History*. Syracuse: Syracuse Univ. Press, 2012.

Sanchez, Rick. "Out in the Open." *CNN Show*, November 19, 2007. http://www.cnn.com/TRANSCRIPTS/0711/19/se.02.html.

Sargany, Khalid el-. "From Alexandria to New York, Uncle Sam in Egyptian Cinema." *WSI Arab Insight* 1, no. 2 (2007): 49–58.

Scheck, Frank. "The Citizen: Film Review." *Hollywood Reporter*, September 26, 2013. http://www.hollywoodreporter.com/review/citizen-film-review-637337.

Schueller, Malini Johar. *US Orientalisms: Race, Nation, and Gender in Literature 1790–1890*. Ann Arbor: Univ. of Michigan Press, 2004.

Seib, Philip. *The Aljazeera Effect: How the New Global Media are Reshaping World Politics*. Washington, DC: Potomac Books, 2008.

Semmerling, Tim John. *"Evil" Arabs in American Popular Film: Orientalist Fear*. Austin: Univ. of Texas Press, 2006.

Sha'ban, Fuad. *Islam and Arabs in Early American Thought*. Durham, NC: Acorn Press, 1991.

Shafik, Viola. *Arab Cinema: History and Cultural Identity*. Rev. ed. Cairo: American Univ. in Cairo Press, 2007.

———. *Popular Egyptian Cinema: Gender, Class, and Nation*. Cairo: American Univ. in Cairo Press, 2007.

Shaheen, Jack G. *Guilty: Hollywood's Verdict on Arabs after 9/11*. New York: Olive Branch Press, 2008.

———. *Reel Bad Arabs: How Hollywood Vilifies a People*. New York: Olive Branch Press, 2001.

Shalhoub, Tony. "Interview at New York Arab American and South Asian Festival." Streamed live on October 11, 2012. YouTube video, 8:18. https://www.youtube.com/watch?v=7YuKXWuK3cI.

Sharabi, Hisham. *Arab Intellectuals and the West: The Formative Years, 1875–1914*. Baltimore: Johns Hopkins Univ. Press, 1970.

Shmeit, Walid. *Youssef Chahine: Hayah fi-l-Sinima*. Beirut: Riad al-Rayyis Books, 2001.

Shohat, Ella. *Israeli Cinema: East/West and the Politics of Representation*. London: I. B. Tauris, 2010.

———. "Reflections by an Arab Jew." Al-Bushra, April 17, 1999. http://www.al-bushra.org/israel/reflection.htm.

———. *Taboo Memories, Diasporic Voices*. Durham, NC: Duke Univ. Press, 2006.

Silber, Mitchell, and Arvin Bhatt. "Radicalization in the West: The Homegrown Threat." New York: New York Police Department, 2007.

Simon, Alissa. "Film Review: 'Detroit Unleaded.'" *Variety*, November 18, 2013. http://variety.com/2013/film/reviews/detroit-unleaded-review-1200852470.

"Sirhan Sirhan: The Testament of an Assassin." *Timewatch*, BBC. (First broadcast in 1989.)

Siu, Lok. "Diasporic Cultural Citizenship: Chineseness and Belonging in Central America and Panama." *Social Text* 69 (Winter 2001): 7–28.

Smith, Jonathan. *The Siege of Algiers*. Philadelphia: J. Maxwell, 1823.

Social Affairs Sector of the Arab League. "Al-Taqrīr al-Iqlīmi lil-Hijra al-dwaliyya al-Arabbiyaa: al-Hijra al-Dwaliyya wa al-Tanmiyya," 2014. http://www.lasportal.org/ar/sectors/dep/PublishingImages/Lists/Versions/AllItems/Migration%20Report%202014.pdf.

Sowers, Jeannie, and Chris Toensing, eds. *The Journey to Tahrir: Revolution, Protest, and Social Change in Egypt*. London: Verso, 2012.

Spiegel, Lynn. "Entertainment Wars: Television Culture after 9/11." *American Quarterly* 56, no. 2 (June 2004): 235–70.

Steet, Linda. *Veils and Daggers: A Century of National Geographic's Representation of the Arab World*. Philadelphia: Temple Univ. Press, 2000.

Stein, June. "Cherien Dabis." *BOMB*, Fall 2009. http://bombmagazine.org/article/3328/cherien-dabis.

Stein, Rebecca L., and Ted Swedenburg, eds. *Palestine, Israel, and the Politics of Popular Culture*. Durham, NC: Duke Univ. Press, 2005.

Stewart, Andrew. "How Cannon Films Demonizes Arabs." Counterpunch, December 25, 2015. https://www.counterpunch.org/2015/12/25/how-cannon-films-demonizes-arabs.

Stockton, Ronald. "Ethnic Archetypes and the Arab Image." In *The Development of Arab American Identity*, edited by Ernest McCarus, 119–53. Ann Arbor: Univ. of Michigan Press, 1994.

Stratton, David. "At the Movies: *Traitor*." ABC.net, June 18, 2008.

Sturken, Marita. *Tangled Memories: The Vietnam War, the AIDS Epidemic and the Politics of Remembering*. Berkeley: Univ. of California Press, 1997.

Suleiman, Michael W. *Arabs in America: Building a New Future*. Philadelphia: Temple Univ. Press, 1999.

Suleiman, Yasir. *Arabic, Self and Identity: A Study in Conflict and Displacement*. Oxford: Oxford Univ. Press, 2011.

Tahawy, Miral al-. *Brooklyn Heights: An Egyptian Novel*. Cairo: American Univ. in Cairo Press, 2012.

tedsltg. "Political Anti-American Agenda." Review of *Traitor*. IMDb, May 23, 2010. https://www.imdb.com/user/ur23304719.

Thabet, Madkour. *Industrie du film Egyptien: Cinema et Monde Musulman. Cultures et interdits*. Paris: L'Harmattan, 2009.

"The Citizen: A 9/11 Story by Sam Kadi and Khaled Nabawy," streamed live on October 31, 2012, YouTube video, 6:10. https://www.youtube.com/watch?v=UzRB9A7Qh_E.

Tirman, John. "Security the Progressive Way." *Nation*, April 11, 2005.

Trafton, Scott. *Egypt Land: Race and Nineteenth-Century American Egyptomania*. Durham, NC: Duke Univ. Press, 2004.

"Traitor—Jeffrey Nachmanoff Interview." IndieLondon, n.d. http://www.indielondon.co.uk/Film-Review/traitor-jeffrey-nachmanoff-interview.

Tsourapas, Gerasimos. "Why Do States Develop Multi-tier Emigrant Policies? Evidence from Egypt?" *Journal of Ethnic and Migration Studies* 41, no. 13 (2015): 2192–2214.

Tuan, Mia. *Forever Foreigners or Honorary Whites? The Asian Ethnic Experience Today*. New Brunswick, NJ: Rutgers Univ. Press, 1998.

Tyler, Royall. *The Algerine Captive; or, the Life and Adventures of Doctor Updike Underhill: Six Years a Prisoner among the Algerines*. Edited by Caleb Crain. New York: Modern Library, 2002.

Valassopoulos, Anastasia, ed. *Arab Cultural Studies: History, Politics and the Popular*. London: Routledge, 2013.

Vogel, Lester I. *To See a Promised Land: Americans and the Holy Land in the Nineteenth Century*. University Park: Pennsylvania State Univ. Press, 1993.

Volpp, Leti. "The Citizen and the Terrorist." *UCLA Law Review* 49, no. 5 (2002): 1575–1600.

———. "The Culture of Citizenship." *Theoretical Inquiries in Law* 8, no. 2 (2007): 571–602.

Wickham, Carrie Rosefsk. *Mobilizing Islam: Religion, Activism, and Political Change in Egypt*. New York: Columbia Univ. Press, 2002.

Wilkins, Karin Gwinn. *Home/Land/Security: What We Learn about Arab Communities from Action-Adventure Films*. Lanham, MD: Lexington Books, 2009.

Witteborn, Saskia. "The Situated Expression of Arab Collective Identities in the United States." *Journal of Communication* 57, no. 3 (2007): 556–75.

Wolfe, Michael, ed. *Taking Back Islam: American Muslims Reclaim Their Faith*. Emmaus, PA: Rodale, 2002.

Wong, Eugene Franklin. *On Visual Media Racism: Asians in American Motion Pictures*. New York: Arno, 1978.

Wormser, Richard. *American Islam: Growing Up Muslim in America*. New York: Walker, 1994.

Yaqub, Salim. *Imperfect Strangers: Americans, Arabs, and US–Middle East Relations in the 1970s*. Ithaca, NY: Cornell Univ. Press, 2016.

Yergin, Daniel. *The Prize: The Epic Quest for Oil, Money, and Power*. New York: Simon and Schuster, 1991.

Filmography

Adventure in Sahara. Directed by D. Ross Lederman. US: Columbia Pictures, 1938.

Adventures of Hajji Baba. Directed by Don Weis. US: Walter Wanger Productions, Twentieth Century Fox, 1954.

Agda' Nas (The Toughest People). Directed by Midhat el-Sherif. Egypt: Tamido for Production and Distribution, 1993.

Air Marshall. Directed by Alain Jakubowicz. US: Martien Holdings A.V.V., Millennium Films, 2003.

Aladdin. Directed by Ron Clements and John Musker. US: Walt Disney Pictures, Silver Screen Partners IV, Walt Disney Feature Animation, 1992.

Aladdin. Directed by Guy Ritchie. US: Walt Disney Pictures, Lin Pictures, Rideback, et al., 2019.

Aladdin and His Wonder Lamp. Directed by Albert Capellani. France: Pathe Freres, 1906.

Aladdin and the Wonderful Lamp. Directed by Chester M. Franklin and Sidney A. Franklin. US: Fox Film, 1917.

Aladdin from Broadway. Directed by William Wolbert. US: Vitagraph Co. of America, 1917.

Algiers. Directed by John Cromwell. US: Walter Wanger Productions, United Artists, 1938.

Ali Baba and the Forty Thieves. Directed by Ferdinand Zecca. France: Pathe Freres, Edison Manufacturing, 1902.

Ali Baba and the Forty Thieves. Directed by Arthur Lubin. US: Universal Pictures, 1944.

Ali Baba Goes to Town. Directed by David Butler. US: Twentieth Century Fox, 1937.

Allan Quatermain and the Lost City of Gold. Directed by Gary Nelson. US–Israel: Golan-Globus Productions, 1986.

Al-Risālah (The Message). Directed by Moustapha Akkad. Libya–Morocco: Filmco International Productions, 1976.

The Ambassador. Directed by J. Lee Thompson. US: Northbrook Films, Cannon Film Distributors, 1984.

American Dreamz. Directed by Paul Weitz. US: Universal Pictures, Depth of Field, 2006.

AmericanEast. Directed by Hesham Issawi. US: Distant Horizon, Zahra Pictures, 2007.

American Hustle. Directed by David O. Russell. US: Columbia Pictures, Annapurna Pictures, Atlas Entertainment, 2013.

American Ninja 3: Blood Hunt. Directed by Cedric Sundstrom. US–Canada–South Africa: Breton Film Productions, Cannon Group, 1989.

American Ninja 4: The Annihilation. Directed by Cedric Sundstrom. US–South Africa: Cannon Group, 1991.

The American President. Directed by Rob Reiner. US: Universal Pictures, Castle Rock Entertainment, Wildwood Enterprises, Columbia Pictures, 1995.

American Samurai. Directed by Sam Firstenberg. US: Cannon Pictures, Global Pictures, 1992.

American Sniper. Directed by Clint Eastwood. US: Warner Bros., Village Roadshow Pictures, RatPac-Dune Entertainment, 2014.

Americathon. Directed by Neal Israel. West Germany–US: Lorimar Filmgesellschaft, United Artists, 1979.

Amreeka. Directed by Cherien Dabis. US–United Arab Emirates–Canada–Kuwait–Jordan: A National Geographic/Imagenation Abu Dhabi release, Levantine Entertainment, Rotana Film Production, et al., 2009.

Amricany Min Ṭanṭa (An American from Tanta). Directed by Ahmed Kamel Morsi. Egypt: Studio Misr, 1954.

Amrīka Shika Bika (America Abracadabra). Directed by Khairy Beshara. Egypt: el-Rania Film, 1993.

Anna Ascends. Directed by Victor Fleming. US: Paramount Pictures, 1922.

Another Dawn. Directed by William Dieterle. US: Warner Bros., 1937.

Antony and Cleopatra. Directed by Charlton Heston. UK–Spain–Switzerland: Folio Films, Rank Organisation, Transac, 1972.

Appointment with Death. Directed by Michael Winner. US: Golan-Globus Productions, 1988.

The Arab. Directed by Cecil B. DeMille. US: Jesse L. Lasky Feature Play, 1915.

The Arab. Directed by Rex Ingram. US: Metro-Goldwyn Pictures, 1924.

Arabian Adventure. Directed by Kevin Connor. UK: EMI Films, British Lion Film, Major Studio Partners, 1979.

Arabian Dagger. France: Pathe Freres, 1908.

An Arabian Knight. Directed by Charles Swickard. US: Haworth Pictures Corp., 1920.

Arabian Love. Directed by Jerome Storm. US: Fox Film, 1922.

Arabian Nights. Directed by John Rawlins. US: Universal Pictures, Walter Wanger Productions, 1942.

Arḍ el-Aḥlam (The Land of Dreams). Directed by Daoud Abdel Sayed. Egypt: el-Shirkah el-Alamia for Television and Cinema, 1993.

Assal Eswed (Bittersweet, also known as Molasses). Directed by Khaled Marei. Egypt: United Brothers Cinema, 2010.

Attack of the Killer Tomatoes. Directed by John De Bello. US: Four Square Productions, 1978.

Back to the Future. Directed by Robert Zemeckis. US: Universal Pictures, Amblin Entertainment, U-Drive Productions, 1985.

Bagdad. Directed by Charles Lamont. US: Universal International Pictures, 1949.

Barbary Sheep. Directed by Maurice Tourneur. US: Paramount Pictures, 1917.

Beau Geste. Directed by Herbert Brenon. US: Paramount Pictures, 1926.

Beau Geste. Directed by William A. Wellman. US: Paramount Pictures, 1939.

Beau Geste. Directed by Douglas Heyes. US: Universal Pictures, 1966.

Beau Ideal. Directed by Herbert Brenon. US: RKO Radio Pictures, 1931.

Beau Sabreur. Directed by John Waters. US: Paramount Famous Lasky, 1928.

Beirut. Directed by Brad Anderson. US: Kasbah Films, Radar Pictures, ShivHans Pictures, 2018.

Best Defense. Directed by Willard Huyck. US: Cinema Group Ventures, Paramount Pictures, 1984.

A Better Life. Directed by Chris Weitz. US: Summit Entertainment, Lime Orchard Productions, Witt/Thomas Productions, 2011.

Beyond Justice. Directed by Duccio Tessari. Italy: Reteitalia, Titanus Produzion, 1992.

The Big Fisherman. Directed by Frank Borzage. US: Centurion, Walt Disney Productions, 1959.

Black Hawk Dawn. Directed by Ridley Scott. US–UK: Revolution Studios, Jerry Bruckheimer Films, Scott Free Productions, Columbia Pictures, 2001.

The Black Stallion Returns. Directed by Robert Dalva. US: Zoetrope Studios, MGM/UA Entertainment, 1983.

Black Sunday. Directed by John Frankenheimer. US: Paramount Pictures, Robert Evans, 1977.

Blazing Saddles. Directed by Mel Brooks. US: Crossbow Productions, Warner Bros., 1974.

Blazing Sand. Directed by Raphael Nussbaum. Germany–Israel: Aero Film, Ran Film, West, 1960.

Blink of an Eye. Directed by Bob Misiorowski. US: Capitol Films, 1992.

Bloodfist VI: Ground Zero. Directed by Rick Jacobson. US: New Horizons Pictures, 1995.

Blood from the Mummy's Tomb. Directed by Seth Holt. UK: EMI Film Productions, Hammer Production, American International Pictures, 1971.

Bloodsport. Directed by Newt Arnold. US: Cannon International, 1988.

Bound in Morocco. Directed by Allan Dwan. Douglas Fairbanks Pictures, 1918.

Broadcast News. Directed by James L. Brooks. US: Amercent Films, American Entertainment Partners, Gracie Films, Twentieth Century Fox, 1987.

Bulletproof. Directed by Steve Carver. US: Cinetel Films, Bulletproof Productions, 1988.

California Suite. Directed by Herbert Ross. US: Columbia Pictures, Rastar Films, Major Studio Partners, 1978.

The Cannonball Run. Directed by Hal Needham. US–Hong Kong: Golden Harvest Company, Eurasia Investments, Twentieth Century Fox, 1981.

The Cannonball Run II. Directed by Hal Needham. Hong Kong–US: Arcafin, Golden Harvest, Towa Productions, Warner Bros., 1984.

Captured by Bedouins. Directed by Sidney Olcott. US: Kalem, 1912.

The Carpet from Bagdad. Directed by Colin Campbell. US: Selig Polyscope, 1915.

Cast of a Giant Shadow. Directed by Melville Shavelson. US: Batjac Productions, Bryna Productions, Llenroc Productions, United Artists, 1966.

Catacombs. Directed by Tomm Coker and David Elliot. US–France: Lionsgate, Twisted Pictures, Catacombs Productions, 2007.

The Cave. Directed by Bruce Hunt. US–Germany–Romania: Screen Gems, Cinerenta, Lakeshore Entertainment Production, et al., 2005.

The Cavern. Directed by Olatunde Osunsanmi. US: Dead Crow Productions, 2005.

Chain of Command. Directed by David Worth. US: Cannon Pictures, 1993.

Chandu the Magician. Directed by William C. Menzies and Marcel Varnel. US: Fox Film, 1932.

Chasing Danger. Directed by Ricardo Cortez. US: Twentieth Century Fox, 1939.

Cheech and Chong's Next Movie. Directed by Tommy Chong. US: Universal Pictures, 1980.

The Citizen. Directed by Sam Kadi. US: 3K Pictures, Why Me Films, 2012.

Civic Duty. Directed by Jeff Renfroe. UK–US–Canada: Civic Duty Productions, Intandem Films, Landslide Pictures, 2006.

Cleopatra. Directed by J. Gordon Edwards. US: Fox Film, 1917.

Cleopatra. Directed by Cecil B. DeMille. US: Paramount Pictures, 1934.

Cleopatra. Directed by Joseph L. Mankiewicz. Switzerland–UK–US: Twentieth Century Fox, MCL Films, Walwa Films, 1963.

Cover-Up. Directed by Manny Coto. UK–Israel: Capitol Films, Cover-Up, Electra Films, 1991.

Crank. Directed by Mark Neveldine and Brian Taylor. US: Lakeshore Entertainment, Lions Gate Films, RadicalMedia, 2006.

Crash. Directed by Paul Haggis. US–Germany: Bob Yari Productions, DEJ Productions, Blackfriars Bridge Films, Lions Gate Films, 2004.

The Crusades. Directed by Cecil B. DeMille. US: Paramount Pictures, 1935.

The Dance of the Seven Veils. US: Edison Manufacturing, 1893.

A Daughter of the Gods. Directed by Herbert Brenon. US: Fox Film, 1916.

The Day after Tomorrow. Directed by Roland Emmerich. US: Twentieth Century Fox, Centropolis Entertainment, Lions Gate, 2004.

A Day without a Mexican. Directed by Sergio Arau. US–Mexico–Spain: Eye on the Ball Films, Instituto Mexicano de Cinematografia, Jose and Friends Inc., Altavista Films, 2004.

Deadly Heroes. Directed by Menahem Golan. US: 21st Century Film, MDP Worldwide, 1993.

Death before Dishonor. Directed by Terry Leonard. US: Balcor Film Investors, Bima, MPI, New World Pictures, 1987.

The Delta Force. Directed by Menahem Golan. US–Israel: Golan-Globus Productions, 1986.

Delta Force One: The Lost Patrol. Directed by Joseph Zito. US: Warner Bros., 2000.

Delta Force 3: The Killing Games. Directed by Sam Firstenberg. US: Global Pictures, 1991.

The Descent. Directed by Neil Marshall. UK: Celador Films, Northmen Productions, Pathe UK, 2005.

The Descent: Part 2. Directed by Jon Harris. UK: Celador Films, Canal+, Cine Cinema, 2009.

The Desert Hawk. Directed by Frederick de Cordova. US: Universal International Pictures, 1950.

The Desert Song. Directed by H. Bruce Humberstone. US: Warner Bros., 1953.

Detroit Unleaded. Directed by Rola Nashef. US: Gas Afterhours, Gravitas Ventures, 2012.

Double Edge. Directed by Amos Kollek. Israel–US: Castle Hill Enterprise, 1992.

DuckTales the Movie: Treasure of the Lost Lamp. Directed by Bob Hathcock. France–US: Disney Television Animation, Disneytoon Studios, Silver Screen Partners IV, 1990.

Eagles Attack at Dawn (also known as *Attack at Dawn*). Directed by Menahem Golan. Israel: Noah Films, 1970.

The Egyptian. Directed by Michael Curtiz. US: Twentieth Century Fox, 1954.

The Egyptian Mummy. Directed by Lee Beggs. US: Vitagraph Company of America, 1914.

El-'Abwaab el-Moghlaqa (The Closed Doors). Directed by Atef Hetat. Egypt–France: Shirkat Aflam Misr el-Alamia, ART Cinema-France, 1999.

El-Ākhar (The Other). Directed by Youssef Chahine. Egypt–France: Misr International Films, Canal+, France 2 Cinema, 1999.

El Cid. Directed by Anthony Mann. Italy–US: Samuel Bronston Productions, Dear Film Produzione, 1961.

El-Doniya Maklouba (Reversed World). Directed by Hany Sabry. Egypt: TV Arabia: Media Channel Network, Art Music for Artistic and Cinematic Production and Distribution, 2015.

El-'Erhab (Terrorism). Directed by Nader Galal. Egypt: Mohammed Mokhtar Films, el-Nasr Films, 1989.

El-'Erhabi (The Terrorist). Directed by Nader Galal. Egypt: Pop Art Films, 1994.

El-Gezira 2 (The Island 2). Directed by Sherif Arafa. Egypt: el-Magmoah el-Faniah el-Motahida, el-Masa for Artistic Production, Sherif Arafa Films, 2014.

El-Naṣer Salah-e-Din (Saladin the Victorious). Directed by Youssef Chahine. Egypt: Lotus Film, 1963.

El-Zuhoor el-Qatila (also known as *Al Azhar Al Momita*) (Deadly Flowers). Directed by Mohamed Karim. Italy–Egypt: SITICA Productions, 1918.

Enough. Directed by Michael Apted. US: Columbia Pictures, Winkler Films, 2002.

Ernest in the Army. Directed by John Cherry. US: Emshell Producers, Active Entertainment, 1998.

Escape from L.A. Directed by John Carpenter. US: Paramount Pictures, 1996.

Escape from Zahrain. Directed by Ronald Neame. US: Paramount Pictures, 1962.

Executive Decision. Directed by Stuart Baird. US: Warner Bros., 1996.

Exodus. Directed by Otto Preminger. US: Otto Preminger Films, 1960.

The Exorcist. Directed by William Friedkin. US: Warner Bros., 1973.

Fair Game. Directed by Doug Liman. US–United Arab Emirates: River Road Entertainment, Participant, Imagenation Abu Dhabi FZ, et al., 2010.

Father of the Bride Part II. Directed by Charles Shyer. US: Sandollar Productions, Taylor-Made Productions, Meyers/Shyer, Touchstone Pictures, 1995.

Fatwa. Directed by John Carter. US: Capital City Entertainment, 2006.

Fazil. Directed by Howard Hawks. US: Fox Film, 1928.

The Final Cut. Directed by Omar Naim. US–Canada–Germany: Lions Gate Entertainment, Cinerenta, Industry Entertainment, et al., 2004.

Fire and Sword. Directed by T. Hayes Hunter. US: Kismet Feature Film, 1914.

Firewalker. Directed by J. Lee Thompson. US: Cannon Group, Golan-Globus Productions, Major Studio Partners, 1986.

First Family. Directed by Buck Henry. US: F. F. Associates, IndieProd Company Productions, Warner Bros., 1980.

Five Fingers. Directed by Laurence Malkin. US: 24fps Productions, Cinema Gypsy Productions, Element Films, Lionsgate, 2006.

Five Weeks in a Balloon. Directed by Irwin Allen. US: Irwin Allen Productions, 1962.

Flame of Araby. Directed by Charles Lamont. US: Universal International Pictures, 1951.

Flame of the Desert. Directed by Reginald Barker. US: Goldwyn Pictures, 1919.

Flightplan. Directed by Robert Schwentke. US: Touchstone Pictures, Imagine Entertainment, 2005.

The Formula. Directed by John G. Avildsen. West Germany–US: Metro-Goldwyn-Mayer, CIP Filmproduktion, 1980.

Foxhole in Cairo. Directed by John Llewellyn Moxey. UK: Omnia Films, Paramount Pictures, 1960.

Frantic. Directed by Roman Polanski. US–France: Warner Bros., Mount, 1988.

Freedom Strike. Directed by Jerry P. Jacobs. US: Royal Oaks, 1998.

Fun with Dick and Jane. Directed by Ted Kotcheff. US: Columbia Pictures, 1977.

The Fury. Directed by Brian DePalma. US: Twentieth Century Fox, Frank Yablans Presentations, 1978.

The Garden of Allah. Directed by Colin Campbell. US: Selig Polyscope, 1916.

The Garden of Allah. Directed by Rex Ingram. US: Metro-Goldwyn-Mayer, 1927.

The Garden of Allah. Directed by Richard Boleslawski. US: Selznick International Pictures, 1936.

Gas Pump Girls. Directed by Joel Bender. US: David A. Davies Production, American Screen Productions, Cannon Film Distributors, 1979.

Gawaz Safar Amrikany (An American Passport). Directed by Ibrahim Zaki. Egypt: Saout Al-Qahira, Cairo Voice for Audios and Visuals, 2003.

G.I. Jane. Directed by Ridley Scott. US–UK: Caravan Pictures, First Independent Films, Hollywood Pictures, 1997.

The Gold Bracelet. Directed by Kavi Raz. US: Emerald Films, K.R. Films Hollywood, 2006.

The Golden Blade. Directed by Nathan Juran. US: Universal International Pictures, 1953.

The Golden Voyage of Sinbad. Directed by Gordon Hessler. UK–US: Ameran Films and Morningside Productions, Columbia Pictures, 1974.

Hallo Amrīka (Hello America). Directed by Nader Galal. Egypt: Shirkat Aflam Misr el-Arabiya, 2000.

The Happy Hooker Goes to Washington. Directed by William A. Levey. US: Cannon Films, Movie Machine, 1977.

Harem Scarem. Directed by Albert Ray. US: Mermaid Comedies, Paramount Pictures, 1932.

Hawmps! Directed by Joe Camp. US: Mulberry Square Production, 1976.

Ḥein Maysara (Until Better Times). Directed by Khaled Youssef. Egypt: Albatros for Film Production and Distribution, United Brothers, 2007.

Hell Squad. Directed by Kenneth Hartford. US: Cinend, Eastern Hemisphere, Cannon Film, MGM/UA Home Entertainment, 1985.

Hill 24 Doesn't Answer. Directed by Thorold Dickinson. Israel: Israel Motion Picture Studios, Sik'or Films, 1955.

The Hitman. Directed by Aaron Norris. US–Canada: Cannon Pictures, Twilight Motion Picture Seven Ltd. Partnership, 1991.

Hollywood Hot Tubs 2: Educating Crystal. Directed by Kenneth Raich. US: Alimar Productions, 1990.

Honeybaby, Honeybaby. Directed by Michael Schultz. US: Heritage Enterprises, Kelly/Jordan Enterprises, 1974.

The Human Factor. Directed by Edward Dmytryk. UK–Italy: Eton, 1975.

The Human Shield. Directed by Ted Post. US: Cannon Pictures, 1991.

I Am Legend. Directed by Francis Lawrence. US: Warner Bros., Village Roadshow Pictures, Weed Road Pictures, 2007.

In America. Directed by Jim Sheridan. Ireland–US–UK: Hell's Kitchen Films, East of Harlem, UK Ltd., Fox Searchlight Pictures, 2002.

Inside Man. Directed by Spike Lee. US: Universal Pictures, Imagine Entertainment, 40 Acres & A Mule Filmworks, 2006.

The Insider. Directed by Michael Mann. US: Touchstone Pictures, Forward Pass, Blue Lion Entertainment, 1999.

In the Army Now. Directed by Daniel Petrie Jr. US: Hollywood Pictures, 1994.

Intolerance: Love's Struggle throughout the Ages. Directed by D.W. Griffith. US: Triangle Film, Wark Producing, 1916.

Into the Sun. Directed by Fritz Kiersch. US: Trimark Pictures, 1991.

Invasion US. Directed by Joseph Zito. US: Cannon Films, 1985.

Iron Eagle. Directed by Sidney J. Furie. US–Israel–Canada: Tri-Star Pictures, Delphi Films, Falcon's Flight, 1986.

Iron Eagle II. Directed by Sidney J. Furie. Canada–Israel: Carolco Pictures, Alliance Entertainment, Canadian Entertainment Investors Number One and Company Limited Partnership, Harkot Productions, TriStar Pictures, 1988.

Iron Man. Directed by Jon Favreau. US: Paramount Pictures, Marvel Enterprises, Marvel Studios, 2008.

Ishtar. Directed by Elaine May. US: Columbia Pictures, Delphi V Productions, 1987.

Iskindiriyya . . . Lih? (Alexandria . . . Why?). Directed by Youssef Chahine. Egypt: Misr International Films, 1979.

Iskindiriyya . . . New York (Alexandria . . . New York). Directed by Youssef Chahine. Egypt–France: Misr International Films, France 2 Cinema, 2004.

The Jerusalem File. Directed by John Flynn. Israel–US: Doron Industries, Leisure Media, Sparta Films, Metro-Goldwyn-Mayer, 1971.

Jewel of the Nile. Directed by Lewis Teague. US: SLM Production Group, Stone Group Pictures, Twentieth Century Fox, 1985.

John Goldfarb, Please Come Home. Directed by J. Lee Thompson. US: Orchard Productions, Steve Parker Productions, Twentieth Century Fox, 1965.

Journey to Jerusalem. Directed by David Maysles. US: Filmways Pictures, Maysles Films, 1968.

Judith. Directed by Daniel Mann. UK–Israel–US: Command Productions, Cumulus Productions, Paramount Pictures, 1966.

A Kid in Aladdin's Palace. Directed by Robert L. Levy. US: Tapestry Films, Trimark Picture, 1997.

The Kingdom. Directed by Peter Berg. US–Germany–United Arab Emirates: Universal Pictures, Relativity Media, Forward Pass, et al., 2007.

Kingdom of Heaven. Directed by Ridley Scott. UK–Germany–Spain–Morocco–US: Twentieth Century Fox, Scott Free Productions, BK, 2005.

King Richard and the Crusades. Directed by David Butler. US: Warner Bros., 1954.

Kiss of Araby. Directed by Phil Rosen. US: Monarch Productions, 1933.

Kitchen. Directed by Andre Degas. US: ITVS, PBS, 2001.

Land of Plenty. Directed by Wim Wenders. US–Germany–Canada: Emotion Pictures, InDigEnt, Reverse Angle International, 2004.

Land of the Pharaohs. Directed by Howard Hawks. US: Continental and Warner Bros., 1955.

The Last Remake of Beau Geste. Directed by Marty Feldman. US: Universal Pictures, 1977.

Lawrence of Arabia. Directed by David Lean. UK: Horizon Pictures and Columbia Pictures, 1962.

Layla. Directed by Wedad Orfi, produced by Aziza Emir. Egypt: Isis Film, 1927.

Laylat el-Baby Doll (The Baby Doll Night). Directed by Adel Adeeb. Egypt Good News Group, 2008.

Laylat Soqūt Baghdad (The Night Baghdad Fell). Directed by Mohammed Amin. Egypt: Nahdhat Misr for Cinema, 2005.

Legion of the Doomed. Directed by Thor L. Brooks. US: William F. Broidy Productions, Allied Artists Pictures, 1958.

Lion of the Desert. Directed by Moustapha Akkad. Libya–US: Falcon International Productions, United Film Distribution, 1980.

The Little Drummer Girl. Directed by George Roy Hill. US: Bavaria Film, Pan Arts, Warner Bros., 1984.

Ma'alish Iḥna Benetbahdhel (No Problem, We're Getting Screwed). Directed by Sherif Mandour. Egypt: Shirkat Nahdhat Misr, 2005.

Made for Love. Directed by Paul Sloane. US: DeMille Pictures, 1926.

The Magic Carpet. Directed by Lew Landers. US: Sam Katzman Productions, Columbia Pictures, 1951.

Maid in Morocco. Directed by Charles Lamont. US: Lupino Lane Comedy, 1925.

Malibu's Most Wanted. Directed by John Whitesell. US: Warner Bros., Karz Entertainment, Big Ticket Productions, 2003.

The Man with the Gold Gun. Directed by Guy Hamilton. UK: Eon Productions, United Artists, 1974.

March or Die. Directed by Dick Richards. UK: Sir Lew Grade, Associated General Films, Columbia-Warner, 1977.

May in the Summer. Directed by Cherien Dabis. Jordan–Qatar–US: Displaced Pictures, Anonymous Content, Durga Entertainment, Whitewater Films, Cohen Media Group, 2013.

The Message. Directed by Moustapha Akkad. Lebanon–Libya–Kuwait–Morocco–UK–Saudi Arabia: Filmco International Productions, Tarik Film Distributors, 1976.

Mickey in Arabia. Directed by Wilfred Jackson. US: Walt Disney, 1932.

Midnight Express. Directed by Alan Parker. UK–US: Columbia Pictures, Casablanca Filmworks, 1978.

Ministry of Vengeance. Directed by Peter Maris. US: Concorde, 1989.

The Mummy. Directed by Karl Freund. US: Universal Pictures, 1932.

The Mummy. Directed by Stephen Sommers. US: Universal Pictures, Alphaville Films, 1999.

Munich. Directed by Steven Spielberg. France–Canada–US: DreamWorks, Universal Pictures, Amblin Entertainment, 2005.

Naked Gun 33 1/3: The Final Insult. Directed by Peter Segal. US: Paramount Pictures, 1994.

Navy SEALs. Directed by Lewis Teague. US: Orion Pictures, 1990.

Network. Directed by Sidney Lumet. US: Metro-Goldwyn-Mayer, United Artists, 1976.

Never Say Never Again. Directed by Irvin Kershner. UK–US–West Germany: Taliafilm Production, Woodcote Productions Limited, Warner Bros., 1983.

The Next Man (also known as *Arab Conspiracy*). Directed by Richard C. Sarafian. US: Artists Entertainment Complex, 1976.

Non-Stop. Directed by Jaume Collet-Serra. UK–France–US–Canada: Studio Canal, Anton Capital Entertainment, Silver Pictures, et al., 2014.

Not without My Daughter. Directed by Brian Gilbert. US: Pathe Entertainment, Ufland, Metro-Goldwyn-Mayer, 1991.

1001 Arabian Nights. Directed by Jack Kinney. US: United Productions of America, 1959.

Operation Delta Force 5: Random Fire. Directed by Yossi Wein. US: Millennium Films, Martien Holdings, City Heat Productions, 1999.

Operation Thunderbolt. Directed by Menahem Golan. Israel: Golan-Globus Film, 1977.

The Order. Directed by Sheldon Lettich. Aruba–US: 777 Films, Millennium Films, Order Productions, 2001.

Patton. Directed by Franklin J. Schaffner. US: Twentieth Century Fox, 1970.

The Pelican Brief. Directed by Alan J. Pakula. US: Warner Bros., 1993.

Perils of Pauline. Directed by Herbert B. Leonard and Joshua Shelley. US: Universal Pictures, 1967.

Power. Directed by Sidney Lumet. US: Lorimar Productions, Polar Entertainment, Twentieth Century Fox, 1986.

Pretty Persuasion. Directed by Marcos Siega. US: REN-Mar Studios, Prospect Pictures, Samuel Goldwyn Films, 2005.

The Prince of Egypt. Directed by Brenda Chapman, Steve Hickner, and Simon Wells. US: DreamWorks Animation, DreamWorks, 1998.

Protocol. Directed by Herbert Ross. US: Hawn/Sylbert, Warner Bros., 1984.

Qubla fi Esaḥra (Kiss in the Desert). Directed by Ibrahim Lama. Egypt: Nadhat el-Sharq for Distribution, 1927.

Rambo III. Directed by Peter MacDonald. US: Carolco Pictures, TriStar Pictures, 1988.

The Recruit. Directed by Roger Donaldson. US: Touchstone Pictures, Spyglass Entertainment, Epsilon Motion Pictures, 2003.

Rehlet el-'Agayeb (Wonder Journey). Directed by Hasan el-Sifi. Egypt: Cairo Film, 1974.

Rendition. Directed by Gavin Hood. US: Anonymous Content, Level 1 Entertainment, MID Foundation, New Line Cinema, 2007.

Riding the Edge. Directed by James Fargo. US: Kodiak Films, 1989.

The Road to Guantanamo. Directed by Mat Whitecross and Michael Winterbottom. UK: Film4, Revolution Films, Screen West Midlands, 2006.

The Road to Love. Directed by Scott Sidney. US: Oliver Morosco Photoplay, 1916.

Rollover. Directed by Alan J. Pakula. US: IPC Films, Warner Bros., 1981.

Rosebud. Directed by Otto Preminger. US: Oting SA, United Artists, 1975.

Ruby Cairo. Directed by Graeme Clifford. US–Japan–UK: Majestic Films International, Miramax, 1992.

Rules of Engagement. Directed by William Friedkin. UK–Germany–Canada–US: Paramount Pictures, Seven Arts Pictures, Munich Film Partners, ROE Production, 2000.

Saadia. Directed by Albert Lewin. US: Metro-Goldwyn-Mayer, 1953.

Saboteur. Directed by Alfred Hitchcock. US: Frank Lloyd Productions, Universal Pictures, 1942.

Sahara. Directed by Andrew V. McLaglen. UK–US: Cabal Film, Cannon Group, Golan-Globus Productions, 1983.

Salome. Directed by J. Gordon Edwards. US: Fox Film, 1918.

Sands of Beersheba. Directed by Alexander Ramati. Israel–US: Mordeor Films, Landau/Unger, 1966.

Scorpion. Directed by William Riead. US: Brent Films, T.S., Summons, William Riead Productions, Crown International Pictures, 1986.

The Sentinel. Directed by Clark Johnson. US: Twentieth Century Fox, Regency Enterprises, Epsilon Motion Pictures, 2006.

Sharaf el-Badawi (Honor of the Bedouin). Directed by Mohamed Karim. Italy–Egypt: SITICA Productions, 1918.

The Sheik. Directed by George Melford. US: Paramount Pictures, 1921.

The Sheltering Sky. Directed by Bernardo Bertolucci. UK–Italy: Recorded Picture Company, Warner Bros., Aldrich Group, 1990.

She's a Sheik. Directed by Clarence G. Badger. US: Paramount Famous Lasky, 1927.

The Shriek of Araby. Directed by F. Richard Jones. US: Mack Sennett, 1923.

Si'di fi el-Game'a el-Amrīkyya (An Upper Egyptian in the American University). Directed by Said Hamed. Egypt: Shirkat Aflam el-Nasr, 1998.

The Siege. Directed by Edward Zwick. US: Twentieth Century Fox, Lynda Obst Productions, Bedford Falls, 1998.

Sinai Commandos: The Story of the Six Day War. Directed by Raphael Nussbaum. Israel–West Germany–US: Aero Film, Ran Film, 1968.

Sinbad and the Eye of the Tiger. Directed by Sam Wanamaker. UK–US: Columbia Pictures, Charles H. Schneer Productions, Andor Films, 1977.

Snake Eyes. Directed by Brian De Palma. US–Canada: Paramount Pictures, DeBart, Touchstone Pictures, 1998.

Son of Ali Baba. Directed by Kurt Neumann. US: Universal International Pictures, 1952.

A Son of the Desert. Directed by William Merrill McCormick. US: F.W. Kraemer Productions, 1928.

A Son of the Sahara. Directed by Edwin Carewe. US: Edwin Carewe Productions, 1924.

The Son of the Sheik. Directed by George Fitzmaurice. US: Feature Productions, 1926.

Sorry, Haters. Directed by Jeff Stanzler. US: IFC Productions, InDigEnt, Independent Film Channel, et al., 2006.

Soul Plane. Directed by Jessy Terrero. US: Metro-Goldwyn-Mayer, Turbo Productions, Boz Productions, 2004.

Source Code. Directed by Duncan Jones. US–Canada: Summit Entertainment, Vendome Pictures, Mark Gordon, 2011.

The Spy Who Loved Me. Directed by Lewis Gilbert. UK: Eon Productions, United Artists, 1977.

Steal the Sky. Directed by John D. Hancock. US: HBO Pictures, Paramount Pictures, 1988.

St. Elmo's Fire. Directed by Joel Schumacher. US: Columbia Pictures, Delphi IV Productions, 1985.

St. Ives. Directed by J. Lee Thompson. US: Warner Bros., 1976.

Surrender. Directed by Jerry Belson. US: Cannon Group, 1987.

The Tales of a Thousand and One Nights. Directed by Viktor Tourjansky. France: Societe de Films, Albatros, 1922.

Talq Sena'i (Induced Labor). Directed by Khaled Diab. Egypt: New Century Film, 2018.

Tayeh fi Amrika (Lost in America). Directed by Rafy Gerges. Egypt: Zoom Films, 2002.

Team America: World Police. Directed by Trey Parker. US–Germany: Paramount Pictures, Scott Rudin Productions, Munich Movie Development & Production, Project KG, 2004.

The Ten Commandments. Directed by Cecil B. de Mille. US: Motion Picture Associates, Paramount Pictures, 1956.

The Tents of Allah. Directed by Charles A. Logue. US: Encore Pictures, 1923.

Terminal Entry. Directed by John Kincade. Norway–US: Intercontinental Films, IRC, SC Entertainment, 1986.

Terror in Beverly Hills. Directed by John Myhers. US: Peacock Films, 1989.

Terror Squad. Directed by Peter Maris. US: Matterhorn Group, Manson International Pictures, 1988.

The Thief of Bagdad. Directed by Raoul Walsh. US: Douglas Fairbanks Pictures, 1924.

The Thief of Bagdad. Directed by Ludwig Berger, Michael Powell, et al. UK–US: Alexander Korda Films, London Film Productions, 1940.

Things Are Tough All Over. Directed by Thomas K. Avildsen. US: C & C Brown Production, Columbia Pictures, 1982.

The 13th Warrior. Directed by John McTiernan. US: Touchstone Pictures, 1999.

A Thousand and One Nights. Directed by Alfred E. Green. US: Columbia Pictures, 1945.

Three Kings. Directed by David O. Russell. US: Warner Bros., Village Roadshow Pictures, Village-A.M. Partnership, 1999.

To Live and Die in LA. Directed by William Friedkin. US: SLM Production Group, New Century Productions, MGM/UA Distribution, 1985.

Tom Mix in Arabia. Directed by Lynn Reynolds. US: Fox Film, 1922.

Towelhead. Directed by Alan Ball. US: Indian Paintbrush, This Is That Productions, Your Face Goes Here Entertainment, Warner Independent Pictures, 2007.

Traitor. Directed by Jeffrey Nachmanoff. US: Overture Films, Mandeville Films, Hyde Park Entertainment, Crescendo, 2008.

True Lies. Directed by James Cameron. US: Twentieth Century Fox, Lightstorm Entertainment, 1994.

Tuyur el-Ḍalām (The Birds of Darkness). Directed by Sherif Arafa. Egypt: Wahid Hamed Films, 1995.

28 Weeks Later. Directed by Juan Carlos Fresnadillo. UK–Spain: Fox Atomic, DNA Films, UK Film Council, 2007.

Underground Aces. Directed by Robert Butler. US: Filmways Pictures, 1981.

Under Siege 2: Dark Territory. Directed by Geoff Murphy. US: Warner Bros., Regency Enterprises, Seagal/Nasso Productions, 1995.

Under the Same Moon. Directed by Patricia Riggen. Mexico–US: Creando Films, Fidecine, Potomac Pictures, Weinstein Co., Twentieth Century Fox, 2007.

Unthinkable. Directed by Gregor Jordan. US: Lleju Productions, SKE/KI, ChubbCo, Senator, Sony Pictures Home Entertainment, 2010.

Valley of the Kings. Directed by Robert Pirosh. US: Metro-Goldwyn-Mayer, 1954.

The Visitor. Directed by Tom McCarthy. US: Groundswell Productions, Next Wednesday Productions, Participant Productions, 2007.

Wanted: Dead or Alive. Directed by Gary Sherman. US: New World Pictures, Balcor Film Investors, 1986.

Warhead (filmed for television as *Prisoner in the Middle* in 1974). Directed by John O'Connor. US–Israel: Buddy Ruskin—Sabra, Worldwide Entertainment, 1977.

War of the Worlds. Directed by Steven Spielberg. US: Paramount Pictures, DreamWorks, Amblin Entertainment, et al., 2005.

The War Within. Directed by Joseph Castelo. US: HDNet Films, Coalition Films, 2929 Productions, 2005.

Waterborne. Directed by Ben Rekhi. US: Drops Entertainment, MTI Home Video, 2005.

Wild Geese II. Directed by Peter Hunt. UK–Australia: Frontier Film Productions Limited, Thorn EMI Screen Entertainment, 1985.

The Wind and the Lion. Directed by John Milius. US: Metro-Goldwyn-Mayer, Herb Jaffe Production of John Milius, 1975.

Wrong Is Right. Directed by Richard Brooks. US: Columbia Pictures, Rastar Productions, 1982.

You Don't Mess with the Zohan. Directed by Dennis Dugan. US: Columbia Pictures, Relativity Media, Happy Madison Productions, FortyFour Studios, 2008.

Zero Dark Thirty. Directed by Kathryn Bigelow. US–United Arab Emirates: Columbia Pictures, Annapurna Pictures, First Light, 2012.

Ziyarat el-Sayed el-Ra'īs (Visit of the President). Directed by Mounir Rady. Egypt: Shirkat Misr for Studios and Cinematic Production, 1994.

Index

Page numbers in italics refer to illustrative material.

Waleed F. Mahdi is assistant professor at the University of Oklahoma. A specialist in US-Arab cultural politics, he conducts research at the intersection of area studies and ethnic studies as he explores issues of cultural representation and identity politics in American, Arab, and Arab American contexts. Mahdi is a recipient of various national and international grants, and he has contributed to the *Journal of Cinema and Media Studies*, *Mashriq and Mahjar*, and the *International Journal of Cultural Studies*.